MAR 2 0 1978

GODS GHOSTS AND MEN
IN MELANESIA

GODS GHOSTS AND MEN
IN MELANESIA

*Some Religions of Australian New Guinea
and the New Hebrides*

Edited by

P. LAWRENCE

and

M. J. MEGGITT

MELBOURNE
OXFORD UNIVERSITY PRESS
LONDON WELLINGTON NEW YORK

Oxford University Press, Ely House, London, W.1

GLASGOW   NEW YORK   TORONTO   MELBOURNE   WELLINGTON
CAPE TOWN   IBADAN   NAIROBI   DAR ES SALAAM   LUSAKA   ADDIS ABABA
DELHI   BOMBAY   CALCUTTA   MADRAS   KARACHI   LAHORE   DACCA
KUALA LUMPUR   SINGAPORE   HONG KONG   TOKYO

Oxford University Press, 7 Bowen Crescent, Melbourne

First published 1965
Reprinted 1972

ISBN 0 19 550147 0

Registered in Australia for transmission by post as a book
PRINTED IN AUSTRALIA BY HALSTEAD PRESS, SYDNEY

CONTENTS

PREFACE TO THE SECOND IMPRESSION

As we state in the Introduction, an initial aim of this symposium was the possibility of stimulating further inquiry into the traditional religions of Melanesia. Although some relevant material has been published since the book first appeared in 1965, it still remains the most authoritative general work on the subject. Hence we are prepared to reissue it. The text of this edition is substantially the same as that of the first: we have corrected some typographical errors and brought the bibliography up to date, but we have retained the original population figures and references to Australian non-decimal currency.

The most important publications on traditional religion in the broad ethnographic area covered by the symposium (East New Guinea and island Melanesia) since 1965 are: Allen's (1967) study of initiation, to which we refer in the Introduction (p. 26, n. 10); Rappaport's (1967) analysis of the relationship between ritual and ecology among the Tsembaga; Burridge's (1969a) analysis of Tangu mythology; Hogbin's (1970) account of the Wogeo; and McArthur's (1971) paper on the Kunimaipa. In addition, Worsley (1968), Burridge (1969b) and Cochrane (1970) have written about various aspects of cargo cult.

These works on their own do not render the symposium obsolete. Indeed, it may now be of no account to try to supersede it. Future editors of a venture of this type should, perhaps, try to produce a different kind of book in at least two ways. First, they should widen the ethnographic area to include such obvious places as West New Guinea and New Caledonia. Works by van Baal (1966) and Leenhardt (1947) in the traditional field alone indicate the resources available. Second, as analyses of purely traditional religion are becoming, in some regions, harder to produce, future editors should be less conservative than we were. They should incorporate accounts of modern religious phenomena which are some of the most crucial popular issues in Melanesia today, such as cargoism and comparable reactions to imminent independence. Much work on problems of this kind is now being done; for example, Dousset's (1970) study of New Caledonia, and recent but as yet unpublished research in the Morobe and southern Madang districts of New Guinea.

P. LAWRENCE, Sydney, Australia

January 1972   M. J. MEGGITT, New York, U.S.A.

INTRODUCTION

The last twenty years have seen great advances in the ethnography of eastern Melanesia.[1] Field studies have been made in the Central Highlands of mainland New Guinea, an area anthropologically little known before 1945, and our knowledge of the Seaboard has been extended considerably. Much of this research is now being published, and the amount will soon be increased. So far the primary emphasis has been on traditional economic, social, and political systems, although there has been some concern for problems of social and political change. The field most neglected has been traditional religion. Undergraduates and lecturers interested in this subject have had to rely on prewar pioneer studies which, however valuable in themselves, are now too few to be truly representative of the total area ethnographically explored.

The primary aim of these essays is to fill this gap: to provide students and teachers with a textbook which is based on the most recent research and will also, perhaps, stimulate further inquiry. We hope that the symposium will have secondary importance for Europeans practically involved with the area and its peoples: for public servants by giving useful background material in their task of planning development programmes; and for missionaries by illustrating the diversity of religious beliefs and practices among those whom they are trying to convert to a comparatively homogeneous creed.

From the anthropological point of view, our specific purpose is to help delineate some of the principal features of traditional religions in Melanesia.[2] At the local level, this is achieved by the individual essays themselves. Yet the publication of the symposium provides an opportunity to make an initial survey of the whole field (not only the material included here but also information from earlier works) so as to draw attention to major similarities and differences.[3] It will be seen that, although all Melanesian religions belong to a single genus, any subdivision of them into separate species, on the basis of their overt features, is bound to be superficial. Examined in depth, similarities and differences show such a random geographical distribution that any

I

insistence on a rigid typology would be naïve. Such a typology would depend on an orderly pattern of diffusion. Clearly no such pattern exists because of the marked ecological and cultural differences which exist often between adjacent linguistic groups, and are fostered by the rugged terrain and consequent lack of easy communication. These differences promote innumerable variations in the general economic and social needs that religion must satisfy. Until these have been finally tabulated and analysed—a goal still very distant at the present stage of our knowledge—no true typology of traditional religions will be possible.

As we are using the essays in the symposium as a starting point for our survey, we first describe the broad conditions affecting the field work on which they are based. This lays special emphasis on the contact situation and the extent to which it has influenced the religions described. Second, we discuss the main aspects of Melanesian secular socio-cultural systems. Third, we suggest a general definition of Melanesian religion. Finally, we examine and compare the most important features of individual religions in the light of this definition. This stresses their geographical irregularity and, at the same time, the complexity of the problems facing public servants and missionaries.

1. CONDITIONS OF FIELD WORK: THE CONTACT SITUATION

Of the nine contributors, five (Glasse, Salisbury, Berndt, Meggitt and Bulmer) deal with peoples of the Central Highlands, and four (Valentine, Lawrence, Burridge and Lane) with Seaboard peoples. The two regions are geographically dissimilar. The Highlands are self-contained: the great mountain cordillera reaching from the Ramu Valley to the West New Guinea border. The Seaboard is extensive: the mainland coast and sub-coast, the Admiralty Islands, the Bismarck Archipelago and islands to the south, the Solomons, and the New Hebrides. What is more important, Highlands and Seaboard peoples were first contacted by Europeans at widely separated points of time and their subsequent experiences were generally dissimilar. By 1950-60, when all the scholars listed carried out their research, the situations in the two regions had developed along different lines.

The first societies to be contacted were those of the Seaboard, which were being subjected to intensive pressures from the more powerful representatives of the Western world by the end of the nineteenth century. As they were often very small and most lacked large cohesive or united groups, they were unable to offer prolonged resistance. They could not force the immigrant Europeans to come to terms with them but had themselves to accept the alien way of life which European entrepreneurs, administrators and missionaries thrust on them, usually without any consideration of its probable consequences. Much of the external socio-cultural order disappeared or was severely modified. Cannibalism, headhunting and warfare were banned. Old patterns of leadership, generally sustained and reinforced by acknowledged mastery of religious secrets, gave way to new forms introduced by Administrations and missions. Official village headmen and native mission helpers soon wielded power in local communities. Old social formations were broken up either by the alienation of their lands or by deliberate administrative reorganization. The old religion—or at least its observable ritual—was either formally replaced or driven underground by Christianity. In many places, the process was well advanced by the 1920s.

The second set of peoples, the Highlanders, were not contacted until very much later and had relatively favourable experiences. The region was not penetrated by Europeans until 1930 and had only limited effective administration by 1945. As it had a densely settled population of about three-quarters of a million, its societies were comparatively large in scale, comprising groups which, in spite of internal quarrels and cleavages, could present a formidable front to the small numbers of immigrants. Moreover, in establishing its authority in the Highlands, the Australian Administration had profited, to some extent, by the mistakes of the past. The old idea of coercive reorganization had been modified. The emphasis now was rather on peaceful and tolerant co-existence, provided the people obeyed certain stipulated conditions, as a prelude to future economic and socio-political development. Thus, although cannibalism and warfare were banned, and official headmen and mission helpers introduced, the Western impact on the Highlands was less severe than on the Seaboard. The native societies were sufficiently big, strong and resilient to absorb the changes. Relations between Europeans and natives were on the whole amicable. The old socio-cultural order was left more or less intact, shorn only of those customs which the Administration and missions found utterly repugnant. As comparatively little land was alienated and the Administration proceeded warily in its dealings with the people, traditional social formations were hardly disturbed. Above all, although mission work was successful in some places, the old pagan religions were

affected only to a limited degree. The number of converts gained did
not mean their substantial disappearance.

Thus, anthropologists who went to the field after 1950 found that
traditional religion had come to represent different things to the peoples
of the two regions. On the Seaboard, it either survived only as a
memory—as at Busama near Lae (Hogbin 1951)—or was preserved
only in competition or even combination with Christianity. For many
Highlands peoples, it was still an accepted and little disrupted part of
the way of life they had always known.

This raises the question of the comparative authenticity of the
material presented from the two regions. There can be no doubt about
the Highlands material. Glasse, Salisbury and Meggitt worked in
almost purely traditional situations. Although Berndt and Bulmer had
to take into account extensive mission activity near Kainantu and
among the Kyaka, they studied the people at a time when paganism
was still a preponderant cultural reality. But inevitably there will be
some initial doubt about the material from the Seaboard: whether it
represents a true picture of the old religions; and whether it can be
compared safely with that from the Highlands.

We can dismiss one case, South Pentecost in the New Hebrides, at
once. Of the 400 islanders, the 130 pagans described by Lane live apart
from the nominal Christians and consciously maintain their old religion
with few alterations. Among the Tangu, Ngaing and Lakalai the issue
is more complex. Although Tangu religion was seriously affected by
contact, Burridge indicates that changes may have occurred as the
result of purely local disturbances well before the establishment of
administrative and mission organization in the 1920s. The material he
presents could be closer to the pre-contact pattern than a first glance
might suggest. After 1933 many Ngaing, like other southern Madang
District peoples, gave up their old religion in favour of Christianity
in the belief that it would satisfy their desire for European wealth.
Fifteen years later, in 1948, when they realized their mistake, they were
able to reintroduce their most important traditional beliefs and rituals
because there were still enough of the older men living to perpetuate
them. The Lakalai, on the other hand, never ceased to practise their
religion, although they came under strong missionary influence after
1922. They maintained it, in a syncretic form, conjointly with
Christianity. Thus, on the whole, with due allowance for modification
or loss, anthropologists can reconstruct many of the Seaboard religions
and use them quite validly for purposes of comparison.

2. THE SECULAR SOCIO-CULTURAL SYSTEMS OF MELANESIA

All Melanesian societies are of the same general type. All are stateless and lack centralized authority. Whatever their special idiosyncrasies, all stress kinship and descent in the formation of important local groupings. Their members are nearly always primarily subsistence agriculturalists or horticulturalists, secondarily pig-herders, and lastly hunters and fishermen.[4] Their major concern is for socio-economic welfare— broadly, the fertility of people, crops and animals, and success in the manufacture and use of artefacts. The ability to promote socio-economic welfare is the essential qualification for leadership.

Yet there are still considerable differences—admittedly of degree rather than of kind—within this collective homogeneity, especially between the peoples of the Highlands and the Seaboard. Read, in his important survey (1954), while stressing that the socio-cultural systems of the two regions have fundamental points in common, asserts that Highlands systems are distinguished by a special concatenation of characteristics which outweigh local variations. These include not only such easily observable features as relatively specialized agricultural or horticultural techniques and very great preoccupation with public distributions of valuables but also a widespread emphasis on physical aggression and flamboyant oratory, and a comparatively marked division and tension between the sexes. Not only are societies larger than on the Seaboard, their members often numbering several tens of thousands, but also their structures are, on the whole, uniform. The most important mode of social recruitment and property trans-mission is always patrifiliation, although in some groups, such as the Huli, cognatic links are given strong recognition. But formalized matrilineal or double unilineal descent is unknown. Even so, according to Read, who has been corroborated by subsequent field workers, within this common Highlands pattern there is a subdivision between the cultures of the east and west. Thus, although men and women everywhere live apart, in the east people usually reside in small villages, whereas in the west dispersed homesteads are the norm. Although the patrilineal clan is a general structural feature, tribal[5] organization pre-dominates in the east and phratry organization in the west. In the east, also, men's clubhouses have a greater social significance, dis-tributions of pigs occur on a smaller scale, and the pervasive hostility between the sexes is expressed more violently.

With a few exceptions such as the Tolai of New Britain (37,000), the Orokaiva of north-east Papua (9,000), and the Motu near Port

Moresby (9,000), Seaboard societies are, as we have stressed, very small. Their members range from a few thousands to a few hundreds. As would be expected in a region open to different cultural influences in the past, its socio-cultural systems are more heterogeneous than those of the Highlands. Agriculture or horticulture has no standard pattern. While most groups attach great significance to wealth for public distribution, not all devote the same amount of time and energy to accumulating it. There are considerable differences of emphasis on physical and other forms of aggression, and on the social division and antagonism between the sexes. There are at least four main types of social structure: patrilineal, matrilineal, double unilineal, and cognatic. Major descent groups range from small lineages, clans, or clusters of cognatic kin to moieties, and political groups from single villages to village confederacies and, among the Orokaiva, tribes. Local organization is based generally on the village or hamlet, within which the family may or may not be a compact residential unit. In some societies, a husband, his wife (or wives), and his children live under the same roof; in others, the wife (or wives) and children sleep in their own house (or houses), while a man sleeps in the clubhouse or a separate dwelling.

3. A GENERAL DEFINITION OF MELANESIAN RELIGION

In Melanesia it is impossible to make any convincing distinction between religion and magic. Certainly none of the three classical dichotomies corresponds with the evidence available. For Tylor (1903) and Frazer (1913), religion was man's belief in superior spirit-beings, whom he endeavoured to placate by prayer and sacrifice, thereby according them freedom of action; whereas pure magic was his belief that he himself, unaided by spirit-beings, could control non-personalized occult forces by means of sympathetic techniques. Yet there are many rituals designed not to placate spirit-beings but to place them in a position where they have to do man's bidding. Again, some sympathetic techniques are thought to derive their power from spirit-beings who gave them to mankind. If we relied on this definition, we should have to allow continually for unsatisfactory hybrid forms.[6] Malinowski (1948), whose approach derived from his field work in the Trobriand Islands, saw the distinction in the goals sought by those engaged in ritual: a religious rite was an end in itself and had no other immediately obvious objective; while the aim of magic, which was especially important for economic production, was 'always clear, straightforward, and definite'. This view is not supported by the work of his successors: every ritual described in these essays has a specific end in view and is so conceived by the people performing it. Durkheim (1947) based the division on the human personnel holding particular beliefs and performing particular rites. Religion was social and collective: its beliefs symbolized, and its rituals reinforced, the social order. Magic was individual and isolative. This position also cannot be maintained: all beliefs are generally held by all members of society, and the personnel involved in any ritual activity depends on the number of people necessary to carry it out efficiently and may vary considerably according to the situation.

It might be argued that this brings us close to the approach of Goode (1951), who sees religion and magic as the two ideal poles of a continuum, to either of which actual beliefs and practices only approximate. Yet nothing is gained by basing a definition on hypothetical categories which not only bear little resemblance to reality but also are not recognized by the people themselves. Neither Highlands nor Seaboard natives have special words for religion and magic as mutually exclusive cultural entities. It is wisest, therefore, to avoid any suggestion of a rigid dichotomy between them.

Yet, although we cannot accept these definitions as they stand, we still draw heavily on them to formulate our own. With Goode, we recognize that any definition of religion must be sufficiently flexible to allow for a variety of forms. From Tylor and Frazer, we adopt an intellectualist or cognitive approach, which sees religion as part of a people's mental life and emphasizes their interpretation of the world around them. With Malinowski, we stress the role of religion in the economic system. From Durkheim we adopt a social approach, which sees religion as a social process and accentuates its relation to society in the way we have indicated.

Thus, combining these views, we start our definition of religion with the concept of world-view: the total cosmic order that a people believes to exist. This order has two main parts: the empirical—the natural environment, its economic resources (including animals), and its human inhabitants; and the non-empirical, which includes spirit-beings, non-personalized occult forces, and sometimes totems. Structurally, it has three analytically separate but functionally interdependent systems: men in relation to the environment and its resources, or the economic system; men in relation to other men, or the socio-political system; and men in relation to spirit-beings, occult forces, and totems, or religion. More specifically, we define religion, as does Horton (1960), as the putative extension of men's social relationships into the non-empirical realm of the cosmos. It must be examined from two points of view: men's beliefs about the nature of spirit-beings, occult forces, and totems, which are contained generally in a series of explanatory myths; and their attempts to communicate with them on the best possible terms by means of ritual. But to see religion purely as a cultural isolate, as we should do by limiting ourselves to this largely intellectualist approach, would be inadequate. We have to examine it also in the context of the whole cosmic order: its involvement in economic production and its relation to the socio-political system (the social approach).

Beliefs about occult forces are of the types analysed by Frazer (1913), although variations are noted in context. Those about spirit-beings and totems need some classification. Spirit-beings fall into three categories. First, there are autonomous spirit-beings such as deities and culture heroes. Some deities are both creative and regulative: they are thought to have been responsible for the whole or parts of the cosmic order, still to live in or near human society, and still to intervene in its concerns. Others are only regulative: they are attributed no real creative role but are said to be important in human affairs. Culture heroes are only creative: after establishing the cosmos, they left human society and took no further interest in it. Second, there are autonomous spirit-beings who have no creative or regulative functions: tricksters, demons, and pucks who wantonly cause annoyance or harm. Third, there are the dead, who can be subdivided into the recent dead (ghosts or spirits of the dead) and the remote dead (ancestors, ancestral spirits, or ancestral ghosts). Totems belong to either of two categories: first, putative totemic forebears of named unilineal descent groups; and totems from which no descent is claimed but which named descent groups adopt as heraldic badges or emblems because of supposed association with them in the past.

Ritual, which often has to be supported by the observance of taboos, may take any of the following forms. For spirit-beings, it may be seen as a substitute for face-to-face relationships and may emphasize or combine any of three approaches: propitiation by prayers or offerings; bargaining with offerings; or what is often called coercion—usually the attempt to create by invocation or spell reciprocal relationships, which are modelled on those in human society and in which spirit-beings should automatically confer material benefits on men. Occult forces are believed to be controlled by sympathetic magic, power being attributed, as already indicated, either entirely to the ritual itself or to the spirit-beings said to have invented the techniques involved. Finally, sorcery is any ritual designed to kill or harm human beings. It may require co-operation from spirit-beings or rely solely on sympathetic magic. No true ritual is performed for either kind of totem apart from the avoidance of destroying, killing or eating.

The function of religion within the total cosmic order is: first, to explain and validate through myths the origin and existence of the physical world, its economic resources and the means of exploiting them, and the socio-political structure; and, second, to give man the assurance that he can control the cosmic order by performing ritual. The extent to which religion is used in these ways demonstrates those aspects of the cosmos about which people feel the most acute anxiety, its importance for achieving prestige and status, and its role in intellectual life.

We now compare the salient features of Melanesian religions in the light of this general definition: beliefs about the non-empirical realm of the cosmos; and the relation of religion to the natural environment, the economic and socio-political systems, and leadership and epistemology.

4. THE NON-EMPIRICAL REALM OF THE COSMOS[7]

Melanesian belief systems have two broad areas of similarity. First, the realm of the non-empirical is always closely associated with, in most cases part of, the ordinary physical world. It is supernatural only in a limited sense. Its most important representatives—gods, ghosts, ancestors, demons, and totems—are generally said to live on the earth, often near human settlements. Although more powerful than men, they are frequently thought to have or to be able to assume the same corporeal form. Even when they live away from the earth, as do the Mae and Kyaka sky people, or have no fixed abode, as in the case of the Ngaing Parambik, they are hardly transcendental. Either their world is a physical replica of the earth or they are assumed to live somewhere on the earth. Occult forces are conceived, of course, as purely terrestrial.

Second, although exceptions are noted below, very many peoples in the area believe in roughly the same types of spirit-beings. Thus all the groups described in the symposium, with the sole exclusion of the Tangu, acknowledge creative or regulative spirit-beings of some

kind (deities or culture heroes). Apart from the Kainantu peoples
(Kamano, Jate, Fore and Usurufa) and the Ngaing, all claim autonomous spirit-beings of the non-creative or non-regulative class (demons
and so forth). Virtually all have some belief in sympathetic magic and
all, without exception, have strong beliefs about the dead.

Yet, as can be seen by comparing the following account with the
map, at a deeper level of analysis there is a great deal of geographically
random variation in these belief systems, especially in respect of the
number and significance of autonomous creative and regulative spirit-
beings, ideas about the nature of the dead, and the presence or absence
of totems. Thus of the peoples in the symposium, in the southern
Highlands, the Huli claim one major god but also many other powerful
deities. In the western Highlands, the Mae and Kyaka, who speak
related languages, both acknowledge numerous sky beings but, while
the Mae ascribe to them an important creative role, the Kyaka regard
them as of little consequence. Indeed, the Kyaka have only one deity,
a goddess to whom they attribute only regulative functions and whom
they imported from the Metlpa. In the eastern Highlands, while the
Kainantu peoples have two very important creative deities, the Siane
acknowledge only one, whose primary function is guardianship of
the dead. On the Seaboard, the people of South Pentecost and the
Ngaing both have a large number of creative beings, while the Lakalai
claim about three gods, only one of whom is in any way significant.

Additional examples from earlier literature increase the irregularity
of the pattern. In the western Highlands, whereas the Metlpa (Vicedom
and Tischner 1943-8) attach little importance to their deities, the
Kuma (Reay 1959) have a contrary attitude to theirs. In the eastern
Highlands, the Chimbu (Nilles 1950) and the Gahuku Gama (Read
1952b), who are fairly close neighbours of the Kainantu peoples and the
Siane, only vaguely recognize or expressly deny the existence of such
spirit-beings. On the Seaboard, creative or regulative spirit-beings are
acknowledged fairly generally from the Trans-Fly (Williams 1936) to
the Sepik region, in the north, and the New Hebrides, in the east.
Yet there are innumerable variations in, and several exceptions to, the
pattern. Thus, around Astrolabe Bay and on Karkar Island, the people
acknowledge two great creative spirit-beings, Kilibob and Manup,
who delegated power to a number of minor deities. The natives of the
Rai Coast beach, who also acknowledge Kilibob and Manup, claim
many equally important and autonomous deities of their own (Lawrence 1964). The peoples of the Bagasin Area, the hinterland of

Astrolabe Bay, have extremely elaborate pantheons (Lawrence 1954). Similar variations could be quoted from elsewhere. There are at least five cases (again with no geographical consistency), in which the deistic principle is largely or entirely ignored and the principal spirit-beings recognized are the dead: the Orokaiva of north-east Papua (Williams 1930), the Ngarawapum of the Markham Valley (Read 1958), the Manus of the Admiralty Islands (Fortune 1935), the people of Lesu in New Ireland (Powdermaker 1933), and the To'ambaita of Malaita (Hogbin 1939b). Yet the neighbours of all these groups have clear beliefs in deities or culture heroes.

In one respect it is possible to distinguish between Highlands and Seaboard peoples on the basis of their beliefs about the dead. Most Highlanders make a sharp division between the recent and the remote dead, and attribute different importance and attitudes (which are discussed in a later context) to each category. Seaboard peoples, however, tend to disregard remote ancestral spirits and concentrate their interest on those of the recent dead. Yet the neatness of the division is partially obscured in another respect. Beliefs in 'reincarnation' are reported irregularly from both the Highlands and the Seaboard, among such widely scattered groups as the Siane, the Kyaka, the Iatmül (Bateson 1936) and the peoples of South Pentecost and the Trobriand Islands (Malinowski 1932). The concept has not been found elsewhere. Furthermore, it does not appear to correlate closely, as might be expected, with social systems in which distinctions of achieved or hereditary rank are strongly emphasized. This structural principle is certainly present in South Pentecost and the Trobriand Islands, but not among the Siane and Kyaka. It exists also in Manam (Wedgwood 1934), Wogeo (Hogbin 1939a), and Manus (Mead 1934b), and among the Metlpa, but not in association with beliefs about 'reincarnation'.

Totemism is not reported from the Highlands,[8] and its distribution on the Seaboard is random. Many groups, such as the Wogeo, Tangu and Bagasin Area peoples, have no totemic beliefs, and there are marked differences between those who do. The Lakalai and people of Lesu claim matrilineal totemic emblems, the one for clans and the other for moieties. The people of South Pentecost claim patriclan totemic ancestors. The Ngaing acknowledge matriclan totemic ancestresses, whereas their neighbours of the Rai Coast beach and the peoples of Astrolabe Bay, who have an otherwise similar social system, recognize patriclan totemic emblems. The Orokaiva acknowledge patriclan totemic emblems, while their island neighbours (as in Dobu and the Trobriands) claim matrilineal totemic ancestresses. In the Sepik District, the Arapesh (Mead 1947) have totemic emblems for their moieties but not their patriclans. Of their neighbours, the Abelam (Kaberry 1940-1) have patriclan totemic emblems, and the Iatmül (Bateson 1936) patriclan totemic ancestors.

5. RELIGION AND THE NATURAL ENVIRONMENT

No Melanesian religion pays great attention to the total natural environment. Most treat it implicitly as something that can be taken for granted. It is no cause for anxiety except on the relatively rare occasions when it is threatened by disasters such as volcanic eruptions. Hence there are no elaborate myths to explain its origin or rituals to ensure its continuance. Those peoples who have little or no interest in creative spirit-beings assume that the earth always existed; but this is true also of others, such as the Huli, Mae, Siane, people of South Pentecost, Arapesh, and Trobriand Islanders, who believe in deities or culture heroes. Other groups, such as the Ngaing and Garia (Lawrence 1954), attribute the origin of the earth to creator gods but dismiss the matter in, at most, a few sentences. The Wogeo (Hogbin 1939a) believe that their island always existed but that their culture heroes created all other places in New Guinea. In yet other cases, contradictory beliefs may be held by members of the same society. Berndt records that among the Kainantu peoples some informants claimed that the earth had always existed and others that it was brought into being by the two great deities. The same kind of division of belief is found among the peoples of Astrolabe Bay.

6. RELIGION AND THE ECONOMIC AND SOCIO-POLITICAL SYSTEMS

Mythology and ritual are generally more explicit and elaborate for the economic and socio-political structures. These are systems in which instability, and hence tension and worry, are likely to occur, and thus they must be validated and reinforced. In the field of mythological explanation, we can divide the religions of the whole area into three types: those attributing the origin of both systems to only one or two spirit-beings; those attributing it to a large number; and those who pay little regard to or ignore the problem. Again, reference to the map will show their irregular distribution. In the first category, we should place the Kainantu peoples, the Kaoka of Guadalcanal (Hogbin 1964), the Lakalai, the people of the Trans-Fly, the Trobriand

Islanders and the peoples of Astrolabe Bay. In the second, we should place the Huli, the Mae, the people of South Pentecost, the Ngaing and their neighbours of the Rai Coast beach, the Bagasin Area peoples, the Arapesh and the Wogeo. In the third, we should place the Siane, the Chimbu, the Gahuku Gama, the Kyaka, the Orokaiva, the Tangu, the people of Lesu, the To'ambaita and the Manus.

Nevertheless, elaborate mythologies are not restricted to groups with large pantheons. Certainly some peoples, such as the Huli and Ngaing, who recognize many deities, have also many myths. Yet the Kainantu and Astrolabe Bay peoples, who each claim only two creator deities, have very complex myth cycles. Nor do elaborate mythologies always explain the origins of the economic and socio-political systems *in toto*. Although this is true of the Mae, Kainantu peoples, the people of South Pentecost and the Wogeo, other groups, such as the Ngaing, have no overall account but only separate myths for particular food plants, animals, artefacts, and socio-political groups and relationships, which are vital to their way of life and must be preserved at all costs.

As already stated, the general needs that religion must satisfy in the economic and socio-political fields are the fertility of crops and animals, success in the manufacture and use of artefacts, and the well-being of society. In the economic field, ritual falls into three broad categories: ritual for creative or regulative spirit-beings, which may involve placation, bargaining or coercion; sympathetic magic; and ritual for the dead. Techniques used in the first two categories (ritual for creative or regulative spirit-beings and sympathetic magic) have little uniformity and are often combined. The Kyaka honour their Metlpa goddess with a special cult, but they have some sympathetic magic as well. Huli and Kuma ritual aims partly to placate and partly to bargain with the deities. The Huli also use sympathetic magic. The Kainantu peoples invoke their two creator deities. The Kaoka of Guadalcanal try partly to placate and partly to coerce their creator god and other spirit-beings. The Lakalai perform ritual to placate their major god but also use a great deal of sympathetic magic. The Ngaing, their beach neighbours, and the peoples of Astrolabe Bay, the Bagasin Area, Wogeo and South Pentecost invoke creative or private spirit-beings in expectation of automatic and immediate success. They also use some sympathetic magic which, in most cases, they say was taught them by their deities or culture heroes. The Arapesh use only sympathetic magic, which they believe to be powerful in its own right. The Mae perform no ritual for their sky people, whom they believe to be impervious to human persuasion or manipulation of any kind. The Siane, Chimbu, Gahuku Gama, Orokaiva, Ngarawapum, Manus, Lesu and To'ambaita, as noted, have at most only weakly developed beliefs in creative or regulative spirit-beings and so perform comparatively little or no ritual for them. All these peoples rely, to a greater or lesser extent, on sympathetic magic.

All Melanesian peoples perform ritual for the dead with economic ends in view: mourning ceremonies, food offerings, and the Male Cult (dances and exchanges of pigs, vegetable food, and valuables). This category of ritual obviously assumes greater importance in those societies which have no elaborate rites for creative or regulative spirit-beings, such as the Siane, Chimbu, Gahuku Gama and Mae in the Highlands, and the Orokaiva, Ngarawapum, Manus, Lesu and To' ambaita on the Seaboard. Beyond this, however, there appear to be two major differences in the ritual of the two regions. First, there are divergent attitudes to the recent and remote dead, to which we have already referred. Highlanders generally expect economic benefits from the spirits of remote rather than recent dead. They regard the spirits of the recent dead as more interested in punishing the transgressions of their descendants. This is especially marked in the case of the Mae, for whom ghosts of immediate forbears are invariably malevolent. Seaboard peoples, on the other hand, tend to regard the spirits of the recent dead as potentially friendly to their living relatives, provided that requisite honour is accorded them—although the Lakalai at least are not convinced that this is always certain. Second, in both regions, the emotional character of ritual for the dead, who are treated as an extension of the social structure, seems to correspond with that of human relationships. Thus, in the Highlands, the ritual emphasizes bargaining and bribery—the social techniques for manipulating aggressive egalitarian rivals; whereas, on the Seaboard, the prevailing view is that, just as the rule of reciprocity should operate in dealings between men themselves, and very often between men and deities, so the fulfilment of ritual obligations should meet with an immediate and equivalent response from the dead. In short, Highlands ritual assumes that the dead have freedom of choice in helping mankind, while Seaboard ritual tries to leave them no option but to do so.

In the socio-political field, religion serves to ensure the well-being of society initially by buttressing key groups and social relationships, and promoting the fertility of human beings. For this, deities and culture heroes are on the whole less important than the dead. Among some peoples, deities or culture heroes and the ritual associated with them symbolize and are believed to maintain specific groups: for instance, sky beings among the Mae, and war and reef gods, and totems among the Ngaing, their beach neighbours, and the peoples of Astrolabe Bay. Again, in Wogeo, each important group in the social structure claims its own specific culture heroes and ritual. Yet, throughout all Melanesia, it is usually ceremonies honouring the dead—especially feast-exchanges solemnizing birth, initiation, marriage and death—that are principally concerned with these issues.[9] The aim of these ceremonies is that the dead should give strength to novices experiencing them for the first time, and guarantee the fecundity of women and the health of children. But their latent function is even more important. They reinforce clans and other groups, by mobilizing them to produce the wealth to be distributed, and hence the affinal and kinship bonds that are the axes of the exchanges between them. They express the social difference, yet the interdependence, between men and women. The prevailing pattern is one of male dominance, men having ultimate control over all major ritual. Yet many societies, such as the Siane and Iatmül, have special rites which stress the indispensable role that women play in society. Again there is no widespread uniformity. In the eastern Highlands, the more extreme male-female enmity is reflected by severe initiatory ordeals and blood-letting which emphasize the values of male superiority. In the western Highlands, where sex antagonism is not so intense and women have a more secure social position, the techniques of initiation and education are less traumatic and repressive. Harsh and obligatory rites give way to the voluntary association of the relatively moderate bachelors' cult. On the Seaboard, sex attitudes range from those of the Bagasin Area and parts of the Sepik District, where women are regarded as vastly inferior to males and ritually dangerous, to those of the Rai Coast, where they enjoy a measure of equality and have their appointed, if less prominent, role in serious religious ceremonies. Initiatory ceremonies for males are generally less exacting than in the eastern Highlands. They involve segregation from women, special taboos, and in many places some form of blood-letting—such as scarification of the body, which is practised in the Sepik District, and penile incision, which is common around the mainland coast. In the Sepik District, novices are often 'swallowed' and 'regurgitated' by a deity who presides over the ceremonies. In many societies, such as the Ngaing and Arapesh, girls undergo first menstrual rites which complement initiation for males.[10]

In some cases, although by no means all, religion makes an even greater contribution to the stability of the social order by explicitly formulating or upholding the moral norms on which it rests. The pattern is clearest in the Highlands. The Kainantu peoples have a secondary mythology devoted to inculcating rules of proper conduct. Datagaliwabe, the major god of the Huli, is the guardian of ethics. The pattern is also implied by the prevailing attitude that deities should be propitiated, and that ghosts and ancestral spirits will respond to ritual only if the laws of clanship and kinship are scrupulously observed. On the Seaboard, the issue is not as transparent. Among some peoples, such as the Lakalai and Manus, spirit-beings are thought to have the greatest concern for human morality. Tangu ghosts admonish and remonstrate with their descendants. To'ambaita, Busama and Garia ghosts punish a limited range of offences: To'ambaita ghosts, adultery and murder of a kinsman; Busama ghosts, trespass and marriage within the forbidden degrees of kinship; and Garia ghosts, trespass. Other societies, however, do not associate religion with morality. Thus among the Kaoka, the people of South Pentecost, the Ngaing and the Wogeo, good conduct is seen as a purely human concern and must be enforced by secular sanctions alone.

In this context, we must consider also sorcery, techniques for which are recognized throughout all Melanesia. Yet its socio-political importance is by no means constant and is not, as might be expected, in inverse proportion to the degree to which spirit-beings uphold codes of ethics. In the Highlands, where the association between religion and morality is general, the Kainantu peoples, Siane, Chimbu, Kuma, Huli, Kyaka, and Saui and Ipili Enga all claim to be successful or moderately competent practitioners. Yet the Mae, who are also Enga, show very little interest in the art. On the Seaboard, sorcery is found both in religions which prescribe and enforce a moral code and in those which do not. It is an obsession in Dobu and among the Tangu, and there is a strong complex in the Bagasin Area (Lawrence 1952). The belief is of considerable importance in the Trans-Fly region, among the Mailu,[11] among the Orokaiva, the Arapesh (Mead 1940), and other Sepik peoples, in Manus, Wogeo, and Busama, on South Pentecost, and among the Kaoka and To'ambaita. Around Astrolabe Bay, along the Rai Coast beach, and among the Lakalai, it has only moderate significance. The Ngaing very rarely use the limited sorcery techniques they possess.

This brief review indicates that we must look for the conditions making sorcery an important institution in another field. There are two immediate possibilities: a religion's degree of intellectual elaboration; and forces within the socio-political structure. The first of these cannot be substantiated. Bulmer suggests, in his contribution to the symposium, the attractive hypothesis that sorcery may receive greater emphasis in societies whose religious systems are incoherent and ill-equipped to account for a wide variety of everyday occurrences. This could be true of the Kyaka, Tangu, and Orokaiva but is contradicted by the evidence from the Kainantu peoples (R. M. Berndt 1958), Kuma, Huli, Mailu, Garia, Wogeo, Kaoka and South Pentecost people, all of whom have well developed techniques for sorcery but at the same time intricate religious systems. In short, wherever there is a need for it, sorcery can be easily incorporated in any religion, incoherent or well organized, because of the variety of procedures available. As indicated earlier, some forms involve harnessing the power of deities, ghosts and ancestors, while others rely entirely on sympathetic magic.

Clearly, as Bulmer also hints, sorcery is motivated by forces in the socio-political system, in which it acts, to use Marwick's (1964) term, as a strain-gauge. Its operation as such can be demonstrated for at least two types of society: those with fluid and those with stable local organizations. In the first type, sorcery accusations are a necessary means of easing tension between individuals who lack the security of membership in solidary groups. Hogbin (1958) has argued that the Dobuan's concern for sorcery can be explained by the continual presence in the same settlement of mutually unrelated persons as the result of a migratory residential pattern—a situation most likely to create strain and tension that must have some outlet. This argument applies also to the Tangu, Garia and Huli, among whom similar conditions prevail. In the second type, local organization is based on permanently settled descent groups or congeries of such groups which, in the absence of wars for territorial or other economic aggrandizement, can preserve their identity only by mutual suspicion, rivalry and hostility. Sorcery accusations act here both as an important medium for expressing enmity and as an excuse for initiating warfare, which is ultimately the most effective means of relieving feelings of aggression. This is certainly the pattern among the Kainantu peoples, the Kuma and the Orokaiva, all of whom have strong military cultures. It is significant that there is evidence that among the Bagasin Area and Kainantu peoples, who represent the first and second types of local organization respectively, the rate of sorcery accusation has risen since the Administration banned feuding and warfare. This is the main avenue left them for easing tension.

Yet this does not explain why two peoples, the Mae and Ngaing, both warlike in the past, never had great interest in sorcery and, what is more important, have not developed it since pacification. A probable answer is that both peoples have always had alternative means for channelling aggression. The Mae were one of the few New Guinea peoples who fought to acquire land. They also expressed inter-group rivalry by means of ceremonial exchange, for which they have always been famous and in which they have intensified their interest since coming under European control. Also, unlike many other groups, they prefer to use the Administration's Court for Native Affairs rather than traditional processes for settling major disputes. The Ngaing had no need for wars for territorial expansion but, like the Mae, much of their energy was devoted to ceremonial exchange. Moreover, since pacification, they have had less hesitation than many other Seaboard peoples in using the Court for Native Affairs and for many years were involved in a cargo movement which diverted their attention from local quarrels.

7. RELIGION, LEADERSHIP, AND THE EPISTEMOLOGICAL SYSTEM

It is self-evident that religion is an important part of the epistemological or cognitive systems of all Melanesian peoples. As we have stressed, every myth and ritual act represent, to some extent at least, a people's understanding of the nature of the total cosmos and of the way in which it can be controlled to human advantage. They tell us about the types and sources of much of the knowledge men believe to be available to them. Moreover, as is obvious from the general view of the cosmos (both its empirical and non-empirical parts) as a unitary physical realm with few, if any, transcendental attributes, the prevailing attitude towards religion is essentially pragmatic and materialistic. Religion is a technology rather than a spiritual force for human salvation.[12]

Nevertheless, from the accounts at our disposal, it is possible that there are different degrees to which religion dominates the epistemological system and that these differences correspond broadly with the two general regions discussed—the Highlands and Seaboard. The Mae and the Ngaing seem to represent opposite extremes. The Mae, while relying on religion—especially ritual for the dead—for general economic and social welfare, still regard purely secular techniques as the only valid avenue to success in many important tasks. They stress hard physical work, and power deriving from personal and military strength, as the primary qualifications a leader must possess. The Ngaing, on the other hand, believe that they can achieve success in major undertakings only if they buttress secular techniques with ritual. For them, work necessitates co-operation not only between men themselves but also between men, deities and spirits of the dead. Only those who show that they can guarantee this total cosmic collaboration can aspire to leadership. This pattern is common to the whole southern Madang District (Lawrence 1959; 1964). On the whole, Highlands peoples (especially the Siane, Gahuku Gama and Kyaka, although probably not the Kainantu groups, Chimbu, Huli and Kuma to the same extent) approximate to the Mae position, while many Seaboard peoples (again allowing for less extreme cases) appear to approximate to that of the Ngaing.

The evidence for this distinction between the tendency towards secularism in the Highlands and towards religious thinking on the Seaboard comes partly from the ethnography and partly from the somewhat different theoretical emphases in the essays in the symposium. In the first place, we must compare the attitude to ritual in the two regions. Highlands secularism seems to reflect the generally close association between religion and morality, and the assumption that success in ritual is not automatic but depends on securing the goodwill of spirit-beings. Deities, where they are important, and ghosts and ancestors are accorded freedom of action: they have to be propitiated or manipulated by bargaining. Man cannot invariably rely on their support and hence is very often thrown back on his own purely human intellectual resources. By the same token, the greater prominence of religion in Seaboard epistemological systems could be attributed to the weaker association between religion and morality, and the more pronounced view that spirit-beings react immediately to ritual correctly performed. Thus man, convinced that spirit-beings are under his direction, regards ritual techniques as the most valuable knowledge in his possession.

In the second place, although the essays fall along a continuum, they accentuate two different approaches which we included in our definition of religion earlier: the social approach, which concentrates largely on the indirect or oblique statements made by belief and ritual to symbolize and reinforce the social order; and the intellectualist approach, which is concerned chiefly with epistemological problems—

man's attempt to explain the cosmos and bring it under his control. Essays by Salisbury, Meggitt and Bulmer tend towards the social approach; those by Valentine and Lane tend towards the intellectualist; and those by Glasse, Berndt, Lawrence and Burridge tend to adopt both. In short, three of the essays on Highlands peoples ignore epistemological issues, while all those on the Seaboard stress them. Yet before this can be accepted as testimony for the general cultural dichotomy we have suggested, future field workers should consider carefully whether the true reason for it could not be found in the personal equations of their forerunners (a factor that should never be ruled out) and, more particularly, in the contact situations in the two regions, which we must now reconsider.

The contact situation in the Highlands, it will be remembered, was less disruptive than on the Seaboard. The people were able to reach a *modus vivendi* with the Europeans, who treated them with some respect, and left their social and religious systems largely intact. They still found their traditional way of life satisfying. Thus the problems facing the anthropologist in the Highlands were relatively straightforward. He rarely had to deal with antagonism to white men, which was normally expressed elsewhere through the medium of cargo cult. Such cargo cults or other 'revolutionary' movements as he met were usually only marginal and of short duration. Obviously, his most important objective was to record, for their own sake, the indigenous sociocultural systems before disintegration should set in (Stanner in Salisbury, 1962: p. v). As we remarked earlier, the old religions were still being used only for purposes laid down by tradition, and for this normal social analysis was quite adequate. Methodologically speaking, there was no immediate necessity for the field worker to adopt an intellectualist approach, for epistemological problems were rarely apparent. In this context, it is significant that Berndt, working in the extreme eastern Highlands, where the people were involved in the only prolonged cargo cult in the region, had to adopt an intellectualist approach to understand some of the problems with which he was faced.

The effects of contact on the Seaboard were, of course, more drastic. The small native societies were soon swamped by, and incorporated within, the new state system. The outward forms of the old religions were replaced by Christianity or driven underground. This could lead to only two kinds of reaction: the complete disintegration of native society and the disappearance of its culture; or, as was more often the case, a resurgence of the society with its organization and ideology deliberately modernized to solve problems created by European rule. The resurgence usually took the form of cargo cult: new social formations, generally wider than those of traditional society, were recruited on the basis of a belief that careful enactment of systematic religious ritual would provide the people with the white man's goods, including very often the military equipment that would drive him from the country. These cargo cults have been far more prevalent and longer sustained than those in the Highlands.

This situation was bound to influence the work of anthropologists on the Seaboard. Their analyses of traditional religions (even where these involved some reconstruction) were intended as serious contributions to Melanesian ethnography. But, beyond this, they were often intended, as was the case with three contributors to this volume (Valentine, Lawrence and Burridge), to shed light on cargo cults and other reactions to colonial rule.

In spite of the extensive consequences of the impact of the West, Seaboard religions have proved far more durable than is generally supposed. The changes introduced impinged mainly on the superstructure of native life, the external form of the socio-cultural order. In most places, the village subsistence economy was barely altered. In spite of the incorporation of native societies within the new administrative and mission organizations, the old systems of social relationships based on locality, kinship and descent remained, even if they no longer strictly followed original patterns. Although indigenous religious life lost many of its more colourful ceremonies, Western secular education had, until recently, little influence. It did not replace the original concept of a cosmic order created for man by spirit-beings and maintained to his advantage by ritual. Thus, although individual social structures and religious systems *per se* might cease to be politically important in the contact situation, most of the socio-economic values and intellectual assumptions underlying them were still current and determined native reactions to the new conditions. In particular, traditional religious concepts lay at the root of cargo cult ideologies. These concepts provided the key to understanding the people's interpretation of Christianity: how they construed the white man's religion so as to elaborate a series of systematically interrelated ideas about the new world order to which they saw themselves as belonging. Thus the anthropologist had to adopt an intellectualist approach to comprehend native attempts to use ritual as a means of coming to terms with the problems of contact. He had to recognize religion's prominent role in the indigenous epistemological system and leadership. An analysis in purely social terms, demonstrating only the systematic connexion between belief and ritual and social relationships in traditional and colonial human society, would have given him a very limited answer to the problem.

It is possible, therefore, that in their need to provide *ad hoc* solutions to the immediate questions in the two regions—the nature of traditional socio-cultural systems, on the one hand, and of contact ideologies, on the other—the anthropologists of the last decade may not have used to the full the two major approaches to the study of religion open to them. They may not have asked all the relevant questions. In the Highlands, the intellectualist approach may have been ignored at the expense of the social and, on the Seaboard, vice versa. If this is true, the dichotomy we have suggested between the relatively secular-minded Highlanders and religious-minded Seaboard peoples, although not entirely invalidated, will have to be revised. This is a serious issue for the field workers of the present decade, as can be seen from the practical implications we discuss below.

8. DOMINANT THEMES OF MELANESIAN RELIGION: PROBLEMS FOR ADMINISTRATIONS AND MISSIONS

Our initial point should hardly need restating: all Melanesian religions are broadly similar but such are their individual idiosyncrasies that any attempt to divide them into neat sub-types on a regional basis would be fruitless. Everywhere religion is regarded as a means to or guarantee of material welfare but, when the situation is analysed in depth, there is no uniform expression of this generalization. Even close neighbours of the same language or dialect group are differentiated on important issues: the classes of spirit-beings they recognize and the ritual techniques they use to contact them.

Nevertheless, even if allowance is made for the exceptions and modifications we have discussed, it is still possible to recapitulate two dominant themes. In Highlands religions, there is universal interest in the dead but rather less in autonomous creative or regulative spirit-beings. There are no totemic beliefs. Distant ancestors are collectively powerful and on the whole beneficent, while recent ghosts are potentially malevolent. There is a close connexion between religion and morality, and ritual for deities, ghosts and ancestors involves the concepts of propitiation, bargaining, and dependence rather than human direction. The epistemological system, although obviously incorporating religious beliefs to some extent, still gives considerable scope to the unaided human intellect. In Seaboard religions, there is strong emphasis on autonomous creative or regulative spirit-beings and also on the dead. In many places, there are totemic beliefs. Distant ancestors tend to be forgotten, while recent ghosts are regarded as the protectors of their living descendants. Ritual for deities and ghosts, although embodying elements of placation, is based on the confidence that, properly approached, they will automatically serve man's interest. Religion, therefore, pervades man's whole intellectual life.

From a practical point of view, these two themes may shed some light on different native attitudes to development by Administrations and to mission work. Where they remain intact, traditional religions may provide obstacles to these programmes; and even if many of their overt characteristics disappear, the basic concepts on which they rest may persist and influence reactions to any innovations impinging on them.

For Administrations, the crucial consideration is native response to economic, political and intellectual development: cash crops and Co-operative Societies; modern democratic government; and primary, secondary and tertiary education. In the Highlands, because of the comparatively secular outlook, traditional religious beliefs in themselves may present few problems; and except in a few places such as Kainantu, where there has been pronounced cargo cult activity, the contact situation has never been such as to make the people self-conscious about or reliant on any religious ideology. In this context, the people's response seems to have stressed physical effort, aggressiveness, and mental astuteness—'life values' most likely to commend themselves to middle-class Europeans trying to promote their welfare. Yet the purely social aspects of traditional religion may yet prove a hindrance to development. As can be seen in most of the essays, Highlands religious beliefs and rituals stand out clearly as symbols of strong group unity. Because the groups themselves have retained their identity under contact, these symbols (however limited their strictly intellectual significance) may obstruct the wider regional reorganization demanded by Co-operative Societies, Native Local Government Councils, and the new national electorates. Local and descent group loyalties, and the belief that leadership, in the past cosmogonically ordained for single groups, cannot spread beyond strictly defined traditional limits, may prevent the formation of new relationships and expanded associations demanded by modern economic and political interests.

In many parts of the Seaboard, however, native responses can be understood in both social and intellectualist terms. Social responses may not be the same as those in the Highlands: they will be based on cleavages within the structure of colonial rather than of traditional society. Long-standing antagonism to Europeans can continue to be expressed in the view that the people still have their own way of life, now symbolized by cargo ideology. This can facilitate the rejection of the new institutions simply because their acceptance implies an increased dependence on the white man. Intellectual responses are frequently determined by both old and new religious considerations. Natives may reject new economic processes because they believe that Europeans have withheld the ritual necessary for their success. They may distrust democratic government because it has only the secular sanction of Administrations and prefer to look for charismatic leaders claiming divine authority. They may regard Western secular education as irrelevant to their way of life, and cling to their conviction that knowledge is not acquired by hard and consistent mental application but through revelation by a spirit-being.

For the missionary, the issue is to convert the people from essentially materialist religions to Christianity, which stresses spiritual values. Among many Highlands peoples, the most likely reaction seems to be either the total rejection of the new religion or its assimilation to the traditional cult of the dead. The first of these responses is typified by that of the secularist Mae, who see no practical benefits to be gained from conversion. The second is typified by that of the Kyaka, who attribute to God many of the everyday punitive functions of ghosts. On the Seaboard, the pattern ranges from almost total and apparently altruistic acceptance of Christianity, as at Busama (Hogbin 1951), to its adoption and adaptation for purely mundane ends elsewhere. But there is no uniform response. The To'ambaita use Christianity as a substitute for sorcery, praying to God to smite their enemies. Other groups have seen in it, as we have stated, the secret of cargo. Yet, even here, there is still room for several different interpretations. Thus the Manus, who always emphasized obedience to a rigid moral code as the means of securing ghostly help in economic ventures, accused their missionaries of withholding the Christian equivalent, which was the key to European wealth (Schwartz 1962). The Garia claimed that they had not been taught the Christian equivalent of their own ritual formulae and hence had no way of actuating God to send them goods. The Ngaing accused their missionaries of hiding secrets about human origins by persuading the natives to accept Adam and Eve as the only totemic forebears of all mankind. They believed they could prove that Europeans, like themselves, really acknowledged multiple totemic ancestresses (Lawrence 1964).

These last examples, however, bring back into focus one cardinal certainty. Although the two themes we have outlined for Highlands and Seaboard religions may serve as a general guide from a regional point of view, they still allow innumerable idiosyncrasies and permutations in each local situation. The anthropologist, the administrative officer, and the missionary ultimately all face the same problem: geographically random and inexplicable diversity. Years of experience have taught us that the pattern in one community will not necessarily be repeated in the next, and that beyond the next mountain or the next river—even in the next village—we must be prepared to record, analyse or come to terms with the completely unexpected.

Sydney, N.S.W.,   P. Lawrence
September 1964   M. J. Meggitt

NOTES

[1] For the sake of convenience, we are departing from strict usage in defining Melanesia as the whole of Australian New Guinea, the British Solomon Islands and the New Hebrides. We have excluded West New Guinea to keep the analysis within reasonable bounds.

[2] Some of the essays refer to the influence of Christianity. In the Introduction, we discuss this only in relevant contexts. The dominant emphasis throughout is on traditional religion.

[3] Space prevents a summary of the entire information available. We have tried only to delineate the main features of Melanesian religions. There is still room for a longer and more detailed examination.

[4] The exceptions to this generalization (for example, the peoples of the Trans-Fly, some Trobriand Islanders and the Manus) are too few to warrant special attention here.

[5] For the sake of convenience, we use this term to cover the formations called tribes by Salisbury and Read (1952a) and district groups by Berndt. For our present purposes, all these groups are sufficiently similar to be included within the same general category.

[6] Frazer (1913) realized this problem, but we cannot accept his evolutionary explanation, which he himself admitted to be hypothetical.

[7] We are indebted to Dr Valentine for drawing our attention to a good deal of the material included in this section.

[8] Nilles (1950) refers to totemism among the Chimbu, but his account suggests that a different interpretation could be placed on the material he discusses.

[9] The Huli appear to be an exception to this generalization, certainly in the Highlands: they frequently combine ritual for their deities and the dead. Among the Ngaing, the god Yabuling is invoked in the Male Cult, but his role is subsidiary.

[10] We have not discussed this subject at length because it has been covered in detail by Allen (1967).

[11] Personal communication from Dr B. Verma, who recently worked among the Mailu.

[12] See also Guiart (1962), who reaches similar conclusions concerning the religions of the New Hebrides.

EDITORIAL NOTE

We should like to thank Dr R. M. Glasse, who served on the editorial panel at the inception of the symposium until he had to withdraw because of pressures of field work, and also Dr Ian Hogbin, who consistently gave us encouragement and advice.

P. L. and M. J. M.

R. M. GLASSE

The Huli of the Southern Highlands

T HIS paper is a study of belief and explanation.[1] It is concerned
with ideas about sickness and health, fertility and growth, and
the fate of the soul in the afterlife. It is specifically concerned with
four concepts which underlie the 'religious' behaviour of the Huli—an
agricultural people of the New Guinea Highlands. Huli call these
concepts *dinini*, *dama*, *gamu* and Datagaliwabe. They conceive *dinini*
to be the immaterial essence of human personality which survives
bodily death and persists indefinitely thereafter as a ghost. In the latter
form *dinini* affects the behaviour of living people and to some extent
the actions of *dama*. *Dama* are gods—extremely powerful beings who
control the course of nature and often intervene in the affairs of men.
Men can directly influence the *dama* by a special form of behaviour
called *gamu* which includes spells, oaths, offerings and other rites. All
forms of *gamu* aim to induce the deities and ghosts to permit a desired
event to occur or to prevent an undesirable event from occurring.

Datagaliwabe is not an ordinary deity, but a unique spirit-being
whose sole concern is punishing breaches of kinship rules. Unlike the
dama, he cannot be influenced in any way, by men, by ghosts or by
other deities. There is no form of *gamu* that can placate, propitiate
or deter him.

1. COUNTRY AND SOCIETY[2]

The Huli live in the Southern Highlands District of the Territory
of Papua. Their country lies on the southern flank of the central
cordillera in the great basin formed by the Tagari River and its tribu-
taries. Its elevation is from 4,500 to 6,000 feet above sea-level and there
are few ridges in the settled area more than 8,000 feet high. Much of
the land is flat or gently undulating. Dense rain forest covers the

27

c

northern and eastern mountain slopes and some patches remain in the settled area.

The climate is temperate with little seasonal variation. There is usually some rain every month but the pattern is irregular. Day temperatures are in the seventies or eighties (F.), and nights are twenty to thirty degrees cooler throughout the year. Fluctuations in rainfall may cause serious harm. One month without rain damages newly planted gardens; two may bring famine and starvation. Too much rain can also be disastrous: rivers flood and tubers rot in the ground. Frost, which occurs rarely, can destroy acres of garden overnight. Nevertheless the Huli environment is generally favourable. The volcanic soils are fertile. Crop yields are high by Highlands standards and arable land is abundant.

The Huli number between 30,000 and 40,000, and occupy an area of about 2,000 square miles. Population density is comparatively low, averaging twenty per square mile and nowhere exceeding about one hundred per square mile. The settlement pattern is one of dispersed homesteads rather than tightly clustered villages, and the family is not a residential unit. Men live apart from their wives and young children because they believe that contact with women impairs their health and leads to premature ageing. Young children reside with their mothers and, after initiation, boys join their fathers' households.

Huli subsist on agriculture and their staple crop is sweet potato. They are skilled cultivators and use effective techniques for clearing forest, preparing the soil and draining their plots. Men do the heavier work, such as felling large trees, but otherwise there is no strict division of labour. They also keep pigs, which everyone needs to meet social and ritual obligations. For example, the bride price is, traditionally, a payment of fifteen pigs, and war indemnities for a single death range from thirty to one hundred and fifty pigs. Hunting and gathering are of little economic importance.

The social structure of the Huli is in some respects atypical of the New Guinea Highlands. There are no corporate descent groups in which membership rights and duties are ascribed solely as a consequence of descent, as among Enga. Nor are there corporate units, ostensibly agnatic, but actually based on patrifiliation and other principles. Instead group membership is an achieved status that can be acquired by any member of a cognatic stock. It follows that every man is eligible for membership in a number of groups. There are no local groups in a residential sense, but there are well-defined territories in which group members, resident and non-resident, have recognized rights. There are some group members who reside exclusively in one parish-territory. Others commute more or less regularly between two or three. And some men fulfil obligations to a group without residing on its land. It is a complex, mobile society. Individuals have great freedom of choice. High status is achieved by acquiring rights in many groups rather than by winning recognition in any one.

Every Huli also belongs to a dispersed, non-corporate clan. Clan members have the same patrilineal surname and observe the rule of exogamy, but they never mobilize for common action, own no property in common and even fight against one another in war.

The personal kindred is also an important social unit though it is not a corporate group. When a man marries, his bilateral kin contribute to his bride price and this payment is divided among the bride's kindred who come together for the occasion. Indemnity payments, too, are provided and distributed on the same basis.

Until the 1950s warfare was the dominant orientation of Huli society. Every boy was taught to fight and every man was expected actively to defend his own interests. People fought to avenge killings, sexual offences and property infractions. A major war mobilized up to a thousand warriors, lasted for four or five months and resulted in fifty deaths. The victors plundered the losers' gardens, destroyed their homes and slaughtered their pigs. Great fighters were highly esteemed and prowess in war qualified a man for leadership in other fields.

A second significant orientation of Huli society is male anxiety about health and physical development. Boys mature slowly and they believe that their growth can be seriously hampered by women, accidentally or intentionally. Menstruating women are considered exceptionally dangerous—if a man should be seen by one his skin will shrivel and his hair will turn grey. Copulating with an unclean woman injures a man internally, even fatally. To avoid these hazards men restrict social contact with women. They cook and prepare their own food and take ritual precautions before coitus. Women, on the other hand, attribute no such baleful influence to men. The extension of this belief in the supernatural order will be discussed presently.

2. DININI

The Huli conceive *dinini* to be the immaterial part of human personality which survives physical death and persists indefinitely in ghostly form. The *dinini* or soul is an invisible vapour which, in the waking state, occupies the space just behind the eyes. As a person becomes drowsy his soul gradually condenses and gravitates to the heart (*lilini*). Thus, a sleeping person should be wakened slowly to allow time for the soul to return to its normal position. Huli also apply the term *dinini* to human reflections and shadows; these are but images of the soul, for the true *dinini* is invisible.

The Huli say that the soul is the vital principle or vital essence of human personality. It is the soul that enables a person to perceive, think and experience emotion. In the waking state the soul spreads from its position behind the eyes so that part of it diffuses to the ears, nose and mouth, thereby making contact with the external world and registering sense impressions. In a state of anger the soul 'turns over', sinks into the heart and then suddenly spurts upwards. When it reaches the throat, anger becomes unbearable and some action must be taken to relieve tension. They explain dreaming as a *dinini* movement; during sleep the soul departs from the body of its own volition, and the dreamer experiences the perceptions of the soul. Sexual desire, too, originates in the soul, though they do not account for it in terms of movements of the *dinini*.

The Huli believe that a dying person can be saved if they seal an invisible opening at the crown of the skull (*dinini homiliaga*) from which the soul departs at death. For this purpose a fringe of hair is left growing over the aperture. When death is imminent, they grasp the tuft tightly, closing the hole, so that the soul cannot escape.

The Huli have little personal interest in the fate of the soul. They have no belief in judgement in the afterlife, and the destination of the soul in no way depends upon a person's character or behaviour prior to death. Their views about the destination or habitation of the soul are in fact hazy and uncertain; they are willing to speculate about the whereabouts of ghosts but the question has no great significance. The fate of warriors or other people slain in battle is an exception. Their ghosts go to Dalugeli, a celestial resting place about which the Huli again have few concrete notions. It is a desirable refuge, for in moments of pique people say: 'Oh, to quit this life and go to Dalugeli'. A slain warrior's ghost goes immediately to Dalugeli, but returns temporarily to the world to haunt the place where death occurred. For this reason, a killer should not utter his victim's name, lest the ghost wreak vengeance against him.

There are several views about the fate of people who die from other causes. Many people believe that the soul continues to dwell among the

living, taking an interest in their affairs. Some people say that a father's
ghost hovers over its former habitation waiting to collect the souls
of his children and his wives. Others say that the souls of the dead
sink into the pools of quiet water at river bends, or that the ghost
travels southward to the country of the Dugube where it finds a circle
of red clay, stoops to collect some and suddenly tips forward into a
black hole. At the bottom of the hole is Humbinianda, a hot, waterless
place where the soul remains indefinitely.

The belief in the persistence of the soul stresses continuity rather than
eternity; there is no positive concept of personal immortality but there
is concern with the fate of ghosts. Curiously enough, ghosts continue
to age even though they have no physical bodies. Their hair turns white,
their limbs stiffen and cataracts form on their eyes. The Huli perform
two rituals to counteract these effects of ageing. *Ega kiliapa* is a leaping
dance performed by two young men. The ghosts are attracted to the
site by the aroma of pigs cooked in their honour, witness the dance and
enthusiastically join with the dancers. The vigorous exercise loosens
their limbs. *Teba* is a rite in which the deities are asked to remove the
cataracts from the eyes of ancestral ghosts. Both rites are performed
for male ghosts only.

Male ghosts are concerned in the affairs of their descendants just as
men are concerned with the affairs of their families. Their interest is
benevolent and protective. A sick man dreams that he is surrounded by
a conclave of his male ghosts, hoary-headed, with long white beards,
who are solicitous for his recovery. No female ghosts appear in their
dreams. Just as women (with the exception of mother) are dangerous
to men, female ghosts are dangerous to their descendants, both male
and female. The Huli attribute to them greed and covetousness, the
worst characteristics of living women. They say that female ghosts
attack their descendants, particularly children, causing sores, boils and
illnesses in order to induce people to sacrifice pigs in their names. They
consider barrenness, too, both in women and pigs, to be the work of
female ghosts. They detect the responsible ghost by divination or
through a medium and dedicate a pig to that ghost. The pig must be
slaughtered at a sacrificial hut (*damanda*) located at the site of an ancestral grave. The slaughtered beast is bled inside the hut, and the ghost,
attracted by the incantation of her name, consumes the blood and the
aroma of the cooking pork. When satiated she relinquishes her attack.

Ghosts of the recently dead have little influence on human affairs
and cannot provoke or intercede with the deities. They are mainly

concerned with the family affairs of their offspring and their contemporaries. People sometimes communicate with parental ghosts through a medium or diviner. One man sought advice from his father's ghost as to whether he should kill a pig inherited from his father in a forthcoming ritual. Another wished to ascertain whether a pig that had belonged to his father had previously been dedicated to any of the deities. In both instances a medium supplied an answer.

Unlike other female ghosts, the mother's ghost never attacks her own children; her concern for her offspring persists after death, overcoming the greed and covetousness common to female ghosts. A wife's ghost is potentially dangerous to her husband, especially if the husband were responsible for her death. If she dies after a long and fruitful union, her ghost is unlikely to attack her husband; but if a couple have not lived happily her ghost may continue to plague him. Accusations against a wife's ghost are rare, for uncongenial marriages often end in divorce. Male ghosts are universally benevolent (except towards their slayers). Fathers' ghosts never assail their children, nor husbands' ghosts their widows.

The degree to which a ghost can affect its descendants for good or evil is largely dependent upon its antiquity. The ghosts of grandparents and more distant ancestors exert more power than those of parents. All male ghosts gain potency generation by generation, but this principle is modified for female ghosts. The Huli most often accuse their near ancestresses of causing sickness and harm, particularly those two to five generations from the victim. The more distant female ghosts, called kepa, are believed to possess great powers, but they exercise them rarely; in fact, only when their names are uttered without sacrifice. Thus, the Huli maintain cognatic genealogies for five or six generations, but beyond this level, only males are regularly recalled. Nevertheless, the names of the wives and daughters of parish founders are sometimes known. They are not kepa, and it is not forbidden to utter their names. The founding ancestors, both male and female, are rather aloof from human affairs. People regard them more as deities than as human ghosts, and refer to them loosely as dama. Specifically they call them dama agali duo, 'half deity-half ghost'. Thus, conceptually, the ancient ancestral ghosts are intermediate between the deities and the recent ghosts and they also function as intermediaries. The remote male ghosts have the power to dissuade the deities from assaulting their descendants. The remote female ghosts, with the exceptions mentioned, attack their descendants and also entice the deities to do so.

3. DAMA

✓   The Huli conceive the *dama* to be invisible deities possessing supra-physical powers. *Dama* control the weather, causing too much or too little rain. They attack humans, sometimes capriciously, causing sickness, infertility or death. At times they punish certain offences, or cause suffering at the bidding of sorcerers. Most *dama* are capable of causing both good and evil, but a few, such as Korimogo, are wholly malicious. *Dama*, like humans, are male and female, though the former outnumber the latter. Many male *dama* have 'wives' and often a female *dama* has several 'husbands' among the gods. There is one male *dama* called Kepei who has no phallus and who is believed to possess enormous power; only continent men may enter the house of Kepei for fear of offending him. Most *dama* attack both men and women, but a few female *dama*, such as Waliporlimia and Dunawali, are aggressive only towards males.

Huli myths (*mana*) explain the origin of the deities and the creation of man. They vary in detail from place to place, but their content is much the same. Myths contain important knowledge of the deities and of *gamu* and must not be related to strangers, to women or to young children. Myths are different from folk stories (*pi te*), and that they are a special kind of knowledge is revealed by the rules of their narration. They are recounted in the men's house at night and the occupants of the house must remain awake. If they fall asleep, the mother of the firekeeper will die. Men do not take this injunction seriously, but they impress it on young boys to ensure that they will pay attention.

—   Myths tell that at first there was land, then the deities, then men, then the bow and arrow, then fire and then water. The first inhabitant of the land was Honabe, a female deity who cooked her food by the heat of her own genitals. Honabe was seduced by a male deity, Timbu, and she later gave birth to five male deities—Korimogo, Helabe, Piandela, Ni, Helahuli—and one female deity, Hana. After a time seven other deities, the first bird and the first possum issued forth from Honabe's menstrual discharge. Today the Huli regard all of Honabe's issue as great deities.

When Helahuli grew up he married an unknown woman who bore him four sons called Huli, Opena, Dugube and Duna. They were the first human beings and each founded the culture group known to the Huli by these names. Another version of this myth tells that Ni seduced the wife of Helahuli, and consequently Ni is the true progenitor of the Huli. Thus, the Huli sometimes refer to themselves as the offspring of Ni (*Ni honowini*).

The man Huli begat many children by an unknown woman and they were the earliest settlers in the Tagari basin, cultivating not sweet potato but taro. Several generations later, the Tagari River inundated the entire basin, killing every living thing. For a time the land was empty. When the floodwaters subsided the deities re-created birds and possums, and they in turn gave birth to human progeny, the founders of the present parish groups.

The same myth describes the origin of the sun and the moon. One day the daughter of Honabe went to the forest, and when she thought no one could observe her, rubbed her body against the trunk of a tree. Unknown to Hana, she was watched by her brother Ni. One morning after Hana's departure Ni went to the forest and inserted a sharp stone into the tree trunk, placing it so that Hana could not see it. When Hana came again, the stone cut a gash in her flesh, and in this way her vulva was formed. When the bleeding ceased, Hana returned to the women's house, meeting Ni who had secretly followed her. She told him of her experience and when Ni asked to see the wound he became sexually aroused and copulated with his sister. Then they were deeply ashamed of their behaviour. Unable to face Honabe, their mother, Ni and Hana ascended to the sky, he to become the sun and she the moon. Ni and Hana had no issue from their incestuous intercourse and later Ni went to live in a cave in Duna country. There he wed a female deity who bore him round black stones. As each issued forth, Ni hurled it away, and thus they were scattered throughout Huli and Duna territory. At present Ni and Hana are both deities of major importance, and the Huli devote to them many rituals with a fertility theme.

A portion of *dama* sometimes becomes embodied in a material object, generally a stone artefact, an oddly shaped natural stone, or a fossil. One *dama* may be associated with many stone objects, yet an invisible residue is omnipresent. When not in use for rituals, the stone objects are buried and the presence of the stone instils the surrounding country with the force of the deity. People who enter these areas must therefore behave with caution. *Ni hariga* is an outstanding example of this—a forest belt ten miles in length spanning the central Tagari basin. It is believed to be the road travelled by Ni on his journey from Duna to Huli territory. No trees were cut from the area and no gardens were cultivated there.

A number of the greater deities, such as Ni, Lindu, Hone, Dindiainyia and Helabe, are associated with stone objects owned corporately by every parish. Other major *dama*, such as Kepei, have several hut-like temples each of which is the centre for the rituals of a group of parishes. The lesser deities each inhabit only one locality, and they are seldom connected with particular objects. A few of the greater deities, such as Korimogo, have no local or object associations at all, except in so far as their evil power emanates temporarily from the body of a person they have slain. The victims of Korimogo are buried with special precautions; the dead man's finger- and toe-nails are removed and their positions reversed to confuse the deity and thwart his attacks on people living in the vicinity.

Nature demons (*dama dagenda*) are a special kind of deity inhabiting the forested ranges. There they attack travellers, causing bruises, sores and bleeding noses. Unlike other deities, nature demons are unnamed and no sacrifices or rituals are enacted to placate them. Travellers try to avert their attack by employing a special vocabulary when journey-ing through their country. This confuses the demons and they hesitate to attack.

The Huli do not generally attribute specific symptoms or illnesses to particular deities. They believe, for example, that the symptoms of pneumonia may be caused by a number of deities acting individually, in concert or in collaboration with female ancestral ghosts. Thus, when a person falls ill, they consult diviners or mediums to discover the identity of the responsible god or ghost. There are exceptions to this. Ni, for example, is solely responsible for causing leprosy (*ge amua*), and three male deities—Matawali, Herabe and Podadeli—separately or in combination cause temporary or permanent insanity. There is only a small number of permanently deranged people (*yambu hara*) in Huli society and, of these, very few are dangerously aggressive. More often, men and women become temporarily insane (*lu-lu*) and frequently one individual has recurrent attacks. The fits last for four or five days and the affected person has to be restrained from wanton violence or self-injury. Men brandish bows and fire arrows indiscriminately at passers-by; women seize digging sticks or lengths of fire-wood, and assault anyone they encounter. From time to time the afflicted person falls to the ground, apparently unconscious, trembling and breathing heavi-ly. The Huli treat the symptoms by killing pigs dedicated to the deity considered responsible.

Another god believed to cause a specific pathological condition is Hugenda. A male deity, Hugenda attacks pregnant women, and as a result of the attack part of the deity lodges itself in the internal organs of the foetus. A child born with blood in its mouth is deemed to have been attacked by Hugenda. It is unfortunate for a woman to bear such a child, but the infant is in no way at fault. Treatment for the child begins three or four months after birth. Using a stone axe the child's mother cuts off the tip of its finger in order to release the 'bad blood'. Later, if the child or a member of its family falls ill, and a diviner further implicates Hugenda, additional measures must be taken. The child's father kills a fruit bat (*kimu*), makes an arrowhead from one of its bones and shoots a pig dedicated to Hugenda, while exhorting him to release the child. A person possessed by Hugenda is potentially dangerous to his family and co-residents for the rest of his life. Any sickness or misfortune suffered by the group may be attributed to Hugenda. The possessed person, however, is never held personally responsible.

Other deities attack their victims indirectly. Four female deities— Waliporlimia, Dunawali, Kapiano and Pinuwali—attack men only, but they do so by first bewitching a woman and (like Hugenda) becoming lodged in her internal organs. Bewitchment is an involuntary process but, once affected, a woman has no option but to use her evil power. A bewitched woman can be detected by her piercing gaze and exceptionally clear skin. Her victims die suddenly or after a very brief illness, and men consult diviners to confirm the cause. If the diviner accuses one of the four deities, the brothers of the dead man act to safeguard themselves from further attack. First, they visit a sorcerer to obtain medicine and spells to protect themselves from the witches' stare. After the corpse is interred, they hide within shooting distance of the coffin platform. The witch is said to visit the coffin at night to consume the dead man's flesh. If a woman approaches during the night, the brothers shoot her and her death is taken to be proof of her bewitchment. Sometimes an apparent witch is wounded, but manages to escape alive. In this event the bowman immediately attempts to unstring his bow; success indicates that the witch will die, failure that she will survive to cause other deaths. No compensation is paid for the death of a witch for she is a public menace.

The Huli do not believe in a hierarchy among the *dama* and disclaim detailed knowledge of relationships among them. They do, however, believe that the greater deities can exert some influence on the lesser, particularly in restraining them from attacking humans. In order to secure the favour of a greater *dama*, a man plants cordyline and dedicates it to him. This act is pleasing to the deity, who then takes an interest in the man. If a lesser deity attacks this man, his family or close kin, the man uproots the cordyline promising to replant it only if the major deity restrains the other from further assault. The man is careful to keep this promise for otherwise he may arouse the anger of his protector.

4. DATAGALIWABE

Datagaliwabe is no ordinary deity and indeed the Huli never call him a *dama* but refer to him only by name. His special province is punishing breaches of kinship and for this purpose he continually observes social behaviour. One man described him as a giant who, with legs astride, looks down upon all and punishes lying, stealing, adultery, murder, incest, breaches of exogamy and of taboos relating to ritual. He also penalizes those who fail to avenge the deaths of kin slain in war. He has no concern, however, with the behaviour of unrelated persons.

Datagaliwabe's punishment can take several forms. Like the deities described before, he causes sickness and accident, such as falling from a tree or drowning. He also causes men to suffer death or wounding in war. While there is no specific test to determine whether or not Datagaliwabe has caused a particular mishap, men suspect him when divination fails to implicate a specific deity or ghost. They also believe that serious breaches of kin rules are sure to provoke Datagaliwabe's wrath. Unlike the deities, Datagaliwabe cannot be propitiated or placated; no pigs are dedicated to his name, no rituals are performed for him and no prayers entreat his goodwill.

5. GAMU

The concept of *gamu* is rather difficult to formulate. The Huli conceive of *gamu* activity not in the abstract but in relation to specific ends. There are *gamu* to forecast the future, to discover missing objects, to treat pathological conditions, to ensure fertility, to promote physical development (particularly in males) and to cause harm to an enemy. *Gamu* is a special kind of behaviour, yet at the same time it is a force or power affecting the ghosts or deities created by that behaviour. Men skilled in *gamu* are successful; successful men are presumed to possess *gamu*. In time, the practitioner of *gamu* becomes personally imbued with its power—no prudent man smokes a sorcerer's pipe. By repeated use of his skill, a diviner personally acquires the power of prophecy.

Not everyone aspires to be a practitioner of *gamu*, for many of its prescriptions are burdensome and exacting. Moreover, certain forms of *gamu* endanger the person who uses them. Arrow *gamu* used in warfare is an example. As a marksman flexes his bow he repeats a spell which causes the arrow to strike the target. But, if he fails to utter the spell (a nonsense formula) correctly, the effect is reversed and the bowman himself sustains a wound. In the same way, sorcery may turn against the sorcerer who fails to carry out its precepts.

The Huli believe that ancient male ancestors invented many of the important forms of *gamu*, such as the cycle of fertility and initiation rites called Tege, and the divinatory rites called *halaga*. Many forms of *gamu* are prescribed in *mana*, the oral narratives created by the deities. Other forms of *gamu*, such as the fertility dance called *dawepeda*, are not Huli in origin; emissaries from Dugube country sold them to the Huli within living memory. The source of many kinds of *gamu* is unknown and no one offers to explain their origin except to say that they are traditional.

The simplest form of *gamu* is the spell (*dawe habe*). A spell may be a collection of meaningful sentences addressed to a particular deity or ghost, or it may be a meaningless utterance addressed to no one. There are spells to counteract illness caused by the attacks of ghosts or deities and spells for women in labour and for the healing of wounds. In one spell, used before a fight, men address the ghosts of warrior-kinsmen at Dalugeli and bid them to intercede with the deities so that the fighting will be brief, the enemy defeated and the casualties few. Another consists simply of the word *nguibe* ('nasal mucus'): when a pig despoils a garden, this spell can bring down sickness on the plundering animal.

Another elementary form of *gamu* is the oblation (*pupu*)—an offering dedicated to a deity or to an ancestral ghost on condition that a wish be fulfilled. The offering may be a pig which the bestower promises to kill in the name of the patron ghost or deity. It may be a string of cowrie shells which is hung permanently in the sacrificial hut. An oblation may not be used for a second purpose for, if it is, the patron deity or ghost will take offence and attack the giver. Thus, an oblation is a kind of provisional contract; in consideration for a fee, the deity or ghost performs a service.

It is possible to distinguish among the many varieties of *gamu* on the basis of the means-to-ends relationship postulated by the Huli. Some forms of *gamu* are considered to be directly efficacious; their action is mechanical or automatic. Provided the prescriptions of the *gamu* are fully carried out, the desired end must be attained. The Huli attribute the failure of this type of *gamu* to careless performance. Arrow *gamu* is an example—it involves no appeal to the ghosts or deities, yet it succeeds only because they uphold it.

A belief in fate or destiny is implicit in the way the Huli interpret natural phenomena as omens (*piyanguma*). If an earthworm appears directly in front of a person, it signifies that a deity will soon attack him. When a pig squeals for no apparent reason, someone will fall ill and men will have to kill pigs to placate the responsible deity. People vary widely in the amount of faith they place in omens. Consulting a diviner is a more reliable means of prophecy. Many techniques are available, and I will illustrate my point with two of them. *Halaga toro gamu* employs the bones of a recently slain warrior, preferably those of a particularly aggressive fighter. Several months after the interment, two diviners collect the bones from the coffin, wrap them in pandanus leaves and deposit them in the divining hut (*toranda*). The two must observe certain taboos. One can lead a normal life but the other, the practising diviner, must remain continent or his predictions will fail. The diviners periodically alternate in their roles. In addition, neither may enter the hut while his wife is menstruating, pregnant or suckling an infant. If either breaks these taboos, the forecasts will be wrong and the offender exposes himself and his close kin to the anger of the deities. Only men consult *toro* diviners, and they pay a fee of a half-side of pork. Their questions must be phrased for a yes or no response. With the package of bones before him, the diviner repeats the questions and then attempts to lift the package, using only his index finger. If he cannot raise it, the reply is negative; if he succeeds, it is affirmative. The bones remain 'potent' for four or five months; if they forecast wrongly, they are buried.

Female diviners employ a technique based on the belief that the ghosts of recently dead relatives, male and female, have prophetic powers. To attract a ghost, some object formerly associated with the dead person, such as a tuft of hair or an armband, is placed in a tiny string-bag (*nu*). The more recent the death, the better the chance of attracting the ghost. Success is also more likely if the dead person is a close relative of the diviner. Once the string-bag has been animated by the presence of a ghost, it answers questions put to it by the diviner, swaying to the right for an affirmative response, to the left for a negative. The average life of a charged string-bag is three months; an exceptionally potent one is five months. When a string-bag forecasts wrongly people believe that the ghost has departed. String-bag diviners serve both male and female clients—receiving for their work a fee of pork or cowrie shells.

Yet the Huli do not believe that a man's lot is fully or inexorably determined. There are some forms of *gamu* through which men seek conditional rather than prophetic knowledge. They are not concerned with the question 'What will happen next?', but 'What will happen if. . . ?' People make many important decisions on the basis of these trials, particularly when the outcome of a course of action is very uncertain. The decision to avenge a slain kinsman by direct retaliation is sometimes taken in this way. A kinswoman of the victim comes to the mourning hut (*tuganda*) where the body is laid out late at night. She lifts the dead man's phallus and releases it. If it remains upright, immediate retaliation will succeed without casualties to the avengers, but, if it falls, the avengers will suffer loss. On the basis of this knowledge, the avengers decide their course of action.

The Huli call on the deities to provide retrospective as well as prophetic and conditional knowledge. Oath-taking (*tera*) is a form of *gamu* whereby two people invoke certain deities to decide issues of fact or of personal responsibility. Each calls on the deities to attest his innocence. Men frequently employ oaths at informal trials or moots and, as oath-taking has jural consequences for the participants, it is an important means of settling conflict.

Only a few men know the appropriate incantations to call down the deities, but for a fee they perform this service for kinsmen and friends. One antagonist must make preparations before challenging his opponent. He enlists an imprecator and at a sacrificial hut slaughters a pig dedicated to nine deities. He cooks the pork, wraps it in banana leaves and conceals it in his string-bag. When discussion in the moot reaches an impasse or turns against him, he dramatically produces the bespelled pork and challenges his opponent to join in taking an oath. If the latter refuses, the challenger argues that the refusal proves guilt. If he accepts, the challenger calls on an oath-giver to invoke the deities and each contender solemnly repeats the imprecation, phrase by phrase: 'If I lie, let my eyes be blinded, my hearing fail, my skin become dry and my penis fall off.' So saying, one smites the other with the pork and in turn accepts a blow.

An oath should take effect within eight days. Any close relative of an oath-taker who falls seriously ill, suffers an injury, or dies in that time is thought to be a victim of the deities. If no serious harm befalls either kin group, the period of danger is prolonged for another six weeks. Casualties that occur during the extended period are more difficult to interpret; the group that suffers can deny that the nine deities are responsible, assigning its misfortune instead to the malice of some other deity or ghost. Should both kin groups sustain injury, the test is again equivocal. There is no precisely defined group of kin implicated by an oath, an ambiguity which poses further problems of interpretation.

A man can also call down the wrath of the nine deities by cursing (also *tera*) but this, unlike oath-taking, is a unilateral action. There need be no issue at stake; usually the curser is retaliating against a specific adversary for some injury. He too enlists the service of an imprecator, sacrifices a pig and invokes the deities. This curse also should take effect within eight days, but the deities do not always act in response to an oath or a curse. If an imprecation fails, it may be repeated or some other form of action, such as sorcery or physical coercion, may be substituted.

Toro gamu, a form of sorcery, is a surer way of causing harm. When overt retaliation is dangerous or impossible, the Huli fall back on *Toro gamu*. They explain its action in quasi-mechanical terms; by following the prescriptions of the *mana* the sorcerer attracts the deity Toro to certain stones in his possession. Imbued with the power of the deity the stones emit a stream of invisible, lethal particles which the sorcerer can aim in any direction but not so accurately as to strike only a particular person. Anyone in their path may also be struck down, including those not intended as targets.

A man wishing to become a sorcerer procures the *mana* story and certain objects from a practising sorcerer, preferably from Duna where the method originated. It is a costly purchase, equal in value to a bride price, and the equipment includes a red string-bag filled with small stones and a bog-iris corm (*podama*) to protect the owner from the deity Toro. The *mana* gives directions for performing the rites and observing the taboos necessary to activate the stones. But mere knowledge of the *mana* is no guarantee of success; the preliminaries must be correctly performed lest the deity turn on the sorcerer himself, or the stones acquire only the power to kill two or three people instead of ten or fifteen. One preliminary requires the sorcerer to run the length of a narrow, slippery platform six feet above the ground without falling.

Toro particles can cause sickness, accident, or injury in war. A corpse may show no outward sign that *Toro* has caused death but, if an autopsy reveals black spots on the dead man's lungs, *Toro* is held responsible.

—— To repel *Toro* emanations the Huli purchase a piece of a tree that grows in Duna country, daub it with pig's blood and bespell and bury it near their houses. The stick (*manago helo gamu*) deflects the stream of deadly particles and thus safeguards the inhabitants of the house.

—— There are other forms of sorcery that do not require the participation of the deities. *Hambu gamu*, recently acquired from the Pai-yela people, is directly efficacious. The sorcerer faces in the direction of the enemy, incants a spell and breaks a small stick into pieces. Each fracture damages the victim's limbs, though the effect is not immediately apparent. Three months later he has fits of shivering and fever; abscesses and boils appear and, unless counter-measures are taken, he dies soon afterwards.

When a person eating pork or some other tasty food fails to offer a morsel to a visitor, a minor breach of etiquette, the affronted person retaliates with *Linki gamu*, sorcery causing temporary disability. The visitor covertly swallows his saliva and mumbles a spell. This propels portion of his own soul through the victim's anus and into his stomach, causing him to vomit and suffer diarrhoea. To give him relief, a kinsman recites another spell which forces the sorcerer's soul to depart. But, before doing so, the kinsman must close the openings in the victim's head to prevent the escape of the victim's own soul.

The Huli employ many kinds of *gamu* (collectively, *hubibi*) for protection against indiscriminate attacks by ghosts and deities, and from the covert malice of their enemies. Before an encounter, a warrior rubs a bespelled stone to make himself invulnerable to his enemies and invisible to the deities. Women recite spells to safeguard their kinsmen and husbands when a fight is imminent. In times of danger men test gifts of food for poison; they hang the food from a bespelled stick and, if fireflies collect around it, they know it is tainted.

There are other varieties of *gamu* that ensure the health and physical growth of males. Some rites are individual; others are organized by the parish group as a whole. The latter include the initiation rites in the *Tege* (*gurumaigiti gamu*) and the bachelors' ritual (*haroli gamu*). About one out of every two youths in the late teens elects to join the parish bachelors' group and to pay an entrance fee of cowrie shells and pork. Each member cultivates a bog-iris to ensure the health and welfare of all members of the group and, if an iris withers, it is thought that a member will fall ill or suffer some other misfortune. The youths believe that such irises do not die naturally but only when a bachelor corrupts the group by breaking the taboo on association with women. Myths connect the irises with female blood and tell of their origin in ground where a woman's blood was shed many generations ago. Each group now owns a small bamboo tube, said to contain a portion of that blood which, together with the irises, protects the bachelors from the evil emanations of menstruating women.

For about two years the new members receive training in a secluded house. They learn *gamu* to make their skins 'firm' and their hair grow, and they are taught to be self-reliant and to disdain physical comfort. At the end of the period they emerge from their confinement wearing the red, crescent-shaped ceremonial wig that symbolizes manhood. Dressed in their finest feathers, shells and possum skins, they paint their faces in traditional patterns with red and yellow clay and their bodies glisten with oil. They parade in single file through their own and adjacent parish-territories for three or four days, rarely speaking to each other or to onlookers. Each carries a strung bow in one hand and an arrow in the other. Men who see them praise their appearance in measured tones; from a distance women strain to catch a glimpse of them, for if they approach too closely the bachelors run away. For about one year the bachelors parade at monthly intervals. Between appearances they live in ordinary men's houses but, like all young men, accept no food from women. In addition they avoid the sight of women and refrain from discarding scraps of food wherever a woman might tread. These precautions are taken to prevent their irises from withering. But the bachelors are still at times exposed to feminine influences and to cleanse themselves they perform monthly purificatory rites, washing their eyes under a waterfall to remove the stigma of the female image. Women greatly admire the young bachelors and regard them as attractive future husbands.

Fertility is the theme of a large number of Huli rites, ranging from personal garden spells (*mabu gamu*) to the Earth Ritual (*dindi gamu*) which took place some thirty years ago. To promote garden fertility a man bespells some leaves of the crops he intends to plant, burns them and turns the ash into the soil. He may also slaughter a pig dedicated to the two deities, Dinditane and Wandatilepu, who are specifically concerned with garden fertility. Not everyone performs these rites. People who garden in newly cleared forest land seldom employ *gamu*, and some men believe that group fertility rites are sufficient. There is

D

one rite (*kimbu gamu*) that ensures fertility in women, pigs and gardens. A man procures smooth round stones from the Tagari River which, when bespelled, acquire the power to instil fertility by contact. Before copulating with his wife for the first time, the man rubs one stone between her breasts, buries a second where his pigs feed and embeds the third in the middle of a new garden.

The *Tege* is a series of rites devoted in part to fertility. The entire sequence is spread over several years, and there are no fixed intervals between component rites. Timing depends rather on omens, such as a violent storm or a drought, on the availability of pigs, sweet potatoes and other foods, and on the current political relationships among participant groups. The cycle begins with the sacrifice of a pig to Ni and other deities by members of the sponsoring parish-section (*Tege tene*). The deities consume the pig's blood and the aroma of the cooking pork. Women, girls and married men eat the meat and fat. The head is reserved for unmarried and continent elderly men. The explicit purpose of the sacrifice is to propitiate the deities. The next rite takes place months later, when another omen indicates that one or more of the deities is again hostile towards the sponsoring group. This rite also consists of a pig sacrifice dedicated to the powerful deity Korimogo. The group sacrifices pigs until the omen departs, consulting diviners or mediums to determine which deity should be placated. Several months after completing six prescribed sacrifices, the *Tege tene* perform the *Teba*, a rite to remove the cataracts from the eyes of their male ancestors, followed by the sacrificial rite called *Himuku*, dedicated to both the deities and the ancient male ancestors.

The culminating rite in the cycle—the *Tege* proper—lasts for six days and five nights. It may be precipitated by a catastrophe, such as an epidemic, or it may be held in acknowledgement of the deities' favour. About a dozen men called the *liduali*, who are versed in the *mana* of *Tege*, direct proceedings. One or two may be members of the host parish-section, but most come from other sections or other parishes. Like *Toro* sorcerers, *liduali* are dangerous because of their association with the deities. They do not lend their pipes to other men; their ghosts are more powerful than those of ordinary men; when they die, their skulls are preserved and anointed together with the stones of Ni.

The *Tege tene* choose two of their members to lead the performance. The pair, called *uriali*, carry out the instructions of the *liduali* and, after officiating twice, become *liduali* themselves. One must be an agnate of the host group, the other a cognate who is not an agnate.[3] This choice simultaneously stresses the structural duality within the parish-section and the complementary relationship of the categories; the agnatic *uriali* receives a payment from the non-agnatic members and the non-agnate receives an equal payment from the agnates.

On the first day of the *Tege*, the spectacular *pulu* dance is performed. Men and women of the *Tege tene* lead the dance, followed by the group that is to receive the prestation. They in turn head a procession of male dancers from surrounding parish groups. There are several hundred participants and about a thousand onlookers, all elaborately decorated. The ancestral ghosts of the *Tege tene* also attend, attracted by the preliminary sacrifices. It is they who influence the deities to make gardens fertile, provided that the rite has been properly celebrated.

Space does not permit a description of the other rites which follow the *pulu* dance—the numerous initiation rites, the exchange and distribution of the food and the subsequent feast, and the rites to ensure the health of the *liduali*. Nor can I describe in detail how men and youths run through a bed of glowing embers or how ritualized fighting erupts among the *Tege tene* for one vindictive hour just before dawn. These events have purposes other than the promotion of fertility, but at the same time they gain for the performers the approbation of the ghosts and deities, without which crops fail, women bear no children and pigs cannot multiply.

The concern with garden fertility which the Huli manifest in ritual may appear extravagant in view of the richness of their soil and the generally favourable environment. Yet rainfall is erratic and from time to time this results in poor garden yields. In addition the Huli believe that fall-outs of pumiceous silt, called *bingi*, have produced great although temporary increases of garden productivity. No living person has witnessed such an occurrence but people, when digging ditches, find lumps of pumice, discoveries that give credence to the myth.

Thunder, lightning and earth tremors herald the coming of *bingi*. The sky darkens and for four days grey silt falls from the sky, covering the mounds of sweet potatoes, choking the streams and destroying unprotected crops. For a time food is scarce, but people quickly plant new crops and these flourish in the enriched soil. When the crops are harvested, the pigs benefit from the superabundance and multiply rapidly. A fall-out of *bingi* ushers in a period of plenty.

The Huli believe that *bingi* has occurred several times and *mana*

tales give practical and ritual precautions to take in the event of a recurrence. When *bingi* appears imminent, men should at once construct
houses large enough to shelter an entire parish with its dogs and pigs
and provide in each house a supply of food and water sufficient for
several days. They should also cover gardens with grass to prevent
their destruction. Ritual precautions are taken to ensure that *bingi*
does not last longer than four days. Sexual relations are forbidden
during the time of the fall-out of silt, and to ensure this all wives
should return to their natal parishes. The only people permitted to
leave the shelter are men who are the last surviving sons of their parents
—other people who do so risk death. If these rules are not followed,
bingi will destroy all life.

The Huli do not attribute *bingi* to volcanic eruptions or other natural
phenomena. They surmise that the deities (*dama*) are ultimately responsible, but they have no concept of a specific causative agent. In
the last two generations they have made two major attempts to secure
a recurrence of *bingi*. About fifty years ago they undertook without
success a traditional pig-killing rite called *Ega Wandari gamu*, which
parish after parish performed in a customary sequence. A generation
later they adapted a rite (*Dindi gamu*) from the Dugube people, which
was also unsuccessful. The Huli attribute the failure of *Dindi gamu* to
an excess of enthusiasm. The finger of a red-skinned Duna child was
to be pricked, his blood mixed with the blood of a pig and the mixture
sprinkled in areas of poor fertility. But, instead of pricking the child's
finger, the Huli butchered him and scattered the dismembered body in
their gardens, a fatal deviation from the *mana* instructions. In 1955
several earth tremors led the Huli to believe that a recurrence of *bingi*
was imminent. Remembering their earlier behaviour, the men who
had killed the child hastily paid compensation to his relatives in Duna,
fearing that *bingi* would otherwise prove catastrophic. *Bingi* is outside
the range of ordinary experience, and Huli beliefs do not adequately
explain it for them. Thus, they are ambivalent about its possible recurrence. On the one hand, they are eager for the putative increase
in garden fertility; on the other, they view *bingi* as a dangerous threat
which could lead to complete devastation.

The Huli supernatural world is populated by the ghosts of the dead,
the deities and Datagaliwabe. The deities strike many of their victims
indiscriminately but certain forms of behaviour provoke them to
attack specific individuals, groups or categories of people. The deity
Toro responds to the sorcerer's injunction and sends lethal particles

in the direction of the sorcerer's foe. There are the nine deities who act when two men join an oath. The greater deities specifically disapprove of certain outrageous acts; they punish the duplicity of the man who avenges a killing, while accepting wergild payment for that killing, and they punish trespassers on dedicated land. A person who utters Korimogo's name will be struck down by that deity unless he sacrifices pigs at the same time.

Yet the deities are not generally concerned with the behaviour of men. They are indifferent to most immoral acts, such as incest or the slaughter of a kinsman. They neither sanction breaches nor regularly reward conformity to the norms. They are aloof from human affairs. Nevertheless, the Huli endeavour to influence them and win their favour by acts of *gamu*. Corporate rituals aim at general approbation; individual rites have more limited goals. *Gamu* is, however, a circular self-fulfilling concept: the successful warrior, the mother of many children, the person who enjoys good health are all presumed to have won the deities' support.

The performance of corporate rites of *gamu* has great structural significance in Huli society. Membership in the parish entails participation in its rituals, drawing together people living in different group territories. A rite not only mobilizes the active members of a parish, it also provides an opportunity for new members to participate. Usually the new recruit belongs to the stock associated with the parish; he converts a potential right to membership status by his action over a period. The opposite process also occurs. A member loses parish rights by failing to meet his ritual obligations. In Huli society recruitment into, and resignation from groups, are continual processes. Rites enable men to demonstrate their personal status.

The soul animates human personality, giving rise to perception, thought and emotion. Released from the body at death it persists indefinitely either in Dalugeli, the celestial resting place for people slain in war, or in Humbinianda, a vaguely conceived though less desirable abode. The living are not concerned with the fate of their own souls. They do not believe in rewards or punishments in the afterlife. The Huli are concerned, however, with the ancestral ghosts, for they cause living people to suffer or gain for them release from suffering.

The powers of the ancestors increase with their antiquity, and the nature of their behaviour depends mainly upon their sex. Male ancestors are essentially benevolent: interested in their descendants, they intercede with the deities on their behalf. If no sacrifices are made for them, male ancestors remain neutral or inactive. Female ancestors, except for the mother's ghost, are indifferent to the well-being of their descendants and inflict sores and illnesses to wring sacrifices from them. This view of the ghosts is an extension of Huli beliefs about human nature. Women are inherently evil owing to their menstrual role, and their wickedness persists in the afterlife.

Humans are descended from the deities, and ancient ancestors are more powerful than recent ghosts because they are nearer the deities. Although they require sacrifices from their descendants, the ghosts, like the deities, do not generally sanction social behaviour. They neither punish breaches of kinship rules nor reward meritorious actions.

Belief in the existence of the ghosts is relevant to the cognatic structure of the parish group. The need to offer sacrifices to the named, known ghosts encourages the preservation of genealogical knowledge, upon which the groups are founded. Every man knows his agnatic parish group, whether or not he is currently a member of it. Most people know of about eight parishes to which they are cognatically related and they are active members of three or four at any given time. Belief in ghosts provides the incentive to conserve this genealogical knowledge.[4]

Datagaliwabe is in no way associated with the ghosts or *dama*. He never acts capriciously, requires no sacrifices and is aloof from human influence. His sole concern is to punish kinship offences. People may commit murder, theft or rape against non-kin without incurring his disapproval but, when a relative is the victim, he automatically punishes the wrongdoer. A man who fails to avenge his brother's murder is equally at fault.

The concept of Datagaliwabe is also pertinent to the structure of Huli society. As every man belongs simultaneously to several parish groups, no single group claims his full allegiance at any time. Because of this, no parish group can wholly constrain a member's behaviour or force him to honour his obligations. Individualistic behaviour prevails and residential fluidity is the rule. There is a high rate of interpersonal conflict, and the responsibility for initiating war falls on a single instigator on each side. This may be compared with the group pressures that prevail in unilineally organized societies lacking institutionalized authority. There clans or lineages can exert influence on an unruly member; they can restrict his property rights, ridicule his behaviour, or ostracize him. A Huli, however, can evade all these penalties by taking up residence with another parish group in which he has cognatic rights. Belief in Datagaliwabe lends support to the machinery of social control. Moral obligations diminish or disappear beyond the range of kinship ties. Datagaliwabe provides moral sanction within that range, and failure to fulfil an obligation towards kin of any parish group goads him into action. A man can escape his obligations in one parish by fleeing to another territory, but he cannot escape the omnipresent eye of Datagaliwabe.

NOTES

[1] The following account is based on anthropological field work which I undertook as a Research Scholar of the Australian National University and as a W. M. Strong Research Fellow of the University of Sydney. I thank both universities for their financial support.

[2] Other relevant information on the Huli is given in Glasse (1959a; 1959b; 1962).

[3] Compare the analogous arrangement made in some rituals among the Ipili to the north (Meggitt 1957b: p. 52).

[4] This argument is developed in greater detail in Glasse (1962).

R. F. SALISBURY

The Siane of the Eastern
Highlands[1]

THIS paper is mainly a description of Siane beliefs and practices
relating to supernatural beings. These beliefs are presented in a
formal way, not because the Siane themselves systematically formulate
dogma, but to show how the anthropologist can infer a coherent
theology from the scattered explanations of particular items of behaviour which informants give. The process of making such inferences
and the disconformities between beliefs and action are left for more
extensive treatment elsewhere. The present formal treatment of beliefs
has the advantage, however, of enabling me to relate beliefs to formal
elements in the social structure, as I attempt to do in section 3,
'Religion and Society'. The generally close relationship between formal
beliefs and social structure throws into relief a paradox which I consider in the final section. I try to explain the great emotional intensity
and mystical reverence associated with women's rites in a society in
which the organization of all social groupings revolves around males.

1. THE SIANE PEOPLES

The Siane are a congeries of tribes living in the Eastern Highlands
District of New Guinea, in the mountainous area just to the west of
the Goroka Plain. They number some 15,000 people and inhabit about
200 square miles of precipitous mountain ridges, deep valleys and limestone chasms. The sovereign political unit in Siane is the clan-village
of 200 to 250 individuals; although there are certain larger named
units, there is no feeling of unity within them. The term *Siane* defines
a linguistic and cultural area which is not demarcated by significant
social boundaries.

The Siane live in villages along the minor ridges of the mountains
at elevations between 6,000 and 7,000 feet: higher up, the mountains

50

are covered by primary moss forest; the uninhabitable valley bottoms are at about 5,500 feet. Each village consists of a 'street' running along the ridge which is flanked by some fifty small round houses where the women and children live. Two or three large oval 'men's houses', where all men live, block the village street at intervals. A fence surrounds each men's house, its complex of adjoining small houses and a large clearing where public activities take place. Each men's house holds between thirty and forty males, whose mothers, wives and children live in the nearest women's houses. A married man usually builds for his wife both a house in the village and a 'pig house' in the bush, away from the village, for her use when she is tending his gardens and his pigs.

The gardens and the pasture for the pigs lie on the mountain slopes on both sides of the village. Cultivation is by bush-fallow methods; small new areas of secondary forest are cleared every three or four months. Each area is cropped over a period of eighteen months and is then left fallow for some fifteen years under *kunai* grass, scrubby bush, or casuarina pines. Gardens are initially planted with mixed sweet potatoes, taro, yams, maize, green vegetables, bananas and sugar cane. Most vegetables yield only once, except that sweet potatoes, the main crop, bear throughout the life of the garden, and bananas and sugar produce crops only shortly before the garden is exhausted.

Productive tasks are divided into men's work (which requires the use of an axe) and women's work. Men clear garden sites, fence them, cut poles to support yams and sugar cane, and cut down banana trees for replanting. Women grub out roots with digging sticks, plant the principal crops, and weed, harvest and cook them. Growing crops belong to the person who tends them, be they 'male' or 'female' crops. Women do the daily tasks of caring for pigs; men bring in newly farrowed piglets from the bush. Men construct houses; women collect straw for the thatch. Men beat out bark for women's clothing; women spin bark thread for making net bags which men wear as aprons. Before the coming of the steel axe the division of labour was equitable.

Although the clan-village is the most obvious group in Siane, there are many other levels of grouping both larger and smaller. The largest of these is the tribe, of which there are sixteen of varying size. Tribes rarely unite for action but they use a common name which basically refers to the land on which the constituent clans reside. Members of the same tribe can, in the most extended usage, call each other 'brother'. Groups of two or three clans who prohibit intermarriage are called in Siane *nenta wenena*[2] ('close people')—a term which I shall translate as 'phratries'. Phratries may be coterminous with the landholding tribe, if the latter is small; but larger tribes have several phratries, which may intermarry and which are the important political and religious units. Phratry myths of origin tell either how they emerged from the land on which they live, or how, following a migration, clans became linked in their present locations. Phratries rarely combine for common activity as most inter-clan activities revolve around marriage, which is impossible within the phratry. Fighting to kill is forbidden within this unit, but a phratry does not unite to fight outsiders. Instead, when one clan is fighting it is dependent on the neutrality of its phratry-mates to facilitate an eventual peace settlement.[3] I shall discuss in later sections the ritual stressing of phratry unity.

The clan level of grouping is the one most discussed by the Siane; idealized narratives of what occurs in ceremonies or in politics have the form 'We, Antomona (clan) did this: they, Waifo (clan) did that.' The clan is patrilineal and localized, usually in one village, with males living with their fathers and wives coming from those near-by clans which are not of the same phratry. 'Sisters' of the clan leave the village in marriage. Males try to retain ties with married sisters by visiting, gift-giving, and ritual, but in daily life they place greater emphasis on incorporating wives into their own group, especially after they have borne children. A wife uses the same kin terms as her husband, she is addressed by teknonymy, she participates in village ceremonials and she is expected to assist her husband's group in warfare against her natal group. Clansmen know the name of the original ancestor and connect him with the phratry origin myth, but they do not know the names of his descendants or a genealogy to relate all members of the clan. Nevertheless they always use kin terms or proper names for each other, and they take corporate responsibility for each other in the blood-feud that follows a death.

Each clan is divided into residential groupings centring about the men's houses. Men's house groups tend to be descent groups like the clans, although no genealogies connect all members and sons do not always reside with fathers.

The smallest Siane level of grouping I term, for convenience, a lineage. Lineages have neither proper names nor a generic term to describe them. Numbering some ten individuals each, they jointly recognize one member of each generation as an 'oldest brother' (*yarafo*) and one as an 'oldest sister' (*atarafo*). An idealized (though objectively inaccurate) genealogy connects members together. The lineage owns the most important land rights, which the 'oldest brother' of the parental generation exercises. He acts as the lineage representative in arranging marriages and in disputes, and pronounces ritual speeches owned by the lineage. I shall refer to him as a 'lineage head'. A man's lineage forms his close kin, who attend all his rites of passage and whose contributions to his payments do not, even informally, require repayment. It is the basic work group for clearing garden plots; it allocates the cleared plots for cultivation by wives; its males receive their cooked food as a single unit. Seniority within each generation determines succession to lineage headship, and all lineage members can hope to be head at some time, though many reach 'retiring age' before doing so.[4]

The role of lineage head is the only ascribed political status. Most power is in the hands of 'big men', of whom there may be seven in a men's house, who have achieved respect by their ability in council, their activity, and their oratorical and financial skills. Many 'big men' are also lineage heads, but there is no necessary connection between the two statuses. Policy, particularly about payments to other clans, is discussed inside each men's house at night, with 'big men' taking the lead. Informal discussions between the 'big men' of several men's houses confirm clan policy, which is executed by each men's house acting separately. One 'big man' represents his men's house in relations with other men's houses (or represents the clan if a member of his house has relations with a member of another clan). Nowadays he is often termed a *bosboi*. He is an organizing focus for the men's house but has no generalized authority. Traditionally no one person always represented the clan, although now the Government appointed *luluai* is assuming this role.

Most representation of the clan involves the presentation of pork and numbers of 'valuables' to the representative of another clan at a dance or feast. The valuables consist of many kinds of shells, bird-of-paradise plumes, bark strips to which have been sewn small shells, and more recently lengths of red cloth and pound notes. They are presented at all rites of passage and at other ceremonies, often in exchange for certain rights over the recipient's clan (for example, a bridal payment is given for rights over the bride's reproductive powers) but also in order to put the recipients in a generalized position of inferiority. The giving of payments is the major means of inter-clan political rivalry in Siane. Collecting payments together and contributing to the payments of others are the major means of achieving status within a clan.

For men already in the system increased participation comes from increasing the rate of circulation of valuables owned; a newcomer can start only by breeding pigs until he has capital. Pigs and their fertility provide the real basis for what is in fact the rapid circulation of numbers of credit tokens.

The logic of inter-group relations underlying the payments of pork and valuables is one of clan autonomy in politics but clan interdependence in obtaining wives. Each clan is related to every near-by clan (except those of its own phratry) as affines (*nitofa*), a relationship involving formal politeness and ceremonial exchanges of valuables, but also the possibility of open warfare. Alliance with, and hostility towards, particular affinally-related clans alternate at roughly ten-year intervals. But, although clans as unit-wholes have these political relationships, each individual within a clan maintains permanent friendly ties with his mother's natal clan.

Personal ties of friendship are used to obtain, in a form of tradepartner relationship, scarce luxuries such as nuts or salt produced in distant areas. Personal ties also facilitate courting and eventually lead to renewing affinal ties (and schisms). Courting is done by small groups of boys who visit the girls of other villages in which one of their number has a mother's brother. They arrive at about 8 p.m. and, if invited in, sing and sleep in the girls' club house. Intercourse rarely takes place and marriages are precipitated when, after a boy has indicated his liking by nightly visits, the girl decides to elope to his village. Courting visits are termed *awoiro*.

To sum up the structure of Siane society, it is one of numerous small sovereign clans, each one composed of several levels of segmental groupings. Each clan is opposed to most other clans through a distributive opposition, phrased in terms of affinal relations, the payment of valuables, and warfare or alliance. Ensuring some form of cohesion between the sovereign groups are the mutual interdependence for obtaining wives, the existence of phratry groupings to facilitate peacemaking, and the cross-cutting ties of individual personal friendship. Within clans, cohesion is based on the alliance of segments against outsiders, economic interdependence of men and women, and close personal friendship between age-mates. Age-mates may come from different segments of the clan but are initiated together and remain socially identified even after death. These are the formal features of the social structure which, as I shall try to show, are symbolized in the religion.

2. SIANE RELIGION

(a) The cosmos

I obtained no Siane accounts of the creation of the world. There is a god, *Oma Rumufa* (Black Way), who existed before men did, and phratry origin myths usually begin 'When *Oma Rumufa* was abroad...' Otherwise *Oma Rumufa* is rarely referred to and no ceremonies are explicitly directed to him. He controls some cosmological events like the daily passage of the sun, but such phenomena happen regularly and need no human prayers. However, a purifying, peace-enjoining ritual occurs in many ceremonies, in which people tear a branch apart lengthwise, calling on the sun to 'break' them as the branch is broken if they disrupt the ceremony. *Oma Rumufa* may symbolize the sun, but I could get no explicit confirmation of this, although as ruler over a land of the dead he takes the form of a circle of white light.

Accepted in much the same way, as immanent in the physical universe but generally indifferent to human actions, are numerous spirit-beings. Some which cause storms have unspecified forms but can be frightened away (or delayed until one reaches shelter) by firing arrows. Others, generically called *reyana*, have the form of snakes or fireflies and capriciously harm humans if disturbed, for example, by inflicting venereal disease.

In general, however, the physical universe is seen as having always existed, as running smoothly without human intervention, under the direction of spirit-beings who are indifferent to man unless he disturbs them.

(b) Man and the supernatural

Man, pigs and certain other animals have both a body and a supernatural aspect, for which I shall use the term 'spirit', though the Siane conceive it as a non-material, non-discrete spiritual essence. In life the spirit in an individual is termed his *oinya*; after death his *oinya* becomes his *korova*; at a later ceremony the spirit becomes part of an undifferentiated 'pool' of *korova*, elements of which later enter another body to become its *oinya*. 'Spirit' is the basic Siane religious concept and the remainder of this section will describe, first the behaviour of spirit in individual forms, then ways in which individuals can directly manipulate individual spirits and finally the ways in which groups influence undifferentiated spirit.[5]

A person's *oinya* is variously thought of as residing in his blood, his hair, his sexual organs, his breath or his shadow. It can leave his body in sleep, when he sees dreams. In its material form it appears as a white mucous secretion called *oko*, and emotions show the movement of the spirit, the blood, or *oko* inside the body. Thus too much spirit makes the belly 'hot', produces undesirable anger, and necessitates an exchange of gifts 'to make the belly smooth'. Sickness may be caused by bad blood (that is foreign *oko*) and is cured by bloodletting. The latter may be real or magical, as when a native 'doctor' bleeds a pig to death to remove bad blood from the pig's owner. Alternatively, cold blood indicates that the *oinya* may become a *korova* and that the individual may die. To remedy such coldness 'heat' is applied in the form of hot liquids, 'hot' food, especially meat flavoured with salt and ginger, or the smearing on of red clay. Headaches indicate an imminent loss of the *oinya* and are cured by securing the *oinya* with a 'strong' object. One can tie a band round the patient's forehead, wrap drops of his blood in 'strong' ferns and bury the bundle in clan land, or insert a lock of his hair in the socket of an arrow shaft and secure it with the head of a man-killing arrow. Used prophylactically these techniques avert the danger of spirit loss and death, as, for example, when a Siane man visits a foreign clan or leaves for indentured labour. Possession indicates the entry of either a foreign *oinya* or a *korova*; I shall discuss possession after describing *korova*.

Korova have human form but have many characteristics diametrically opposed to those of humans. They are white and insubstantial, emerge only at night and like cold and quiet while disliking strong smells and sexuality; humans are black and material, and love daylight, warmth, noise, odours and sex. The *korova* of a newly dead person continues the actions of the person when alive. It frequents the same places, associates with the same people and worries about unpaid obligations. It is angry at being separated from its body and may 'hit' its associates or its enemies, the *korova* of women being more capricious and vindictive than those of men. When incorporated into the undifferentiated body of ancestral spirits, *korova* lose all personal vindictiveness. If they 'hit' humans it is construed as being, in some inscrutable way, for the general good.

When *korova* hit people and they become possessed (*turiye*), the first sensation is of a cold wind passing. This presses on the eardrums and produces deafness, which may not be complete but gives a feeling of detachment from the world. The possessed person takes on a fixed look and responds to no physical stimuli, but only to the spirit inside him. If a foreign *oinya* or a newly-dead male *korova* possesses him, he runs berserk and is approached only by daylight, or he invades houses and needs forcible restraint. A newly-dead female *korova* appears to him as indistinguishable from a live woman and seduces him into running through the bush until he is torn to pieces by thorns, has fallen to his death in a limestone fissure, or has discovered a priceless new salt spring. Such is the capricious way of women.

If the possessing *korova* is a long-dead one, the behaviour is less violent but of longer duration and must be tolerated and humoured (unless it is homicidal or suicidal). It may range from over-masculinity in an elderly woman, whose aberrations are treated as humorous even when materially destructive, through recurrent episodes of kleptomania, to chronic psychoses where the possessed person dances and sings incoherently and wanders from village to village being treated as a pet. Included in this form of possession are girls who elope to force a marriage, as were the first European explorers whose white skins caused them to be greeted with cries of '*We turimo*' (Leahy and Crain 1937: p. 145).

Ancestral *korova* are of greater importance in human affairs for their general beneficence. They are identified with the land from which they originally emerged and to which they are relinked by the mortuary rites. They make the land fertile and in return receive portions of all crops. They are associated with the clan valuables and the spirits of the clan pigs, and so they bring success in ceremonial exchanges. In return, valuables are displayed for the *korova* in dances, and pork is often fed to them. It is from the stock of ancestral *korova* that the spirit enters the bodies of infants; in return children are named after dead ancestors to give them material form once again. *Korova* make children grow strong and tall; in return, actions hateful to *korova* must be avoided, especially by growing children.

In short, *korova* provide humans with the good things of life, yet they depend on human work to realize those benefits. The living and the *korova* are in partnership in everyday life, and the assiduous performance of communal ceremonials ensures the successful continuation of the partnership. But, if ritual ensures communal welfare, more specific techniques are available to individuals to obtain the support of the spirits for their private ends. I shall discuss these techniques before discussing communal ritual, as some of the techniques also form elements of the communal ceremonies.

(c) Individual manipulation of spirits

Some techniques for influencing *oinya* have already been described as cures for disease. Two other techniques, which appear to be like exuvial magic and simple witchcraft, are also in fact means of influencing *oinya*. For the first, termed *kimfi hiyaiye* ('to burn a bundle'), personal leavings are wrapped in leaves and burned to cause pain or death. The leavings are those which are the seat of the *oinya*—hair, fingernails, or semen—but a person's name (which is usually known only by fellow clansmen) may be spoken into a leaf and used instead.

The second technique is called *kumo* ('something secret' or 'shut') and in it men, either singly or in groups, pronounce formulae while inhaling or exhaling cigarette smoke. This makes a white secretion (*oko*, the material form of *oinya*) pass through the air and affect the victim's *oinya*. As the *oko* passes through the air it emits a white light, which becomes stronger when many men perform the ritual together. *Kumo* can cause death or the migration of the victim's valuables into the *kumo*-worker's possession. *Kumo* can also be beneficial, used as a prophylaxis before youths make *awoiro* visits, as a cure for disease caused by foreign *kumo*, or in ceremonials. Thus, in the Pig Feast it is performed over a pig and a board (*gerua*), representing the spirits of all village pigs, to avert pig disease at the beginning of the religious cycle. But although *kumo* is well integrated into the religion, the technique itself is new. It was brought from tribes to the north-east within living memory, probably between 1900 and 1915, perhaps as the initial introduction of tobacco (cf. Riesenfeld 1951). There is evidence that ritual cannibalism was the previous *kumo* technique.

The *korova* of a newly-dead man may be influenced in several ways. If the death was caused by sorcery, divination makes the dead body reveal the name of the killer. Sacrifice of a pig placates the *korova* if it has been worrying over unpaid debts and so causing misfortune to relatives and dreams to the next-of-kin. That the important aim is to placate the *korova* and not to repay the debts is shown by the way in which the pork is eaten. The carcass is cooked whole and the entire clan eats by tearing off lumps with their teeth, each person taking his turn. The original debt is not repaid and no single person becomes indebted to the sacrificer of the pig. Such pigs are called *korova weraneta* or 'spirit food'. Exorcism removes newly-dead *korova* from the village and from people who are possessed and violent. All the things regarded as abhorrent to spirits are used—blackness, heat, smells, noise and sexual symbols. The person undergoing exorcism is smeared with charcoal, sits next to the fire and is touched at every orifice with scented herbs. Noises (especially the explosion by heat of lengths of green bamboo) and female symbols such as rats and sweet potato leaves drive out the spirit, which departs in a sneeze. Scratching the skin may retain some spirit in the fingernails, so sticks only may be used for scratching during an exorcism.

Ancestral *korova* also have pork offered to them as 'spirit food' to induce them to cure puzzling sickness and also during rites of passage. Techniques like those of exorcism protect individuals from spiritual danger during initiation and first menses ceremonies. Another technique for obtaining specific favours from them is to 'be a *korova*' (*korovaiye*) by voluntarily assuming the deafness and detachment symptomatic of possession. Dancers 'are *korova*' when performing formal dances at ancestral ceremonies (for example, boys and girls at a First Fruits ceremony); but anyone may 'be a *korova*' informally on such occasions. He may rush about calling 'sh-sh-sh' (a way to call pigs or talk to spirits), wave sweet potato leaves or flap a pandanus-leaf mat (childless women seeking children commonly do this); in the *gerua* dances a woman may catch hold of a cord hanging from the board which a dancer carries, and pretend to pull down on it hand over hand.

(d) Ceremonial—communal manipulation of spirits

The individual manipulative techniques already described operate either directly on the spirit or on the body in which the spirit resides. In the ceremonials now to be described, the influencing is through communal action directed towards *symbols* of the spirits. Consequently, I must describe both the observable phenomena and the symbols. For simplicity I shall discuss only the 'ideal' forms of the three main classes of ceremony in Siane—rites of passage, First Fruits ceremonies and Pig Feasts; and for each I shall first give the rationale of the ceremony, then list the symbols used and finally describe the observable sequence of actions.

(i) *Rites of passage*. At conception a child is composed of paternal spirit in the form of semen and maternal spirit in the form of blood. Early male rites of passage (I shall treat female rites later) are to remove the maternal spirit, when it has done its job of causing early growth, and to replace it with paternal spirit. This permits the ancestral *korova* to cause full adult growth. At the person's death his spirit is appeased; later it is incorporated into the body of ancestral spirits.

E

In the various rites, maternal spirit is symbolized by female objects: milk, sweet potatoes and their leaves, opossums and rats. Paternal spirit is symbolized by male objects: notably male clothing, bows and arrows and pork. Blood, hair and other seats of the spirit may be maternal or paternal depending on the context. In addition the paternal *korova* appear as flying foxes and as sacred flutes. These simple flutes, about three inches in diameter and of varying lengths, are made in pairs (cf. Read 1952a: p. 5). Two men play them together, one man inhaling as the other blows; and by varying their timing, lipping and muting they can play simple motifs. The name of a bird (for example, *nema famti*, 'the greater bird of paradise') is given to each pair of flutes and its distinctive tunes. *Nema*, the generic word for 'bird', is used for all flutes, their tunes and dances and songs connected with them. Women are told that monstrous birds cause the sounds. These birds, of which the most fearsome is 'The Mother of the Birds', would kill the women if seen by them, but they are restrained by the men.

Birth, the first rite of passage, is marked by the child's father giving the mother a meal of pork and opossum's meat on her emergence from confinement, and by his placing in the child's hand an arrow that has been used to kill an enemy (or a digging stick if it is a girl). The pork (and a number of valuables) actually goes to the mother's brothers as a secular payment; but the opossum's meat returns maternal spirit to the mother while the arrow puts paternal spirit in the child's hands.

The second rite of passage, weaning, occurs between the ages of three and six at the second Pig Feast following birth. The child's clanmates kill pigs as 'spirit food', cut off the child's hair (a site for maternal spirit) and dress him or her in clothing of the appropriate sex. A boy must now sit with other boys at ceremonies, and not with his mother.

A boy is initiated into his father's group at the Pig Feast which occurs when he is aged between seven and ten. The men seize him as well as other eligible boys and take them all to a men's house to dress them in new clothes and arm them. Amidst the screams of the women, who say their children are being stolen to feed the birds, the men, all armed, parade the boys through the village and back to the men's house, where they reveal the secret of the flutes. They swear the novices to secrecy on pain of death, lead them into the men's house and seat them cross-legged close to the fires. They tie 'strong' leaves to the posts of the house which are associated with the novices' lineages and all the men grasp the posts in turn. This 'fastens' the novices' lineage *korova* to the house and the men to the *korova*, and it puts everyone in a taboo condition. The heat and fragrant herbs now exorcise the novices' maternal spirit, while the flutes infuse paternal spirit, by being placed in the novices' laps when not being played. At least one pair of flutes belonging to each men's house plays constantly for several days, during which the novices may not sleep, speak or scratch themselves and must listen to formal speeches describing the duties of men and the purpose of initiation. 'Your mothers' food has made you grow until your skin is tight,' they are told, 'now only male food and the *korova* can make you grow further to full adulthood'. They also learn that the placing of each pair of flutes in their laps has made them 'Father' of that particular 'bird' (for example, *nema famti merafo* 'Father of the greater bird of paradise').

A novice's connection with his mother's brothers is not yet completely severed, for they bring their own *nema* to place in his arms and give him pork as his first food since seclusion. The novice's fathers deny this assertion that the boy is inhabited by maternal spirit by repaying the gifts of pork many times over, and they kill other pigs as 'spirit food' and feed them to the novices for the rest of their seclusion.

When the mothers' brothers have returned home, the novices demonstrate their manhood in a deliberately provoked formal battle. On the next day they are told they will see the 'Mother of the Birds'. Singly they enter a men's house where a man of the grandfather's generation sits on one side of the fire, holding cradled in his arms two lengths of bamboo, decorated with cassowary plumes. The novice sits down opposite him in a similar posture and both begin swaying to and fro in unison. With a jerk of his arms, the old man tosses the bamboos into the air. The novice catches them in his arms and continues swaying uninterruptedly. After several tosses back and forth the bamboos remain with the novice. The old man then splits them open and reveals cooked meat inside. The meat is supposedly of the flying fox, and the boy is told he has been given, and must now eat, his ancestral spirits. The novices now join in the main ceremonies of the Pig Feast.

When the last visitors to the Pig Feast have left, the youths begin to expel the last maternal spirit from inside themselves—their blood. On the pretext that they must rescue an unsuccessful war party, some older men lead the youths singly to the stream bounding the tribal territory, where they suddenly come across four bloody 'bodies', lying half submerged. Each 'body' has an arrowhead in its hair, armpit or mouth, and the novice must pull out the arrows. Three come out easily, but the fourth, held firmly in the teeth, proves difficult. As he struggles, the three other 'bodies' come to life, seize him, force his head back and thrust bundles of reeds up his nostrils. The blood pours forth and, as it mingles with the water of the stream, the boy is told that his mother's blood 'is being washed away'. When all the novices have been bled, they are dressed in new clothes and the party returns to the village, singing of the heroic war exploits of the boys. The women bring abundant cooked food for their 'victorious' sons (the novices) to distribute. But before the boys can touch the food they must fetch water for their fathers to drink; they may not eat until everyone else has eaten. This ritual, in which the novices eat their first 'female' food after months of eating only 'male' food, teaches them their place in the men's authority system and their duties of sharing with every member of their clan.

During adolescence, youths voluntarily let their own blood at regular intervals. Some use Gahuku techniques (cf. Read 1954) of inducing vomiting to remove maternal food. Others, as they practise flute-playing in the distant bush, have their tongues rubbed with nettles—an ordeal which forms an integral part of Chimbu initiation (cf. Schaefer 1938). Among the Siane these are merely additional techniques for acquiring real manhood. To avoid alienating the *korova* the Siane adolescent must not eat food cooked by women whom he might marry, must abstain from sexual intercourse and must not eat certain female foods, such as rats and opossums. If he breaks these rules, his growth will remain stunted, but he suffers no secular punishment except, perhaps, ridicule by his peers for his weak-minded pursuit of momentary pleasure. Marriage does not alter his status, for he must avoid his wife entirely until he reaches formal adulthood.

Formal adulthood, marked by his father's killing several pigs as 'spirit food', occurs either at the Pig Feast following the youth's marriage or when he 'grows hair on his chest'. He now begins cohabiting with his wife but still is warned of the danger to his *oinya* of sleeping with her too often; if he does so, his skin will shrivel and he will quickly age and die.

Only an old man may neglect these dangers, sleep with his wife as he wishes, eat the 'hottest' portions of a pig (such as sausages made of blood), or even eat his own pigs which contain his own spirit.

The rites of passage at death have four phases: mourning to appease the spirit; disposal of the body to give the spirit a home and to make it favour its clanmates; payment of foreign mourners to settle all its obligations; exorcism of the spirit from the village to enable everyday life to resume.

Mourning involves showing that one wishes one could join the dead person, by making oneself white (like a *korova*) with wet clay, by cutting off a finger-joint or earlobe, by holding the dead body and rubbing oneself in its juices, or by committing suicide by hanging. The last two variants occur rarely, being performed mainly by widows. Usually all the deceased's clan mourn intensely for a short period, then dispose of the body quickly before foreign mourners arrive.

Disposal of the body is also variable. The spirit of important men is spread over the whole clan territory by the separate burial of each limb, or by cremation and the scattering of the ashes. Corpses whose spirit is unwanted are summarily thrown down deep limestone chasms. Most commonly a body is interred in low-lying ground, reclining on its back in a foetal posture. The grave is lined with twigs, straw and branches, making a box with 'floor', 'walls' and 'rafters'. New clothing and a few shells and plumes are put with the body and earth is heaped over them. Above the grave is built a flimsy structure of five-foot poles termed a 'grave-house'. Round it are set decorative shrubs, bamboos and a fence to keep out pigs. A belt, some 'dress' clothing and personal objects such as a pipe or jew's harp are hung from the posts of the 'house'. Thus, the spirit obtains a home in a cold, damp area, which *korova* like, and clothing and articles for its personal needs.

Only a dead person's closest kin help in the burial, for the dead man's juices (*oko*) on their skins contaminate them and they must observe stringent taboos (for example, on entering the men's house) for three months. One of them commonly keeps watch on a new grave to make sure that no pig or foreigner, but only *Oma Rumufa* (in the form of a white light or thunder) comes for the body.

The principal foreign mourners who are repaid are the mother's brothers' clan of a dead man or the brother's clan of a dead woman, although sisters, other relatives and even non-relatives may come to mourn as individuals. The mourning clan feigns an attack to avenge 'their child' who has been 'killed', but in reality they bring contributions to the mourning feast and are soon mollified, bathed in oil and fed delicacies. The deceased's clan kill large numbers of pigs, break a branch to enjoin peace and enumerate to the spirit those who have provided the pigs for the feast. They pay the mourning clan and any unrelated mourners for the concern they have shown, but they give the bulk of the pork to their own married sisters 'for the sisters' sons of the dead man'. Smaller portions go as 'spirit food'. Thus the dead man repays his obligations and gives food to all his clan and its spirits, to ease his acceptance into the spirit world.

The spirit is not exorcized until all foreign mourners have left the village; until then no clan member may leave the village (except to gather food) and close kin of the deceased may not eat or drink. The exorcism is carried out at the women's house of the deceased by age-mates of the next-of-kin, who use the most powerful exorcising techniques. The next-of-kin is not free of the spirit for a year or more but the *korova* now has ties only with its grave-house.

The ultimate rite of passage is the inclusion of the spirit into the body of unnamed ancestral *korova* at the next Pig Feast. When the head of the deceased's lineage makes the board representing the lineage spirits to carry in the dances, he attaches to it a small personal object of the dead man, such as an armband. After the dances the dead man's *korova* has no further individual existence.

(ii) *First Fruits ceremonies*. When a garden first bears crops, or finishes bearing, a distribution of the crop is made to recognize symbolically the contribution of the spirits. The most elaborate ceremony occurs every three years, when a clan prepares a large garden (or harvests a large crop of nuts) in order to make an immense distribution of food to another clan. Generically such ceremonies are called *numukefa*, but individual ones may be called by the crop distributed (for example, the yam-taro ceremony). All are designed to 'make the *korova* enter the gardens' (that is, to produce crop fertility), though much of the symbolism also relates to human fertility.

The *korova* appear in the ceremonies in the form of the sacred flutes, simple gourd masks and pantomimic acts portraying gardening activities or spirit-beings such as the wind, sun or snakes. Boys and girls temporarily 'are spirits' while dancing and while performing a ritual called *gimagama*. Throughout the familiar symbols of male and female dress, food and tools are used.

Numukefa starts when the maize in the prepared garden is ripe. The clan flutes are played and carried in procession around all the clan lands. In the new garden the men take all the maize (technically still the property of the women who grew it) to eat and for decoration. They explain that 'the birds' took it, thus asserting the spirits' primary right to all the crops.

Next the feast-givers invite another clan (usually a distant one with few affinal ties) to be 'their wives'. When the main crop is ripe, the 'wives' (the unmarried girls of all ages of the guest clan) arrive for the main ceremony. To mark their special status they wear male clothing over their normal female garb. They are entertained as the wives, not of individuals, but of men's houses. For up to seven days they and the youths of the host clan carry out a ritual cycle—*gimagama* by night, sleeping near a river by day, dancing and watching panto-mimic acts at evening.

Gimagama takes place inside the men's houses from which all the beds are removed. The girls squat in a circle round the central fires and the boys form a larger circle round them. Each girl has a partner and both sway in time from side to side, chanting. Gradually they lean towards one another until their noses meet and they are swaying in unison. After each chant the boys change partners by shuffling one place to the right. A girl may place her hand on a particular boy's wrist to indicate that she wishes to sleep, when the *gimagama* finishes, cradled in his arms.

Such sleep is short and is as free of overt sexuality as is the nose-rubbing. At dawn the boys and girls dance in groups to the river bank where they sleep and decorate themselves with leaves. In the late afternoon they return from this abode of spirits to dance in the village. The boys shuffle steadily in a circle and are joined by their 'wives' who slip their hands into the boys' hands and dance beside them.

While they 'are *korova*' the boys and girls attract little attention from the adult spectators, for the latter eagerly watch a succession of panto-mimic episodes which follow each other like music-hall acts. The host clansmen perform most of them, but guest performers from other clans may be invited to participate as an honour. The repertoire of acts is large and varies from area to area; prestige accrues from im-porting a new act. Two typical ones are a gardening act, 'putting down the dividing strips', and one portraying a water snake called Vuno in Emenyo tribe. In the first act a man divides a garden plot he has cleared between his two wives. They fight; he attempts to pacify them; eventually they combine to beat him with digging sticks; he flees followed by the wives. Suddenly all three turn on the audience and pretend to copulate from the rear with anyone they catch. All gestures and costumes, especially those of the men playing the wives, are the grossest caricatures and evoke screams of laughter.

In the second act two men holding the ends of a pliant branch to form an arch are the snake. They wear masks and are smeared with red clay. As they move slowly along, the arch moves up and down sinuously. Two other dancers circle the snake, occasionally dancing through the arch. The dance is to make the snake push up water for the crops through the red earth.

The cycle is repeated day after day, until the girls' parents arrive. On that day there is no visit to the river. Instead, the hosts pile uncooked vegetable food in the clearing by the men's house and, after feasting the 'wives' and their parents with cooked food, they present the heaps to the guests amidst profuse speeches. The parents leave, each carrying about one hundred pounds of food, and walk down a corridor formed by the host youths and their 'wives'. Everyone weeps and sings mourning songs—the hosts because 'their wives will soon leave', and the guests because 'they will never again see such fertile land'. When their parents have gone, the girls break the line and rush, sobbing, for the exit; the boys enter the men's house.

The ceremony is thus a dramatic portrayal of how the spirits obtain wives, marry and produce crops (and children). Only in some phases is it explicit that the boys and girls and the pantomimic acts 'are spirits', but this is implicit throughout. The lack of realism of the spirit portrayers (the age of the 'spouses', the asexual nature of their marital relationship, the lack of affinal ties between their clans, and the caricaturing in the pantomimes) makes a vivid contrast with the realism of what the spirits produce—the immense piles of food.

(iii) *The Pig Feast*. This ceremony, the most spectacular in Siane, involves at its climax several thousand people dancing around some two hundred brilliantly painted *gerua* boards. Each phratry performs one ceremony every three years. The object of doing so is not clearly stated; it is 'for the ancestors', 'to make the pigs grow', 'so that we may eat pig'. All purposes are evident as the celebrants induce the ancestral *korova* to enter the village, perform dances in their honour and then feed pork to them (and to all living phratry members).

One set of *korova* symbols are the sacred flutes and a horn three feet long, made of telescoped lengths of bamboo joined to a curved gourd. Cassowary plumes make the joints airtight, and the instrument is referred to either as *nema orafo*, 'the Mother of the Birds', or as *we kirofo*, 'the Old Man'. Each phratry owns one horn. A second set of symbols are the *gerua*—boards on which designs are painted. Most important of the many types of *gerua* are those six feet high and painted with a stylized anthropomorphic design[6] of a diamond body (*afaniki*, 'hand of the moon'), a circular head (*fo numuna*, 'house of the sun') and vee-shaped limbs at the side (*oma*, 'the way'). These are called *wenena gerua* ('people *gerua*'), and each lineage has its own traditional designs which it must paint on a new board at each feast. Smaller *gerua*, termed *korova gerua*, bearing simpler designs of triangles or circles and rays, may be made by individuals acting privately.

The Pig Feast has five phases: the announcement, the preparation, the dancing for the *gerua*, the killing of pigs and the putting away of the flutes. Rites of passage are usually synchronized with the Pig Feast. Initiation precedes the second phase, weaning and coming of age rituals occur in the fourth phase, while the initiation ordeal follows the last phase.

The announcement starts when the men of one clan play *harafa nema* (a 'bird' with a long, slow call), 'to ask the other birds to come'. The men choose as the specific occasion for this a time when the women have misbehaved (for example, fought among themselves). They tell the women that the birds are angry, are assembling in the men's houses and can be appeased only by pork and by the women's diligence in gardening and pig-care. The men kill pigs, perform a peace-enjoining ceremony over the carcasses, and distribute them as 'spirit food' to all members of the clan, including wives, married sisters and the *korova*. The latter's pork is placed 'in the mouth of the birds' (that is, in the flutes' sound-holes). After the distribution several flutes begin playing, as they do every day at nightfall for the next ten months. That night the men perform *kumo* over a live pig and a small pig-*gerua* (termed *ruwefa*) to ensure the pigs' growth and health. Other clans of the phratry follow suit immediately.

Secular preparations are made, involving the cultivation of large gardens and the rebuilding of the whole village. Nine months after the announcement and one month before the killing, the ritual preparation starts as the 'Mother of the Birds' arrives. The guardian of the phratry horn uncovers it, and its resounding bellow tells all near-by clans that the killing will be at the next full moon. The *gerua* boards are cut and the flutes are taken in procession to other villages to invite the people to dance for the *korova*. During the procession individuals of other clans can become fictive kin (*emona we*, 'sister men', or 'ceremonial friends') of the *korova* by giving them shells or valuables. The gifts entitle the 'sister men' to share in the spirits' pigs.

Two days before the full moon the men perform *yafo nema* (pig song) to pacify the pigs' spirit and to ensure that it will transmigrate into the piglets which are kept for future breeding. The spirit of a large pig is exorcized into a *ruwefa gerua*, and the *gerua* is carried in procession through the village.

Next day each lineage kills a pig and 'animates' its *wenena gerua* by placing on it a crown of human hair, the valuables given by 'sister men', and objects associated with the recent dead of the lineage. The lineage head plaits strands of bark thread into his own hair. The *gerua* is then placed on his head and tied in position with the threads. *He* is now the *gerua* and he may not remove the threads during the ceremony, though he may untie the board. Nor may he remove the woman's clothing which he wears over his normal male attire. He, as *gerua*, is fed salted pork liver and is ready to dance.

At first the lineage *gerua* dance desultorily in the clearing of their own men's house. Gradually they are joined by drummers and *korova gerua*. Women who 'are *korova*' flap mats at the *gerua* or simulate pulling on cords suspended from them. The cords are termed '*gerua* umbilical cords', and women say they are 'pulling down the birds', thereby stressing the role of women in childbearing and as links with the spirit world. As the evening wears on the *gerua* begin dancing from one men's house to the next, and by dawn they have all danced at every men's house in the phratry. At dawn the two hundred or so *gerua* assemble in one large clearing and dance with the six hundred other members of the phratry, including wives and married sisters. The object of the dance is vividly expressed as 'showing everyone to everyone'. Solidarity being thus affirmed, the *gerua* disperse to their respective men's houses.

The next day and night are the spectacular climax of the feast as invited dancers come from all near-by clans, accompanied by their wives, to dance for the *gerua*. In parties of thirty they move from men's house to men's house, dancing continuously in front of the parading *gerua*, while gifts of pork, sugar cane and sweet potatoes entice them on their way. The full moon adds to the spectacle.

At dawn the dancers leave and the pig-killing starts. Before the dancing *gerua* and to a crescendo of flute and horn playing, each men's house kills some twenty pigs. The carcasses are set in a line. Then an old man recites for the spirits the names of those who provided the pigs and gives the tails of the pigs—their spirits—to the owners.

These pigs are for 'married sisters of the clan'. In fact 'sister men' (fictive kin) are included as married sisters, while non-kin may on special occasions be treated similarly. Thus, in 1952 Yamofwe tribe invited a Yauna clan to receive 'sisters' pork' as a corporate unit because Yauna men had been killed twenty years previously, while fighting as allies of Yamofwe. When all 'sisters" pigs have been distributed, more are killed as 'spirit food' for resident members of the phratry. Each clan dances for every other clan, turn and turn about, and the dancers receive their hosts' 'spirit food' pigs. The animals are contributed by individuals who are validating rites of passage.

Five days after the gifts to 'sisters', the latter return, bringing uncooked vegetables. While they are present the 'birds' leave the village. The flutes and horn go through the village in procession, while all the women hide. Outside each woman's house the flutes halt and ask the owner if any pigs remain unkilled. In answer she holds out an empty hand and receives on it a sharp blow from a cassowary beak. Lineage leaders remove the bark thread from their hair; the *gerua* hair is removed and the boards are placed in bamboo thickets (old burial sites) to decay. Only the refuse and rancid pork remain.

The living have fed the spirits with pork and entertained them with a spectacular ceremony. The spirits have lent their presence to private rites of passage. Now, secure in the knowledge of the spirits' benevolence, the living return to their everyday tasks.

3. RELIGION AND SOCIETY

I shall now consider the preceding data as illustrative of Durkheim's proposition that religion portrays society itself 'in an enlarged, transformed, and idealized form' (1947: p. 421). More specifically, I shall try to show how people, by interpreting apparently unordered social behaviour in terms of a systematic set of religious symbols, are enabled to see order in society.

Most Siane religious symbolism is ordered around three dual oppositions—between body and spirit, between living and dead, and between male and female. Any object or action has characteristics which classify it in terms of these dichotomies. In the religion the systematic nature of this classification appears, for example, in the way in which hair signifies 'spirit' whether the referent is *gerua* animated by hair, pig-spirits retained as tail hairs in the Pig Feast, or human spirit exorcised by haircutting at weaning. Or again, system appears in the use of night as being 'dead' and day as being 'living' in the symbolism of flying foxes (*korova*) which appear at night, in the time of emergence of the flutes at a Pig Feast announcement, or in the dangers of contact between the two worlds in the evening when spirit-possession occurs.

But the religion does not merely classify symbols as opposites; it shows them to be interdependent. Spirits need bodies just as bodies need spirits; the living need the dead; men and women need each other. That the latter relationship is not classified as one of superior to inferior appears most clearly in the First Fruits ceremony with its transvesticism, comic acts and symbolic marriage. Bateson (1936) has analysed in detail the way in which such clear-cut differentiation of symbols, coupled with occasional ritual reversals of sex roles, implies interdependence. It also appears in the importance of female ritual acts such as 'pulling down the birds' in Pig Feasts, or welcoming home the novices after initiation ordeals.

Each pair of symbols is independent of, though closely similar to, the other pairs. Three similar pairs of oppositions occur in the formal structure of society—the opposition of one's own clan and foreign clans, of the individual and the corporate group, and of men and women. It is my thesis that, in Durkheim's sense, the pairs of symbols 'idealize' the pairs of relationships. The body-spirit symbols parallel the interdependence of one's own clan and foreign clans, from which one receives the bodies of wives. Fellow clansmen's actions are determined by spirit: one must respect their actions and be responsible for one's own. Foreigners are body; to them one has no responsibility and can be physically violent, restrained only by fear of their expected violence. The living-dead symbols parallel the relationship between the individual and the corporate clan. The clan, like the *korova*, is the ultimate source of the individual's health, wealth, children, food and security from attack. Finally the male-female symbolism is like the relation between the sexes, as it was before the introduction of steel axes unbalanced it by halving men's work.

The religious symbols do not merely reflect actual social relations; they clarify for the individual how he is to interpret inconsistent social behaviour. The best example of this is given by the relationships with women. In the secular marriage ceremony a woman is exchanged for valuables and pork and is thus classed as female and body by the groom's clan, foreign but useful to men. Her brothers, in exchanging her for pork, also class her as body, but on all other occasions they emphasize her spirituality by giving her 'spirit food' as a member of their own clan. Her husband's clansmen always emphasize her female-ness—her dependence on them and their need for her. On most ceremonial occasions they give her 'spirit food' to indicate that they wish to treat her as spiritual and of their clan; when they wish to treat her as 'body' or foreign, they produce spirit symbols (flutes at a Pig Feast announcement or the start of a First Fruits ceremony) or they exclude her violently from spirit actions (the theft of boys in initiation). The inconsistent real actions can be interpreted as being consistent in so far as the symbolic contexts indicate that they are directed to different social persons.

The theme of 'the birds' is another set of religious symbols which clarifies for the individual the relations between groups and possibly even his relation to nature. Men treat the tale told to the women, that the flutes are real but monstrous birds, as a joke. Yet they also discuss with great seriousness the various flute-birds, their calls, and the importance of 'fathers' of particular birds, especially the 'Mother of the Birds', which may be variously the horn, the cassowary, or the phratry ancestor. Their songs tell how the birds dwell with their Mother in *Fomai* ('there is the sun'), or in the virgin forest to the south-east. The songs vaguely link the 'Mother of the Birds' with the sun, while *Oma Rumufa* (as a circle of light and the puller of the sun) and the heads of *gerua* ('houses of the sun') are also linked to the sun. There seems to be some link between the symbols of the social and of the natural worlds.

The birds symbolize social groupings more directly. Most lineages must guard, 'feed' and produce when needed one pair of flutes. Lineages, which have no secular symbols for their unity, no name, no insignia, no separate dwelling, have the flutes as religious symbols. Every lineage's symbol is qualitatively different, yet all are variants of a single form—birds—and all variants are needed for the performance of each ceremony. Thus the symbols emphasize not only the individuality and equality, but also the interdependence, of lineages. Phratry unity is symbolized by the single phratry 'Mother of the Birds'. This unity must be maintained to preserve the phratry's important political functions (cf. p. 52); yet there are no secular means of doing so. Religious symbolism and ritual exchanges of pork fill the gap.

Age-mate bonds also have a 'bird' counterpart. Boys initiated together become 'fathers' of the same set of 'birds', as the same set of flutes is placed in their laps. Each group of age-mates has a unique set of flute-group loyalties, as different flutes are brought by mothers' brothers to each initiation. As boys are often initiated in men's houses other than those of their fathers, each flute has 'fathers' from different lineages and men's houses. Flute-group loyalties cross-cut descent-group loyalties. If space permitted similar analyses could be made of the qualitative variety but underlying equality and interdependence of the other symbols of lineage unity—(the *gerua* designs, the posts of the men's houses and the formal prescriptive speeches).

With regard to the 'birds', however, these symbols also provide an expression of the ties which make Siane a political entity within which disputes are settled, even though there is no consciousness of wider unity, no centralization of power and no boundaries—what I have elsewhere called a 'fragmentary society' (Salisbury n.d.). Among the villages the specific flutes, songs, *gerua* designs, dances and other elements of ceremonial differ, yet all are variants of general patterns. In spite of the differences, each village recognizes what other villages do, admits any initiated man to its ceremonies regardless of his clan, seeks strange foreign dances for its ceremonies, invites 'birds' from maternal clans to come to initiations. There is a recognition of cultural unity, within which religious diversity, even competition, is encouraged; political unity is an acceptance of cultural rules that regulate warfare and ceremonial exchanges, and so permit competition for prestige.

4. WOMEN AND RELIGION IN A PATRILINEAL SOCIETY

I have already discussed the symbolic significance of women in communal ritual—their interdependence with men, and the way intergroup rivalry is expressed as competition over women. In rites of passage, where the individual is treated as a vessel for patrilineal spirit, we might expect daughters, who provide offspring for foreign groups, to receive little attention. Yet their rites receive great attention, qualitatively different from that given to the male and communal rites. The latter are times of festivity to which outsiders are welcome; the attitude to the former is one of reverence, emotional intensity and secrecy. I shall attempt to analyse this anomaly, which runs counter to the neat explanation given for other ceremonials.

A girl's first menses are treated as a form of pregnancy, heralded similarly by her swelling breasts, but giving birth to blood alone. As this is paternal blood, magical and practical precautions are taken to ensure that the 'birth' occurs on clan territory. The girl's father 'fastens' a lock of her hair and prepares a herbal infusion to rub on her. She 'gives birth' lying in her mother's house, secluded behind a partition of aromatic branches erected by her eldest brother. Small groups of older men from other villages are invited for each of five nights to sing *awoiro* songs in the outer 'room' of the girl's house to

protect her spirit with their noise. She is further protected by the
blazing fire and the smoke of cigarettes which the singers are given
by an attendant male of the girl's clan. At dawn the singers receive
strongly seasoned vegetables, and a portion is placed on the girl's
lips for her to suck.

On the sixth evening the partition is removed, the girl comes forward
to the fire, and the senior wives of the clan instruct her in her duties
as a woman. Then the youths of her own clan enter, singing *awoiro*
songs and led by the girl's lineage head and other important men.
The lineage head, using techniques familiar from male initiation,
teaches her to submit to men and to cook for them, by tricking her
into trying to drink water from an empty water container. By tossing
her a bundle of sugar cane to eat he hands over ancestral spirit. 'The
fire that has burnt you comes from the clan's enemies', he says. 'Eat
the powdered skulls of your ancestors, their arms and legs. This will
bar the road to enemies. Do not forget this.' She eats the sugar, and
all night her 'brothers' sing to her.

Next afternoon the girl and her attendants emerge from seclusion.
The girl then symbolically cooks a previously prepared meal which
includes a cut-up pig and an opossum or rat, killed by her eldest
brother. She eats the small animal and the brains of the pig and gives
the rest to her attendants, her 'mothers' and the foreign singers. For
the next two months she may not leave the village; but thenceforth
she is a privileged person, told by her mother not to work, and she
sleeps every night with other nubile girls in a woman's house which,
pro tempore, becomes a girls' club house.

The first menses ceremony generally parallels male initiation, with
its symbolic handing over of ancestral spirit, its teaching of adult
duties, and its period of seclusion while exorcism keeps away dangerous
spirits. But there is, in addition in the first menses, concern over the
possible loss of paternal blood, and the eating of the small 'female'
animal.

A second exclusively female rite is the departure for marriage (I
shall not discuss the predominantly secular ceremony of marriage
itself). A girl precipitates the ceremony by eloping to the men's house
of her chosen groom. The men purify themselves by letting their
own blood and eating it as 'spirit food' cooked with herbs, and they
purify the house by playing the sacred flutes—the most drastic
purification possible in Siane. The bride temporarily returns home.

For the departure her eldest brother carves a *gerua* eighteen inches high, called *vau*, and paints it with rays radiating from a central oval hole. He cooks a pig and salts it, using ash made by burning some of the bride's hair. Before nightfall he uses aromatic herbs to exorcize her spirit. After dark, in front of an audience of clan wives and married sisters, he takes the pork and *gerua* as though to give them to the bride as symbols of a new body and spirit. He places the pork in her arms, but at the last moment he gives the *gerua* to a younger girl instead. The spirit is transmitted into the young girl amidst dancing, the waving of sweet potato leaves and much sh-sh-shing; the remaining pork is eaten by the *gerua* carver and by all the women. The ceremony is clearly to retain the girl's spirit in her natal clan, although the Siane say it is intended to stop the village pigs from following the bride.

The third 'female' ceremony is the special ritual which occurs when the 'oldest sister' of a lineage (cf. p. 52) first menstruates. The normal first menses sequence is followed; but, instead of the girl's oldest brother killing an opposum or rat for her emergence, all men of the clan kill flying foxes.

The men purify themselves by breaking branches and immure themselves behind a leafy screen in a special limestone cave. After putting down pork for the *korova*, each lineage waits in the darkness near its own crevice and clubs flying foxes as they settle. No man speaks, so that the animals (that is, the *korova*) will not know who is killing them. Men may leave the cave in pairs to sleep and eat, but they may eat only flying fox, and that only outside the cave. The only people they may see are their unmarried daughters who come to collect the carcasses. The slaughter continues for four days and nights.

On the last evening all women, except the girl and her attendants, also leave the village to avoid contact with foreign singers. At dawn the next day the men emerge and carry the carcasses (some 1,600 in the ceremony I attended) to a less sacred, but still secret, place for distribution. The women, and any man accompanying them, must be purified before attending. I myself was allowed to attend only after extensive purification, although I had been freely admitted to all other ceremonies. I never saw a sacred cave.

The flying foxes are divided between the menstruating girl (who receives about one hundred), all the men's houses of the phratry, and all married and unmarried sisters of the phratry. Wives receive meat from their husbands. That night the menstruating girl emerges from seclusion, and next day she receives her flying foxes in lieu of pork and opposum meat.

Throughout the ceremony people assert that they are 'eating their ancestors'; yet they say this with exhilaration and not with the distaste expressed when a young man eats his own pigs—the same action in a different context. They express clan (and even phratry) solidarity, not by exhibiting to others a single symbolic object as in the Pig Feast, but by an inwardly-focused communion of the entire group, both living and dead members.

In the Durkheimian terms used earlier, the female rites all express the imminent loss to the clan of part of its stock of spirit; they mobilize clan solidarity and by ritual prevent the loss. Yet this formulation throws no light on the mystical intensity surrounding these ceremonies. This goes deeper than concern for the loss of a particular spirit; it is a concern for women in general. It appears when a man rapes a minor of another clan (thereby making her 'blood run down' prematurely), or when a man commits incest with a clan sister, even though there is no loss of spirit by his clan. In both cases there is a reaction of horror, and the delinquent male is publicly beaten by his own clansmen, often until he dies. Completely unrelated clans join in expressing this horror. More generally the mystical nature of womankind is expressed by the Siane phrase: 'Women see the *korova's* skin'. This may be translated freely as 'women see spirits in tangible form', while men are aware of them only indirectly. Women, although themselves purely material, capricious and unpredictable, continually produce spirit in the form of blood and may at any time become purely spirit without men being able to see any difference (cf. attacks by female *korova*, p. 56). They are the ultimate ideal of society. Thus, in a concrete example, the 'oldest sister' is the *atarafo* (literally, 'house post person') of the lineage; she *is* the lineage and her first menses are a threat to the clan of losing a lineage. Man, an earthbound mixture of spirit and body, is mysterious woman's contact with the real world.

This is Siane ideology. It must be reconciled with the social reality that there is no way to prevent the physical departure in marriage of female children, for only by sending daughters away can valuables and brides be obtained and the clan be perpetuated. The Siane cannot periodically restate the ideology, using a simple symbol to point out the aspect of everyday reality which is taken to be significant, because everyday reality must be denied. They must state the ideology in a ceremony of such emotional impact that both they and the onlookers are convinced that the statement is true, though all the evidence of the senses denies it. The impact on the departing bride must be all the

F

greater, as no further ceremonies can be held to reinforce her conviction. In this light, the emotionality and mystical intensity surrounding female rites in Siane appear, not as paradoxical, but as only to be expected in a predominantly male-oriented society.

5. CONCLUSION

I have presented an outline of Siane religious beliefs and practices and have tried to show how the systematic nature of the religious symbols enables people to perceive social reality, which the symbols represent, as having a systematic nature. In Durkheim's terms, the symbols teach, through periodic communal rituals, the 'collective representation' of society, or those aspects of social reality which are ideally significant.

Yet Siane female rites suggest that a social ideal may have almost no basis in reality; it may be, not an idealization of actual conditions, but a reversal of reality, logically demanded but in deep conflict with other ideals. In these conditions to represent the social ideal in public ritual would expose its unreality. To assert publicly that women are superior to men and are the sources of men's spirit would be intolerable in a society so dependent on male political authority and patrilineal inheritance. Yet the logic of conception and of the nature of *korova* demands a recognition of the importance of women.

What we find in Siane are dramatic public ceremonies symbolizing the behavioural realities, and relatively private rites surrounded by great mystical intensity and emotional involvement, in which the unreal ideal is stressed. The general hypothesis suggests itself that intensity of emotional involvement, and restrictions on participation in a ritual vary with the social unreality of what the rite tries to accomplish. At least the Siane case suggests that the division between individual mystical beliefs and public symbolic rituals needs as much study in so-called primitive religions as it is currently receiving in Christian theological controversy (cf. Barth 1960).

NOTES

[1] The field work on which this study is based was done during twelve months in 1952–3 as a Research Scholar of the Australian National University. Funds supporting the writing of the paper were provided by the Institute of International Studies, University of California.

[2] Siane terms are spelt phonemically as explained in Salisbury (1956b).

[3] For a more extended discussion of the role of the phratry in peace-making see Salisbury (n.d.).

[4] A more extended discussion of lineage structure is given in Salisbury (1956a).

[5] The terms 'ghost' and 'ancestral ghost', used generally throughout this book, convey a sense of discrete individuality which is often inapplicable in a translation of the concept *korova*. As the same term, *korova*, is used to denote ghosts, ancestral ghosts, and generalized supernatural power, it is felt desirable that a single English term with multiple meanings should be used. Hence the term 'spirit' or its plural 'spirits'.

[6] For an illustration and analysis of the design see Salisbury (1959).

R. M. BERNDT

The Kamano, Usurufa, Jate and Fore of the Eastern Highlands

IN this region[1] of about 1,000 square miles, within the administrative sub-districts of Kainantu and Goroka (Bena), a population of over 42,600 is spread among four language units: Kamano, Jate, Fore and Usurufa (the smallest both territorially and numerically). These names serve as a basis of social identification but do not imply either political unity or collective action. Despite local variations, including language differences, these units share a common cultural background, which means that the behaviour of all their members is roughly predictable even on the part of those who have no direct contact with one another. In the present discussion the emphasis is on this common background, as more important for an overview of local religion than consideration of the differences which exist within as well as between language units, particularly among the Jate and Fore. The most intensive field work was carried out among the Usurufa, southern Kamano, eastern Jate and northern Fore. Despite the social significance of language identification, no one of these units could have been artificially isolated for study without distorting the picture of social reality in which linguistic cleavages are offset by closeness of social ties, cultural similarities, and common assumptions and expectations.

Each language unit comprises a number of districts ('big names'), which for most practical purposes can be regarded as separate political units. A district is made up of several villages and/or hamlets. Each of these, except among the Fore, is broadly synonymous with a local clan, plus adherents (women married into it): two or more named patrilineages of shallow depth, the male members of which share a common house while women and children occupy smaller houses near by. Gardening land is held ultimately in the name of the lineage but in practice is divided among its members.

Inter-district fighting, before the Administration suppressed it, involved temporary alliances on the basis of expediency and bribery; retaliation took the form of fighting sequences and sorcery accusations and counter-accusations. This was a see-sawing process, in which from time to time members of various villages or districts would drop out as refugees until they had regained their fighting strength. Each district was caught up in a network of relationships with others, interaction being most frequent and varied among neighbours, weaker in regard to those farther away, and virtually non-existent outside a certain (undefined) range. Fighting, intermarriage and participation in religious rituals and secular ceremonies were among the ways in which members of various districts could express opposition on the one hand, co-operation on the other; in alignments formed for these purposes, linguistic affiliations were largely irrelevant.

1. THE PROBLEM OF 'WHAT IS RELIGION?'

Attempts to define religion in hard and fast terms tend to be self-defeating, owing to difficulties in pigeonholing 'borderline' material. Yet there is an area which we can arbitrarily distinguish as involving religious phenomena, and on which there would probably be general agreement among anthropologists. Beliefs relating to the place of man and society in the cosmos are religious in so far as they are relevant to moral attitudes and value-orientation patterns. This is of course saying, with Durkheim, that almost every aspect of social and cultural life which reflects such attitudes and patterns is of a religious nature. The broadness of this approach to the field of religion is congenial to many anthropologists. As against it there are suggestions that it would be better to start off afresh with a more neutral term, like Honigmann's 'ideational culture' (J. Honigmann, cited in Kroeber 1953: p. 509; see also his approach in 1959: pp. 509, 653).

In this essay the label 'religion' is interpreted rather flexibly and not sharply differentiated from magic. The phenomena identified here have to do with critical issues directly relevant to the welfare of these people and with the sphere of the non-empirical, including the super-natural, involving belief in the sense of commitment to action. Because this covers such a wide field, it cannot be explored at all fully here. Some of it, however, is already treated elsewhere. (For further details, see R. Berndt 1962: for example pp. 39-113.)

2. THE IDEOLOGICAL BASIS OF ACTION

Relatively standardized narrative material in this area falls into three roughly distinct categories. The first sketches the main features of the natural environment, with some reference to the social dimension. The second, a series of episodes which together make up an 'origin' myth or cycle, centres on two major figures sometimes called Jugu-mishanta and Morufonu.[2] A section of this (see (c) below) covers some aspects of ritual action but does not include practical instructions for performing it.[3] The third consists of 'secondary' or non-sacred my-thology.

(a) Cosmological beliefs

There are several local versions of the formation of the world, although none of the statements recorded from women begins at this point. One holds that the ground with some natural features always existed, like a wooden plate completely surrounded by water. Another suggests that a large tree grew out of nothingness, its thick spreading branches forming the ground, again in the shape of a large wooden plate. At the base of this tree sit Jugumishanta and her husband Moru-fonu, in one of their manifestations, holding the world steady. The tree rests on the shoulders of Morufonu; when his body pains with its weight he moves slightly, causing earth tremors. A version perhaps more generally accepted holds that they fashioned the ground from their faeces, then made a domed roof of stone to protect it. This is the sky, on the other side of which live anthropomorphic beings somehow related to these two.

During this creative period they already had two adult sons: the elder, Wajubu, the Moon, married to Tagisomenaja, the Evening Star; the younger, Wainako', the Sun, also known as Pisiwa, a bird of paradise, married to Moa'ri, a special red stone. Several stories centre on these two brothers. In one Jate version, Wainako' and his wife live under the earth. Every morning, in opposition to his elder brother, he comes up through a hole on the eastern edge. Holding his bow and arrows he climbs up a tree into the sky, and his arrows, held fanwise, are the rays of the sun. After travelling across the sky to the west he climbs down again, his wife meets him with food, and together they return to the east to sleep. A few stories, usually couched in terms of sibling rivalry, tell of their encounters with human beings. One visitor treats the Sun's wife courteously and receives gifts; his brother, jealous, tries to bully her. In one version (Jate and Kamano) the jealous brother is burnt to death by the Sun man, and from the billowing smoke come the first clouds.

Next in importance are stories about Hafoza, the Lightning and Thunder Man (Jate). Others about various stars, including the Milky Way, and about the Rainbow are mostly short and treated rather casually. Rain falls when Jugumishanta and Morufonu urinate after eating quantities of sugar cane. The wind, not identified as an anthropomorphic deity, is virtually independent of the main creators: it is sometimes said (Jate) to have helped in the creation of man by blowing life into the bodies they had made.

(b) The creation of man

Jugumishanta and Morufonu emerged from a swamp somewhere in Fore territory, most often identified as Rivetiga, or Arigi, in Oka. Jugumishanta is identified with the earth, but her husband receives less emphasis. From here they journeyed roughly north toward the Markham Valley. There are dozens of unco-ordinated versions, differing in social perspective according to the district and linguistic affiliations of the speaker; but most tell how they peopled the countryside, established gardens, introduced creatures, plants and trees useful to man, and various behaviour patterns, ritual and ceremonies. All people (including Europeans) are 'children of Jugumishanta'. This bond of common origin, embracing particularly although rather vaguely all within the cultural bloc, was no deterrent to inter-district warfare. The social units making up the region were linked as much through their oppositions as through shared enterprises or agreement on specific issues.

(c) The mythology of ritual

An extension of the creation mythology gives reasons for the use of certain special objects and the performance of ritual actions. Its principal concern is with the sacred flutes (in several named varieties) and with cane-swallowing. Jugumishanta and Morufonu are involved, along with a number of unnamed story people (kaiteni waja'mogi), in other words the sort of characters who appear in the secondary mythology. The myths in this series outline the origin of particular rites, how each was first instituted, and what it means. A concluding statement tells what people should do about it now. All these myths open with women playing a dominant part but conclude with control having passed to men. For instance, men take over the most important sacred objects. Morufonu steals the first flute, the original prototype, from his wife, who had made it; a man disguised as a woman deceives a number of young girls and steals their flute; two young men climb up a greased slope to where two girls are playing their flute, persuade them to let them blow it, and one runs away with it. Also, it is women who show men how to cane-swallow effectively to induce vomiting, a rite now kept secret from women.

(d) The secondary mythology

Kaiteni are stories known to, and told by, both men and women, in which the characters are human beings ('place' or village people) and non-human personages of various kinds, including ghosts.

Whereas the other categories of mythology are rather narrowly focused, despite the existence of many versions, the *kaiteni* allow much more scope for personal selection, revealing awareness of plot and of their value as entertainment. They are oriented along practical lines. Each ends with a moral injunction, to the effect that 'we, story characters, have done this; you, men, should not'. In many cases men behave as the story characters do, and not as the moral dictates. But generally speaking this type of myth deals (negatively) with what people should not do, rather than (positively) with what they should. For instance, a tale may tell of a man who behaves selfishly toward his brother, tricking and perhaps killing him. The concluding maxim may point out that this relationship should be one of mutual help, that brothers should never fight or kill one another. Here is a conflict in values, and in the actual situation sibling rivalry is common. The standards expressed in this series are presented as a matter of alternatives and can be drawn on to validate almost any course of action. (Whether this validation is socially acceptable is another matter. Mythological precedent alone carries little weight.)

(e) Significance of mythology

The cosmological myths are *aipa*, meaning base or foundation. (The same word is used for the myth-series dealing with the creation of man, the adventures of Jugumishanta and Morufonu, the institution of various forms of ritual and so on.) They place the world in human perspective, linking man with other aspects of nature, establishing a working relationship with the forces which are believed to control man's destiny. Whereas at one level harmony is established between man and his physical environment, at another there is evidence of uncertainty, even of fear. This can be overcome to some extent through propitiation. But the world revealed in these tales is fundamentally similar to the world of men, although the statements themselves are framed symbolically. In the first place, although they perform super-human feats and possess superhuman powers, the gods behave essentially as human beings do. In the second place, man is shown pitting his ingenuity and strength against them, and he often emerges triumphant.

In the mythology concerning the creation of man and the social and cultural order which is inseparable from him, we are really at the core of sacred belief; and such knowledge appears to be shared by most adults. It deals primarily with the growth of all living things, expressed both directly and symbolically in a variety of ways. The breaking of the ground with digging sticks in gardening is likened to the impregnation of the earth mother, Jugumishanta, and parallels the mythical scene where Morufonu and Jugumishanta had sexual relations in a garden before the creation of man. Gardens are a popular place for intercourse. Also, at the appropriate season, the growth of new crops is encouraged by spinning small ('penis') tops. On certain occasions libations of pig and human blood are splashed on the ground. Gardens are the burial places of local dead. Bodies which were not eaten were 'given to the earth'; but the others were nearly always cut up and cooked in gardens, and the bones buried there. Most of these are everyday acts, not singled out as being ritual in the more formal sense; but the mythology expressly states that the performance of additional ritual is essential. Life can continue only on that condition.

Jugumishanta is manifested also in red crotons and indigenous salt, both vitally important in a variety of situations. These are among her alternative names. The red croton symbolizes her blood. Salt, used for prophylactic and purificatory reasons as well as for seasoning food, is considered to be her body or essence. Through eating it people derive strength; and the act itself, in whatever context, has a sacramental quality.

In combination the two Creators symbolically represent the forces of nature, upon which these people are directly dependent. The mythology built up around them provides a framework justifying much of social activity, without detailing its actual content. In this body of knowledge, as in the cosmological beliefs, we are dealing with basic assumptions. There is no suggestion here of conflict with actuality, only an interpretation of it; a statement, in summary, of that way of life.

All the mythology of ritual can be classified as religious, or sacred. Usually such myths, with accompanying injunctions, are told during men's initiation rituals. They point out why these are necessary, asserting that there is a fundamental cleavage between the sexes. In so doing they underline the essential dependence of men on women, for much ritual is oriented in the direction of purely female activities. Co-operation between the sexes is important, not only in the ritual sphere but also in ordinary social living. Yet, despite exceptions, women are subordinated to men in a wide range of affairs. Men are in a position to give and enforce orders to women without necessarily specifying reasons. It is this aspect of their relationship which is specifically dealt with, and validated, in the mythology. Men are the wielders of the arrow, both literally, and metaphorically as the penis. (The flutes are also symbolic of male dominance and strength and are of phallic significance, in relation both to their individual owners and to the general constellation of beliefs concerning fertility.) In this respect the inequalities between the sexes are more obvious in the literal sphere, much less so in the symbolic: sexual intercourse represents a form of 'fighting' in which women are sometimes said (by men) to be more aggressive and more ready to take the initiative.

Cane-swallowing, although carried out in the course of certain other rituals, is viewed mainly as a personal matter, a means of ensuring internal cleanliness and physical well-being. All women are considered dangerous to men at certain periods, notably menstruation and childbirth, and cane-swallowing is one way of combating their influence. But frequent cane-swallowing is said to make a man irresistible to women. There are contradictions here. In contemporary life, as far as we can gauge, men refrain from sexual intercourse with their wives during their menstrual periods. Nevertheless there are reported cases of women's receiving lovers in the seclusion hut, and after this a man might take no precautions apart from washing himself externally. It is only if the blood is taken internally that action is called for, and in local terms food becomes 'like blood' if handled by a woman in that state; menstrual blood itself is not dangerous, although it is regarded as sacred.

In contrast to the other categories the secondary myths, *kaiteni*, are not foundation stories in this fundamental sense; they do not elaborate on matters of origin and creation, or the meaning of ritual. But they are important in two ways other than those I have mentioned. Firstly, there are special occasions for telling them: after sundown, only in the wet season when new foods are growing, and usually in the gardens. Their actual recital, apart from the matter of content, is a rite instituted by Jugumishanta to promote the growth of garden crops. Secondly, they constitute a complex belief system, flexible enough to accommodate a certain amount of variation and innovation. Also, they represent an extension of the real world, blurring the distinction between ordinary everyday living and the range of experience which from one point of view could be called non-empirical or extra- (or super-) natural.

3. MYTHOLOGY AS A SYSTEM OF BELIEF

This is a tradition-oriented society. A great deal of local knowledge is phrased in non-empirical terms, especially in regard to those areas of living which are of critical importance. We might expect to find here not just values which are significant in the course of everyday living, but also particular emphases which could provide an abstract statement about the society and culture. These are difficult to identify unless measured against the actual situation; to consider them alone without some basis for their selection would invite distortion. Mythology as such is not subjected to empirical inquiry and testing. It is regarded as true, as having a reality of its own which is not at all levels separable from the reality of social living. It validates whole areas of social action, not only ritual, providing the social order with legitimacy in Weber's sense.

The mythology centring on Jugumishanta and Morufonu, their creation of man, and the institution of social life, has a much more obvious or direct social relevance than the cosmological material. It is couched in such terms as 'This is the way in which the gods and ancestors behaved; they did this and that', none of it seriously questioned even when there are, as there must be, discrepancies between mythical and everyday behaviour. Nor is it a matter of contrasting ideal with actual. However contradictory, however strange such actions may be, they are not viewed as incompatible with human actions; both are part of the same universe of reality.

The beings who appear in this part of the mythology are considered to be real, in the sense of having an independent physical existence. This is less obvious as regards the *kaiteni* characters. Jugumishanta and Morufonu and others who appear in the cosmological as well as in the creative and ritual-oriented mythology are sacred; those in the secondary mythology are merely supernatural. The distinction rests not on the content of the myths in which they appear, but on their importance in controlling the physical and natural environment of man and in providing the means (the ritual key) by which the basic necessities of life as these people know it may continue to be available. All mythology deals with explanation and meaning, but the first represents a different order of explanation from the second. The one is preoccupied with the meaning of life, its origin and its maintenance, and has specific reference to the creation of men. The other treats in story form such issues as man's place in nature but does not dwell on them.

A number of statements express concern not only with the origin of life but also with the contrasting theme of death. As they moved northward Jugumishanta and Morufonu grew older and finally died, in other words ceased to exist in the same physical shape as before. In so doing they founded the (or a) land of the dead, which for the Kamano, the eastern Jate, and some of the Usurufa, lay beyond the Markham River. (See R. M. Berndt 1962: pp. 46-7; C. H. Berndt 1966.) But despite what appears to be general belief in the persistence of life after death, views about the nature of such life are vague and not always consistent. Existing alongside the notion of a specific land of the dead, as well as independently of it, is the suggestion that for an undefined period after death a ghost may communicate with living kin through dreams, either voluntarily or in response to a request from the dreamer: chewing *himeru* bark before sleep is said to be a way of getting in touch with the dead, to seek their advice or help in personal problems. The role of ghosts in cargo cult manifestations in this region has been indicated elsewhere (R. M. Berndt 1952-3; 1954a). Apart from rumours and accounts of what purport to be contemporary incidents, ghost stories of a more dramatically entertaining sort are couched in the framework of *kaiteni*, often concluding with the explicit injunction that the dead must not return to disturb or threaten the living. Much of this ghost lore, however, is not directly pertinent to the present theme. What is relevant is the merging of individual ghosts, losing their personal identities, into the category of ancestors and mythical characters associated with various local sites. As such they are invoked in the course of certain rites, with offerings of food and fresh blood; and their presence during the playing of the sacred flutes, each tune owned by a specific lineage, is vital to the growth of pigs and the success of the Pig Festivals.

The major deities are viewed as eternal and indestructible. They assume different manifestations, are called by different names, but are still essentially unchanging. Although they may be killed, this means merely that they assume another shape. The same applies to some of the partly anthropomorphic inhabitants of the bush and jungle. But ghosts and characters in the secondary myths, including giants, ogres and apparitions of several kinds, appear to be almost as vulnerable as man is himself.

Part of the cosmological mythology, but particularly the secondary mythology, deals with inter-personal relations. In the cosmology, where social relations are subsidiary to the main emphasis, a given mode of action may on one occasion bring rewards, on another retribution: but it is not invariably condemned just because in one mythological setting it leads to punishment. Within a certain range, one cannot be sure what course of action a character will adopt or how other characters will respond to it. Up to a point this is so in the secondary mythology too, but in that case the final maxim may evaluate certain features of the situation as good or bad. In drawing out the implications of any of these stories, as summarized in the maxims, despite some general agreement a narrator is not bound by any hard and fast rules. The stories consist of sets of plot-elements which various narrators reshuffle into more or less different combinations. This process is not acknowledged: they are regarded as fixed units, transmitted unchanged from one generation to another.

In the mythology concerning the creation of man and of his social setting there is no evaluation in local terms, only acceptance. The basic knowledge referring to the cosmos, too, taken as a whole, involves accepted ways of acting and of viewing situations, accepted sentiments and standards.

4. RITUAL ACTION

Radcliffe-Brown (1952: p. 155) suggested that 'in attempting to understand a religion it is on the rites rather than on the beliefs that we should first concentrate our attention'. Ritual is viewed as primarily social action, leading to an analysis in terms of structure, but in his approach is emphasized at the expense of belief. I prefer to view ritual in a general sense as belief transformed into action, while recognizing that this says nothing about the intensity of such belief and that such action may be performed by individual persons for a variety of reasons. Because there is no exact correspondence between the two, considering one does not necessarily help us to understand the meaning of the other.

Certainly myth provides a positive sanction for ritual, even though the
mythology just reviewed includes no clear-cut statement as to how
it should be performed. Yet mythology and ritual are concerned with
broadly the same symbolism and the same values. To Leach (1954:
pp. 13-14) '. . . myth . . . as a statement in words "says" the same thing
as ritual . . . as a statement in action'. But, in this area at least, each
appears to say something different about the same thing, and what they
say about social relations is only a part of this.

The ritual to be discussed here refers back to the creation mythology.
It does not concern cosmological beliefs relating to the origin of the
world; there is no ritual connected with these. Nor does it relate to
the secondary mythology. Following Firth's definition (1951: p. 222),
we can restrict ritual to socially approved regularized action directed
toward the control of human affairs by non-empirical means. This
need not be labelled sacred or religious, and it might very well include
not only sorcery but also birth, marriage and mortuary ritual, and
subsidiary acts relating to ghosts and minor guardians of local sites.
It also embraces other actions directly or indirectly involving the
creators: fertility rites such as blood libations, cannibalistic meals and
the burial of bones or complete corpses in gardens, the spinning of
tops, and preventive and propitiatory rites such as taking salt, planting
crotons and, again, blood libations. 'Archaeological' stones are buried
in gardens to make crops grow, and herbs, wild ginger and other plants
are used for protection against malignant spirits.

However, the importance of ritual in this context might be taken
to lie in the way it contributes to the efficient working of a society
(Nadel 1954: p. 114). It does so through the fairly regular occurrence
of patterned co-activity, with more or less clearly articulated aims[4]
which are part of the process of socialization—inculcation and affirma-
tion of traditional values and emphases on the one hand, maintaining
social alignments on the other. This is not to imply that all the actors
in a ritual sequence could give equally coherent accounts of such aims
or of the symbolic significance of their actions. But I would not say,
as Wilson does (1954: p. 236), that we cannot predict what symbols
will be used in ritual. Certainly the same symbol may represent several
things to the same person; the context in which it is used or expressed
helps to shape its meaning and form. However, we speak of social
symbols because they are agreed upon by the group involved, although we recognize that their meaning depends on such factors as
social alignment. If not, then we are not dealing with social symbolism.

Ritual, as the term is used here, is not synonymous with ceremony. Ceremony is no less important, for it may be oriented toward ends which are not explicitly recognized by the people involved. Moreover, it need not be devoid of symbolic representation: it often represents the wrapping of ritual.

The principal ceremonies in which ritual takes place in this region are all associated at one time or another with various stages in the initiation of youths, but not exclusively so. Although they serve as a vehicle for the formal teaching of the young, they also involve the full participation of adults.

(a) The Pig Festival

For some months before the final climax is reached men play sacred flutes at intervals to encourage the growth of pigs. Women and un-initiated youths are forbidden to look at them, under threat of death. Although the flutes themselves are male symbols, the sound they make is, in a general sense, the voice of Jugumishanta. Women, who know more about the flutes and associated rites than one would suppose from listening to men, sometimes call the flute 'co-wife' and speak of it as a 'flute woman'. During this period men swing bullroarers, also kept secret from women. As they go through a village they may seize young boys and take them off to a secluded place where cane and rough leaves are forced up their nostrils to make blood flow. On other occasions the novices are ritually shown the sacred flutes.

The festival itself may take place each year or at longer intervals of up to five years or so, depending on the number of pigs available. The preliminaries are in the hands of male members of a village or district, but for the main festival members of adjacent districts are invited. Huge quantities of garden produce are collected and prepared. Pigs, from various villages in the district, are killed one after another by a blow on the snout to the accompaniment of flute playing, so that blood flows from their nostrils to the ground 'like men having their noses bled'; as men cut the pigs they sing, offering blood to the ground, to Jugumishanta. New flutes are made in the men's houses and anointed with the fresh pig blood; and while the meat is being cooked in the ovens old men split the blood-stained croton leaves, waving them as they invoke the ancestors associated with various localities, to whom the spiritual essence of the feast belongs.

Because conflicts occurred so frequently, it seems that only rarely were more than six or so districts involved at any one time. But each can be viewed as the centre of an interactory zone, in which the host on one occasion may be a receiver on another and so on, the visitors in each case forming a slightly different constellation. The assumption is that between any two districts concerned expenditure and receipts eventually balance, even though this may not be attained for a generation or so, after which the cycle presumably starts again. There is the deliberate building up of a surplus, which is then conspicuously displayed and disposed of; and in accepting it the recipients acknowledge their obligation to reciprocate in the same terms. Competition and rivalry at such festivals are not confined to relations between districts. Within the host district, prestige accrues to the man or lineage killing the most pigs or distributing the most food.

(b) Avagli

The ritual and ceremony of the sweat-house are substantiated on the one hand by a pseudo-historical tale and on the other by a myth closely resembling some included in the secondary mythology. Adult males of a village gather in their communal houses where special leaves are mixed with bark, ginger and other leaves and salt. After preliminary nose-bleeding and tongue-scraping the mixture is passed around, each man chewing a little. They remain there for several days, singing, around a blazing fire, while the avagli sweat trickles in patterns down their faces and bodies. At intervals their womenfolk, singing special songs, bring water and cooked edible leaves. Finally, the men decorate themselves and come out singing and dancing, carrying bows and arrows, to enjoy a feast prepared by the women.

The more obvious and extensive the avagli pattern, it is said, the greater the warrior, for this is an indication of magical power, a sign of strength: the really 'big' men with shield designs on their chests are protected as if by a magical shield. This is a ceremony entailing ritual which is designed to improve a man's physical condition, to increase his fighting prowess. And in so doing, it enhances a man's attractiveness to the opposite sex. No secrecy is associated with the actual ritual, although sexual abstinence is enjoined and men do not move from the hut during this period.

(c) The initiation rituals

The following rituals are far more closely associated with initiation than the two outlined above, although one could equally well stress their connection with adult religious activity. The following is a sketch in summary.

(i) *Nose-bleeding*. Men with drawn bows surround a site away from the village, near running water, where novices are confronted with men bleeding their nostrils, cane-swallowing and vomiting. Novices are accused of menstruating and told to eat the blood. Then they are shown the guardian of the flutes, masked, with an arrow piercing his foreskin. In a bush shelter behind him flutes are being played, and behind that again a bullroarer is swung. The novices are seized and their nostrils forcibly bled. There is feasting, with food distributed to all the participants. The novices are instructed as to what they should and should not do. From this time on they sleep in the men's house, and no longer in the women's houses with their mothers.

(ii) *The charcoal period*. For several months the youths are rubbed all over with charcoal, while admonitions similar to those during the end of the first rite are repeated. This is the first part of their formal training as warriors. It begins with further nose-bleeding, when bamboo slivers smeared with salt are twirled in their nostrils, followed by cutting and scraping the tongue and rubbing the penis apex with rough leaves. All this is to test their strength and teach them to bear pain, on the assumption that such endurance is a way of achieving strength. Later the adult method of nose-bleeding is adopted: two packs of bound cane and leaves are pushed up the nostrils and twirled. Like all ritual shedding of blood, this is a libation to Jugumishanta and also to the ancestors.

(iii) *Penis-bleeding*. By this time a youth will have been shown the sacred flutes, although he may not own one until he is regarded as fully adult and (in the traditional setting) has proved himself as a warrior. Also, the charcoal period is a prelude to the *avagli* rite. At about eighteen to twenty years a novice is introduced to penis-bleeding.

Again a creek is the scene of the rite, because running water can dispose of blood and other exuviae which might otherwise be used in sorcery. It is usually carried out by men of one or two villages or hamlets, occasionally from others within the same district, less often from outside it. A length of cane is pushed up the urethra and twirled, removed and sprayed with salt and the process repeated until blood flows. Then larger bundles of tightly bunched leaves, about the size of a pencil, are employed, so that gradually the youth is conditioned to the adult procedure. This operation is said to have a strengthening

G

effect: if a man's penis is strong, his arrows will be strong too. Finally there is a ritual presentation of a banana cake, symbolic of maleness.

(iv) *Variation*. The sequence varies even within one area; but most performances include these basic operations, except that among the Fore there is no penis-bleeding or cutting of the penis apex. The most notable additions not mentioned above involve drawing blood from under the fingernails, and beating novices until blood flows when they first see the flutes. There are two other interesting aspects. Just before the novices enter the village on their return from the initiation ground, surrounded by men, they are ambushed by a party of women dressed as men and holding shields and bows with drawn arrows. A mock fight takes place, in which the women accuse the men of alienating and spoiling their sons. The second feature is the use of dramatic scenes to teach the novices the right and wrong ways of behaving: these accompany the admonitions and may include short summaries from the secondary myths.

(v) *Puberty rites for girls*. These relate principally to menstruation and childbirth and centre around the seclusion hut conventionally closed to men. They include both nose-bleeding, and vaginal insertion of a wad of rough leaves twirled around and pushed up and down to draw blood: this, like coitus, is said to induce menstruation. Both rites are said to strengthen the girl and make her physically attractive. To maintain these qualities they must be repeated intermittently, for instance after menstruation and childbirth, and at any major personal crisis.

(d) Implications

The Pig Festivals are directly concerned with fertility and with the basic assumptions which appear in the Jugumishanta-Morufonu mythology. Fertility, associated with the whole range of blood-letting operations for both males and females, represents one dominant theme.

Another such theme is the relations between the sexes. Many of the ritual acts carried out by men, like nose- and penis-bleeding, are explicitly likened to menstruation and are not significantly different from the puberty rites of women. Yet there is a fairly rigid dichotomy between the ritual activities of both sexes, despite their interdependence. For men, symbolic interpretations or simulation of menstruation and childbirth are means of achieving strength. They are this for women,

too, but without the same emphasis on symbolism. Opposition between
the two is expressed in terms of contrast or difference, but in fact more
attention seems to be paid to similarities, or would-be similarities.

Woman's participation in male ritual is, necessarily, of a subsidiary
kind. They join in dancing, prepare feasts and make gifts, but they
are never present at the principal rites and never see the sacred flutes.
The stress on strength and physical well-being, especially for men,
appears in almost every aspect of ritual action: for example, the flutes,
the *avagli*, the penis- and nose-bleeding, as well as cane-swallowing.
It has been developed to such an extent that it could be called a major
preoccupation. Complementary to it is the fear that this strength will
be damaged: women can, if they so desire, render a man ineffectual
as a warrior and vulnerable to the arrows of his enemy. He must be
constantly on guard and, if at all suspicious, should use his vomiting
cane, which will purge and purify him. In the injunctions at initiation
this is continually reiterated. It is even taken so far that youths are
warned against having sexual relations with girls, and adult men
against indulging too frequently in such relations, particularly with
women not their wives. Conventionally, then, an attitude of antagonism toward females is built up and sustained, on the one hand through
ritual practice and on the other through ordinary everyday activity.
In regard to the latter it should be recalled that inter-district hostility,
either potential or actual, was a more or less constant state of affairs.
In construct terms, men were expected to regard their wives with
suspicion because in many cases they came from enemy or potentially
enemy districts, and because of the strong ties between them and their
brothers, as well as their close cross-cousins. But the actual picture
does not always correspond. More generally, the admonitions are
often ignored in practice.

The contrasting themes of male ritual on the basis of female physio-
logical features, and the fear that strength built up in that way can
be harmed by females, are highlighted in still another way. In the
avagli, penis- and nose-bleeding, and cane-swallowing, erotic elements
are conspicuously present. This aspect receives considerable attention
right through the religious sphere, as well as in everyday activity. Its
appearance in the ritual and mythology underlines the basic assumption
that, in primary terms, religion has to do with the necessities of human
existence and the relations between the sexes, with sex itself as a focal
point. Any religion which concerns itself with the welfare of social
man must take all this into account. What is more, it emphasizes the

balance between independence and interdependence which, weighted in one direction or the other, permeates all male-female relations.

5. RELIGION IN SOCIAL PERSPECTIVE

—What does religion mean to these people? Generally, while admitting that beyond a certain point it possibly means different things to different persons, it appears to mean a great deal if we take into account their preoccupation with the topics already indicated. Fertility, strength, fighting prowess and prestige, within the context of what is perceived as an inherent antagonism between the worlds of men and of women, are pervading themes which have a direct relevance to their total way of life; and it is obvious that they are linked not only with economic affairs, with the cultivation and disposal of crops and the acquisition and distribution of wealth, but also with marital relations and warfare, among other features. But although the measure of their interest in these themes indirectly reflects their faith, it is not easy to say that they are a religious people. Much depends on one's definition, and certainly the one employed here is wide enough to permit this. Yet, on the same showing, it is plain that much ritual activity is frankly a matter of self-interest. 'God helps those who help themselves' might well be the dictum here, as it is perhaps in most ritual. The lengthy period leading up to the culmination of the Pig Festival is one of articulating ritual practice, flute-playing, for instance, with gardening activities and the lavishing of attention on domestic pigs. Novices undergo physical training co-ordinated with bow and arrow practice. The theme of 'enduring pain to achieve strength' is a further example. Personal well-being is thus explicitly emphasized, even within the framework of the Pig Festival and the initiation sequence. Only obliquely is the common good accentuated, and then primarily in regard to the political unit. The vague acknowledgement of a common origin, a common traditional background, expressed in the phrase 'children of Jugumishanta', seems to have little practical relevance. But if interpreted in terms of male sibling rivalry, another major theme both in the secondary myths and in everyday activity, it makes more sense.

Another useful way of looking at the situation is to consider the attitudes of these people toward their deities. Although it is frequently said that the rituals and blood offerings are performed primarily for them, Jugumishanta and Morufonu are spoken of quite casually at times and are often very much in the background. The focus is on what can be got out of the situation, rather than on establishing a personal relationship between man and his gods. One has the impression that these are regarded virtually as equals, possessed of superior power and additional knowledge but not very dissimilar to man in spite of this. Certainly they are in a position to do man ill as well as good, but then other men too are in the same position. This is not an authoritarian religion. Rather, at least as far as men are concerned, it is egalitarian, as is essentially their social system: authority and leadership can be achieved through strength, and hypothetically this is available equally to all. The rituals are open to all adult males; and all youths go through the initiation sequence, although certain operations may be modified to allow for individual differences.

Although much religious practice is the concern of lineage members and may be restricted to one district, it is true that relatively large groups are formed on occasions, during a Pig Festival or at an initiation. The numbers, however, depend on circumstances, the most telling being consideration of warfare. When the genealogical ramifications of festival groups were examined, the majority of the participants were seen to be closely linked by ties of kinship.

Distinguishing sacred from secular spheres of interest and activity is difficult when the ramifications of this religious system are explored —and only part of it is discussed here. Although this is a tradition-oriented society, a good case could be made for the growth of secularization through the tremendous emphasis on strength and personal achievement. However, any division we might make should not be in terms of male activity=sacred, female activity=profane. It is not really a matter of divergent spheres of interest, even though male ideology has built up a barrage of antagonism as far as women are concerned. Men play the executive role in ritual, but it is a co-operative undertaking. They keep various ritual objects secret, particularly the flutes, but their use in ritual necessarily brings in women. Women's use of the term co-wife for the flute indicates the closeness of their involvement and incidentally tells us something about their attitude toward men's ritual, for the co-wife relationship is notoriously one of strain. Women are acquainted not only with the cosmological knowledge and the secondary myths but also with nearly all the sacred mythology, including accounts of creation, even if they are not aware of all the symbolic meanings. Only certain sections of ritual and some of the objects, as well as esoteric explanations, remain the special possession of men. But even here women surreptitiously know much of what goes on.

Religious belief in its regulatory aspect is best seen in relation to the initiation complex. It receives its main stimulus in this sphere, because this is the principal medium for the transmission of knowledge relating to religious matters, for the inculcation of cultural values, and for emphasizing certain social relations rather than others. It is also the medium through which youths are, or were, specially trained for a life of intermittent fighting. A corollary of the concept of strength is the positive value accorded to aggression. Elaboration of this theme is associated with a fairly wide range of toleration as far as certain kinds of behaviour are concerned. This is supported by the presence of conflicting values, most notably demonstrated in the secondary myths, in the lack of fit between the incidents dealt with in these stories and their moral injunctions, and between these and everyday life. It is directly relevant in regard to the admonitions which are part of initiation procedure. These do not rest on simple statements such as 'Do this' or 'Don't do that'. Rather, through the medium of a dramatic performance a youth is shown the likely consequences of a given action and told to make his choice. He must, in the final count, rely on himself. These performances take place also during secular ceremonies, where it is said that they reinforce what has been taught in a more formalized way in the course of initiation. The system in this respect, as in others, has the appearance of being permissive and flexible.

The religious ideology, in supporting the theme of strength for all, is also underwriting not only the ideal of the strong man but also the struggle between adult men for ascendancy, the more or less continual jockeying for position which goes on in everyday life. This is seen as rivalry between lineage siblings and age-mates within a village and district, and in terms of physical aggression outside it. Within the district, the struggle centres on wealth on the one hand and sexual adventures on the other, and open violence is discouraged but not entirely prevented. Because no absolute limitations are placed on aggressive action carried out by a strong man, this means that religious belief can indirectly support political power and authority either in the indigenous situation or within the setting of alien influence. Much depends on where we draw the line between the sacred and secular spheres. But power and authority in this situation can, traditionally speaking, be maintained only through a display of physical strength or through prestige continually reinforced by lavish distribution. Religious sanctions, in the sense of supernatural powers, esoteric knowledge and so on, do not seem to be significant. A man who is forceful enough can act very much as he pleases, overriding the opinions of others. For such as he the range of permissible behaviour is considerably extended; and this applies in a lesser degree also to women. Yet the contexts in which strength and physical prowess are derived and sustained are mostly ritualized; the ways in which they are applied, in fighting, quarrelling, discussion and feasting, belong mostly within the secular sphere.

Religion can thus be said to support the structure of this society, virtually the whole social order. But how is this done? Its relationship to the authority system and to the formal sex dichotomy has already been noted. This last must be seen not just as opposition between men and women as such or between husband and wife, but between ingroup and outgroup—the political unit in contrast to all similar units or, to some extent, lineage kin against all affinal kin. Jugumishanta and her husband are said to have established a religious system shared by all members of the Kamano, Usurufa, Jate and Fore. Yet because the ideology was not confined to matters relating to fertility, but emphasized menstruation and blood-letting in conjunction with male strength, it inevitably involved conflict and rivalry.

When these two Creators in the beginning travelled across the country, in each place at which they stopped they placed a male and a female; this was the archaic nucleus of the local unit. They also instructed these first people in the arts of living: in gardening, ritual activity, fighting and so on. In other words, Jugumishanta and Morufonu showed them how to be independent and relatively self-sufficient. The ways in which people perceive their past indicate how they perceive their present: and mythology is one field in which such views are expressed. But this is an assumed relationship. The lineages and the districts show no direct link with the creation mythology. Etymologically, their names often refer to pseudo-historical incidents and to secondary myths but only rarely to Jugumishanta and Morufonu. There is a relationship only because all of this belongs within a common epistemological framework; but within this configuration of ideas there is marked compartmentalization. The binding linkage is in the system of values and basic assumptions which ensures some sort of coherence and relative consistency. In terms of style, the parallel is quite striking when this is compared with what we might call a segmentary social system, made up of a constellation of small political units (districts), in potential opposition to one another, and interacting within limited spheres of competition and co-operation—separateness within a setting of common expectations.

The religious system serves as a vehicle through which values are mediated, and the ramifications of ritual and ceremonial behaviour have more or less straightforward implications for social action generally. Certainly it is pervasive. Nevertheless, the secularization of dominant themes may set limits as far as religious influence is concerned. This is difficult to interpret. For instance, the main focus of religious belief and action concerns the Pig Festival and the significance of the flutes for fertility. If we were to speak impressionistically about degrees of sacredness and religious feeling, we might expect to find it at its maximum within this context. This area, a crucial one, will be mentioned below in relation to alien contact. In social terms, Durkheim's effervescence and collective representation are directly relevant. Yet on other religious occasions it is the political unit which is the co-acting group; and on others again it is a matter for the individual, with his nose-bleeding and his cane-swallowing. We could possibly say that religious belief and action are stronger in some spheres than others, and that this corresponds with the number of participants. But we could say just as well that the theme of strength, upheld by the religious system, has a specifically personal relevance; the rites associated with it are indeed more often carried out separately, by individual performers. This could be seen in terms of 'doing good for the community' in contrast to 'doing good for one's self'.

Flexibility is especially apparent in the secondary mythology. This is within the framework of the belief system, but close to what we can call the secular end of the continuum, and is an area possibly less 'sacred' than any other dealt with here. Setting out as it does alternative lines of action and conflicting moral injunctions, it reflects more accurately the difficulties of everyday social interaction. This is a critical sphere, particularly in circumstances of alien contact, but it is critical in rather a different way from that of the Pig Festival and flutes.

6. ALIEN PRESSURES

Europeans first turned their attention to this region in the years following World War II; irregular patrols touched some districts from 1947-49. By 1949 and 1951 the country as far south as Kogu (Usurufa) and Moke-Busarasa (Fore) respectively was declared to be under control, which meant that inter-district fighting was at least officially suppressed; but farther south, at the time of our field work in 1951-52, 1952-53, the area was 'restricted' and retained fundamentally an indigenous flavour. Throughout there were varying degrees of sophistication in alien terms. It was particularly evident near Kainantu, which was established as an administrative patrol base in 1930-31, and where two missions were operating: Seventh Day Adventist and Lutheran. Apart from the neighbourhood of Kainantu and the mission stations (with an outstation at Taramu in Jate country), most alien contact had been indirect or had been filtered through native evangelists and native police, neither of whom were numerous in this region when we carried out field work there. Nevertheless their influence was considerable, for they were regarded as 'strong men' and were thus in a position, in a society where strength was regarded as the primary criterion of authority, to manipulate the situation.

Before Europeans entered the region, however, the local people were subject to waves of rumours about them; they were viewed as spirits of the dead, and propitiatory and protective rites were performed on their account. Some time later the whole region was affected by the *zona* 'ghost' wind, which involved spirit possession and shivering. In all these, the emphasis was on possessing introduced goods as well as indigenous forms of wealth and on using them to obtain increased prestige. In nearly all cases, the prime movers were warrior leaders. Although these activities were definitely a response to alien impact, the ideology underlying them was wholly traditional. No feature of the belief system or ritual as outlined above was affected; there was only reassembling of elements already present, in response to a special situation. In this respect it differed from the movements taking place north-east of Kainantu, toward the Markham, where Christian and also millennial features were involved.

From 1947 onward in some districts fairly drastic changes took place almost overnight. The cessation of inter-district warfare, the appointment of alien-sponsored *luluais*, *tultuls* and boss-boys, and the suppression of cannibalism and other subsidiary features had repercussions on the organization of activity, the autonomy of the political unit, the maintenance of law and order, and the whole question of relations within the sphere of interaction extending outside the district. Without the people themselves understanding at once what was happening, there was a shift from independence to dependence and incorporation within the alien administrative framework; from being relatively free they became a subject people. The main reasons these changes could be effected so rapidly lay on the one hand in the people's emphasis on strength; they respected this in others, giving way to it as a matter of practical expediency, while expecting that their chance would eventually come. On the other hand, they expected tangible rewards in return for conforming to outside pressures. We could almost say that their indigenous religion supported capitulation in the first instance, while the second relates to another basic theme on which this discussion has hardly touched. Wealth could buy security as well as prestige, especially in the shape of friendship and help in times of threat. This aspect came to the fore in the cargo cult manifestations and represents a popular topic in the secondary mythology.

In spite of all this, the basic value orientation seemed to have remained virtually unaltered. People might perform different actions, but the ideological contexts in which they did so were not appreciably different. The newly-appointed leaders were often warrior leaders. Even when they were not, the indigenous authority system was structured loosely enough to accommodate this without much strain. But there was a shift toward the secularization of authority; it no longer rested on the same premises as before. Some dramatic changes were taking place. The palisades around villages and hamlets were being thrown down, informal courts were developing, men found themselves suddenly 'unemployed'.

In these circumstances native evangelists became active, even in parts of the 'uncontrolled' region which officially they were not permitted to enter. They were largely from other areas, plus a few of the northern Kamano. Members of the upper ranks of the native evangelical hierarchy were mainly Kâte speakers from the coast. Mostly they could communicate only haltingly with the indigenous people, except through local interpreters. The introduction of Kâte by the Lutherans as a lingua franca had serious disadvantages, although use of it, even of no more than a few words, was taken as a sign of at least a foothold in the new order. On the whole these native evangelists had only sketchy ideas about Adventist or Lutheran forms of Christianity; their own experience and education were extremely limited. Here, of course, is a division of authority in secular and sacred terms.

Two incidents highlight the effects of alien impact, and specifically of missionary activity, on the indigenous religious syste:.i.

The first (recorded 26-7 February 1952 from eye-witnesses; not observed personally) occurred at Bamio (Kamano) near Jagana and Ki'o. Spokesmen for this district had expressed their willingness to be accepted into the

Lutheran fold. During the dedication ceremony the sacred flutes were brought out on to the village clearing and shown to the uninitiated, the women and children.[5] They were exhorted to eschew their savage ways: fighting, sorcery, adultery. Part of the appeal went something like this: 'See these flutes which you make so much of? They are only hollow pieces of bamboo. The flute is the mother of Satan; it makes poison come up. When you keep it away from women, it only makes them want to see it; and if they do you kill them or work sorcery on them. Take the flute to the village clearing and show to all, and let the women and children play. Do away with this pretence, for a new way has come with the mission.'

I do not know how these people were persuaded to show their flutes publicly. The women, especially, are reported to have been terrified, and many visitors left to spread the news of what had happened at Bamio. When the news reached Kogu, where we were living at the time, the whole area became disturbed and men prophesied disaster for Bamio. But other northern districts followed suit. Native evangelists, along with missionaries, insisted that the indigenous religion must be done away with entirely, and that exposure and ridicule were the best means of bringing this about. Once the flutes were shown to women their power was said to be rendered ineffective. The flute-playing and Pig Festival in those districts were immediately abandoned. So was the whole sequence of initiation ceremonies and ritual, including the *avagli*.

This remarkable *volte-face* epitomizes the far-reaching changes which are occurring in all aspects of life in this area, and not just in those intimately associated with the flutes. Further, it demonstrates vividly the importance of the flutes themselves, the fact that they seem to be central to the religious system. In this respect there is no rapprochement with the alien religion; nor, probably, would one expect there to be.

Indigenous religion, as broadly defined here, however, incorporates the secondary mythology, and it is in this context that some rapprochement is indicated.

The second example relates to Kogu (Usurufa) (recorded 10 February 1952). Through the efforts of several native evangelists a small, rather crude church was built at Maira(pa) in this district. Soon afterward it was decided to hold an 'open door' ceremony, said to signify the acceptance of Christianity by all district members, as well as the dedication of the church. People from that district and from others converged on Mairapa along one road: all other approaches were blocked. At each side of the village barriers of branches and brush were placed across the roadway, leaving an opening which was guarded by evangelists. Each district group danced toward the opening, passed through and continued on to the village clearing. All the dancing, singing and decorations were of a traditional nature. When all were assembled the evangelists began to harangue their audience, in much the same way as in the first example. This was followed by short dramatic performances or morality plays, designed to emphasize good as against bad kinds of behaviour. A few of these were based on the secondary myths. After that a church service was held, followed by feasting.

This case points up the fact that, although indigenous religion is being directly attacked and supplanted, much of what can be called traditional is being drawn upon to support the introduced religion. The secondary mythology and dramatic scenes, both used in the contexts of initiation and secular ceremony, could readily be adapted to suit the current situation.[6] But in emphasizing this aspect of the belief system alien impact, while sustaining one part of indigenous life, is also shifting the significance of these mythologically-based performances, crystallizing moral values while narrowing the framework of choice, and altering local conceptions of religion. It is probably only a matter of time before new media for the transmission of religiously-oriented values will take their place.

7. CONCLUSION

At Sonofe, a Kamano district a few hours walking distance from Kainantu, by 1952 Jugumishanta had been replaced by 'God', or Anutu in Kâte. It was only after some hours of intensive discussion that a group of leading men admitted to knowing anything about traditional accounts of creation.[7] In Kogu during our first visit the flutes were played almost incessantly; during the second they were scarcely heard. Throughout most of the southern part of this region, however, the indigenous system still operated. Nevertheless, the trends I have mentioned are fast gaining ground; and the Okapa Medical Post (established to study kuru disease, or kuru sorcery) and increasing mission and mission-sponsored activities must surely intensify them.

Up to the time I left the region, one type of non-empirical belief and action (Christianity) had been struggling to supersede the other (the traditional religious system), and doing so quite effectively with the full support of the Administration. Christianity is not designed to fit the society it attempts to evangelize. It may adapt but not alter its basic ideology; and adaptation is insufficient as far as the native society is concerned. Christianity is a way of life, not just a relationship between man and his God; the traditional religion was (and is) this too. And rapprochement, although apparent in some respects, is far from permanent.

The very fact that evangelization was making an impression implies that the belief system was being re-oriented. Its flexibility, especially in relation to the secondary myths and dramatic scenes, suggests that it was potentially receptive to new ideas and could readily be manipulated to suit changing conditions. It means that Christian beliefs, if not action, can be interpreted through traditional media—but not necessarily through traditional religious media.

Notwithstanding this, the core of traditional religious practice, once its symbolic representations are publicly exposed, almost invariably collapses without a struggle. But the cessation of ritual activity, collective or individual, does not mean that the beliefs which have been associated with it automatically disappear. Furthermore, the forced abandonment, or virtual abandonment, of traditional religion does not inevitably mean acceptance of Christianity. The 'open door' ritual and the church represent a change in ceremonial context and not necessarily a change in belief.

The situation superficially indicates rapid change, with the introduction of a new religion and with increasing pressures from the Administration toward conformity over a fairly wide field of behaviour. The position, however, is more complex than this. There are suggestions that a fairly high degree of adaptability and flexibility was a feature of the traditional situation. But rigidity is also apparent. In what other way do we interpret the collapse of the flute-playing and all its interrelated rituals? There is no accommodation or adaptability in this respect. It is possibly much easier to alter the form of a society than to change its basic values and cultural orientation. At least it seems that in this situation, although it has not been possible to present here the evidence for saying so, alien impact had had little real effect where these are concerned. Rejection was not feasible because of the overriding pressures of joint Administrative-Mission impact, especially as Christianity and Europeanization presented a vista of new ways of obtaining wealth and power. Christianity is reconcilable, I would suggest, only in so far as it can fulfil these needs. But Christianity as such does not impinge on the traditional religion, except in so far as both *are* religions.

The lacuna created by the conscious abandoning of traditional religious ritual can be filled in a number of ways: by the adoption of Christian forms, by more frequent performances of secular ceremonies, by ritualized football matches and so on. But these activities are linked with others which are not of a traditional kind. The introduction of Christianity involves the introduction also of a new social organization and structure, incompatible with those we may call indigenous. A non-literate society of this kind, however flexible its religious system or however well integrated its social system, has little chance of retaining social and cultural integrity in the face of the concerted onslaught of a way of life which in spite of many points of convergence is hostile to its fundamental tenets. It seems true, however, that such a people have more opportunity to adjust to and to develop an alternative way of life if their value orientation admits of rephrasing and manipulation, if authority and power rest on achieved rather than on ascribed status, if the range of tolerated behaviour is not restrictive, and if their social organization generally is of a segmentary kind. Conversely, because of these features there is less likelihood that traditional aspects will survive. One does not expect to find complete consistency in any social or religious system, and one does not find it here.

NOTES

[1] Field research in this region was carried out in 1951-52 and 1952-53, under the auspices of the Department of Anthropology, University of Sydney. Unless otherwise stated, reference in the main body of this chapter is largely to the 'ethnographic present' of 1951-53. For convenience all native words, personal and place names are in Jate, although any of the other languages would have served equally well.

[2] To avoid confusion they will be referred to by these names here. Throughout the region there are statements about creator beings who performed actions of the sort described, but they are not always known by identical or similar names even within the same language unit. The question of variation in myth and in social perspective is taken up in a study which focuses specifically on the *kaiteni*, but includes more general aspects as well (C. H. Berndt: n.d.).

[3] Myth may provide an 'explanation' of ritual, but not necessarily in terms of dramatizing the activities of certain mythical personages, such as one finds in Aboriginal Australia. 'Explanation' in this context means local explanation in a mythological framework. See Parsons (1952: p. 398); Nadel (1954: p. 262).

[4] I am dealing here with manifest aims and not with inferences about them. Cf. Merton (1957: pp. 19 ff.).

[5] For reference to the smashing and burning of sacred flutes by native converts in the western Goroka area, toward Chimbu, and subsequent local unrest, see Patrol Reports No. 7 and 7A of 1950-51, Department of District Services and Native Affairs, New Guinea. Read (1952b: pp. 8-9) also comments on this incident.

[6] The Lutheran missionary at Raipinka, however, is said to have given orders (in 1947-48) for the banning of singing and dancing, with particular reference to the Kamano area: these orders were countermanded by the Administration. See Patrol Report No. 5 of 1947-48. Farther west, in the Goroka area, there were reports of the ritual burning of ceremonial emblems (that is, as used in the secular ceremonies); I was subsequently shown coloured slides of one such scene.

[7] This was in contrast to the position in 1953 in two Jate districts, where it turned out that a number of men who had been using the name 'Anutu' in discussing events relating to the creation were really talking about Jugumishanta.

M. J. MEGGITT

The Mae Enga of the Western Highlands[1]

I. MAE SOCIETY[2]

THE Enga live in the Western Highlands District of the Australian Territory of New Guinea, among mountains that rise from about 6,000 to over 11,000 feet above sea-level. Most of the population is concentrated in river valleys at altitudes ranging from about 4,000 to 7,500 feet.

European explorers first met the Enga in 1933. Government officers made sporadic visits until 1942, when they set up a permanent patrol post at Wabaga. Four more patrol posts were established in neighbouring valleys by 1960, when the European population of the Sub-district numbered about ninety.

The culture of the western Enga (generally called the Mae) differs from that of the eastern Enga (the Laiapu). The Mae are further divided into Yandapu and Mae proper (who together include some 30,000 natives) and the Laiapu into the Syaka and Laiapu proper (together about 25,000 natives). The four comprise the central Enga, whose population density is on the average about 110 to 120 per square mile and in places exceeds 250. The population density of the fringe Enga is much lower—averaging perhaps thirty per square mile.

The central Enga are primarily gardeners but also keep pigs and fowls. Sweet potatoes are the staple crop, and cultivation of the valley floors and lower slopes is intensive. In the central valleys clans have occupied all the usable land, and land disputes are common.

The people belong to named and localized patriclans that are elements of segmentary lineage systems. The clan territory, which has sharply-defined boundaries, is generally between one and two square miles in area. The Mae clan parish (that is, the local group of clansmen, their wives, children and certain attached non-agnates) usually has about 350 members, although the range is from about 100 to 1,100.

The people do not live in villages but in homesteads scattered about the clan territory. As a rule, each wife shares her house with unmarried daughters, infant sons and the family pigs, whereas the husband and older sons reside with other male agnates in a small clubhouse.

Ideally the clans are exogamous, and about ninety-two per cent of marriages conform to this norm. About fifteen per cent of married men are polygynists. Land and other important property should be inherited patrilineally within the clan; and on the average about eighty-six per cent of the men of a Mae clan parish are putative agnates, who trace descent through about seven generations from the eponymous clan founder. The clan parish is a relatively autonomous group, which organizes its own rituals, ceremonial exchange relationships, payments of homicide compensation and, until recently, military operations. There are no hereditary or formally-elected chiefs or headmen; the direction of clan activities is mainly in the hands of wealthy and energetic men who have acquired 'big names'.

A cluster of contiguous clans (generally about eight) forms a named phratry, whose founder is thought to have been the father of the clan founders. Although the men of a phratry regard themselves as 'brothers' and may witness each other's clan rituals, they rarely act together as a group. Sometimes one phratry engaged in formalized warfare with another, but ordinary inter-clan fights seldom mobilized whole phratries. Moreover, although intra-phratry warfare was deplored, it often occurred.

Each clan comprises several named sub-clans, whose founders are taken to have been the sons of the clan founder. Sub-clan domains exist within the clan territory, and members tend to live on their own lands. The sub-clan as a corporate group is mainly concerned in payments of death (as distinct from homicide) compensations to maternal kin and in regular performances of purificatory rituals for bachelors. Occasionally large-scale gardening operations call on all the men of a sub-clan.

The sub-clan in turn is divided into named patrilineages, whose founders were the putative sons of the sub-clan founder. Patrilineage lands are dispersed through the sub-clan holdings, but men of the patrilineage commonly live together in one or two clubhouses. Patrilineages generally mobilize for the exchanges of wealth that accompany marriage, for the payments of compensation following injury, for the building of houses for their members and, less often, to provide gardening aid.

Within each lineage, most of the family heads are the putative great-grandsons of the patrilineage founder. The cultivated and fallow land belonging to the patrilineage is divided among these families, so that the head of each administers an estate in trust for his male heirs. He portions off each son from the estate to enable the latter to marry and found his own family. The elementary family constitutes the basic gardening and pig-raising unit in Mae society.

2. THE SKY PEOPLE

The Mae believe that long ago the land was uninhabited. The only quasi-human beings then living were the sun and moon, 'the father and mother of us all'. Eventually they had many children, 'the causal or originating people', who reside in the sky in conditions similar to those on earth. These sky dwellers (whom we may include in the broad category of deities) in turn have had many descendants, who, although pale-skinned, resemble Enga; they are organized into patrilineal descent groups and they marry, feud, grow crops, raise pigs, pay death compensations and so on.

After a time the sky beings colonized the earth. Each sky phratry sent a member to found a terrestrial phratry homologous with his own. Present-day accounts of how this was done differ from clan to clan.

In some cases the sky person simply appeared at a particular locality, where he met a woman (whose presence there is unexplained) and took her as wife. They settled, cultivated gardens and reared sons. As the latter grew up, their father gave them land, and they married daughters of neighbouring families that were also descended from the sky. In this way were founded the clans that legitimately occupy land inherited from their progenitors. Sometimes, too, the behaviour of the clan founders when receiving land and other property from the father is held to have determined for all time the skills, temperaments or personalities of their descendants.

Occasionally a married couple came from the sky and had sons who, after adventures involving cannibalism and parricide, begat the founders of present-day phratries. Some founders originated first in animal or insect form, then married ordinary women and raised human sons. Other sky men arrived carrying 'eggs of the sun', stones from which their wives or children sprang. Such stones are now the residences of phratry or clan ancestral spirits.

The last situation is the (conceptual) norm for, although not all

H

central clans possess this form of the myth of origin, most have stones that are the foci of rituals designed to propitiate clan ghosts in times of adversity. Some clans have small pools that function in the same way, and a few have both pools and stones.

Despite local differences in beliefs, most Mae agree about certain features of the establishment of phratries and clans. They say that all the groups were founded at about the same period, some seven or eight generations ago, and have maintained social inter-relations ever since. Each phratry founder brought with him ritual knowledge and paraphernalia, which his descendants use to preserve not only clan welfare and fertility but also the health and prosperity of individual clansfolk. The existence of the rituals confirms the members' belief in the continuity of the clan, and in turn the myth of origin validates the group's claim to the land it occupies.

The terrestrial society is thought to be isomorphic with the celestial society of the causal people. Every phratry and clan below has a structural homologue above and, indeed, some men describe the earthly system as the shadow of the other.

Although the Mae believe that observable interaction between the two systems is now intermittent and in some ways inexplicable, they assume that ultimately the sky dwellers control man's fate. Because of the behaviour of the sky beings in the past, it is the lot of the Mae to be gardeners and warriors. Men must toil to wrest a meagre livelihood from a harsh environment in which violent death is (or was until recently) an everyday occurrence. Human wishes can no more alter this situation than they can change the course of the sun, the symbol of the sky world. Whether men refer to a military defeat or to a successful pig exchange, they sum up the inevitability of desirable and undesirable events alike in the statement: 'this is the work of the sun'. It is true that other factors, such as the actions of ghosts or demons, the use of magic, or the application of human skill, may also be concerned in the situation; but basically these too must conform to the ends ordained by the sky people.

A man has no way of influencing the decisions of the sky dwellers; he cannot evade his destiny. At best he can employ divining techniques in order to discover his fate. Thus, a man who correctly reads the omens that appear in dreams or follows the preparation of a special oven may learn whether he is to become wealthy and important or is to remain poor and obscure, whether he will die young or enjoy a vigorous old age, whether he is to die peacefully at home or violently in battle. But few men really want such information, and serious divining to this end is rarely practised.

The causal or sky beings also dispense individual good and bad luck. Men attribute to actions in the celestial world the occurrence of the unpredictable in earthly affairs, the intrusion of circumstances that normally they can ignore as extraneous. Thus, it is bad luck when a skilled axeman cuts himself or a careful householder loses a pig; it is good luck when a man dodges an arrow fired point-blank in a skirmish. Although some people assert that a dishonest man is more likely to experience bad luck than is an honest man, they do not believe that the sky beings are concerned consistently to punish the evil and reward the good. The popular tendency is to define right and wrong behaviour in terms of what currently serves the particular interests of corporate groups in the lineage hierarchy.

Nevertheless, the causal beings are not wholly capricious, and they take a mild interest in some fields of human activity. For instance, they control meteorological phenomena so that in general people may expect to produce enough food. But even here their behaviour is not wholly dependable; droughts may occur, sharp frosts destroy the sweet potato plants, or heavy rains prevent adequate tilling of new gardens. People can do nothing to avert such widespread misfortunes. The sky beings for reasons of their own have simply failed to maintain normal conditions, and the Mae must cope as best they can with the situation until the ordinary state of affairs recurs.

The sky dwellers are also indirectly responsible for the presence of certain kinds of portable wealth in Mae society, for they planted shell-bearing trees in distant lands. There other natives harvest the shells, some of which they export to the Mae. But, if this flow of valuables is interrupted, the Mae have no way of inducing the sky beings to re-establish it.

In view of the Olympian indifference imputed to the sky beings, it is not surprising that they enter little into people's calculations. Indeed, they are rarely mentioned, except by older men discussing Mae cosmology. For practical purposes the causal beings are so far outside the immediate socio-physical environment that the men invoke them only to account for circumstances that many people take to be fundamentally inexplicable.

3. GHOSTS

On the other hand, not a day passes but someone refers publicly to the activities of ghosts. The people attribute almost every injurious

event of consequence to ghostly malice, and they employ a variety
of ritual techniques to divine the intentions of ghosts, propitiate them,
or drive them away. Indeed, much of Mae behaviour remains inexplicable to anyone ignorant of the pervasive belief in ghosts.

The Mae believe that only some creatures possess an individual
spirit or breath as well as a passive shade or reflection. These include
people, pigs, dogs, cassowaries and possums—all of which are socially,
ritually or economically significant in the culture. But only a human
spirit can become an active ghost, able to consume or manipulate the
spirits of the other animals when they die.

The popular theory of human conception asserts that semen and
menstrual blood combine to create a foetus, which after four months
is animated by spirit and given a personality. This spirit is not a reincarnation of any individual ghost; but in some way it is implanted
by the totality of clan ancestral ghosts and expresses their potency,
which is located in the clan fertility stones or pool.

In discussion people place little emphasis on the father's biological
role in conception and are more concerned with the child's acquisition
of a spirit, and later a social identity, through the clan membership
of the father. The father's agnatic affiliation legitimately relates the
child by descent and through ritual to the clan ancestral ghosts. But
people constantly stress the mother's part in forming the child's
body; her blood, they say, really makes the child's flesh and skin.
Consequently, men should retain an interest in their sister's children.
They have the right to demand compensation when the ghosts of
dead agnates of the sister's offspring injure the bodies that the children
got from their mother. This view that agnatic spirit and ghosts are
somehow opposed to maternal flesh and blood relates to the general
Mae belief that masculinity and femininity are antithetical.

When a man dies, his spirit leaves his body and becomes a ghost.
It stays near the corpse until burial, after which it wanders freely
around the clan territory. Such ghosts have no special places of assembly
and are dangerous by day or night. Material barriers do not halt
them; they can know human thoughts immediately these arise, so
that mere intention to act in a particular way can cause a ghost to
attack the offender. Waking people usually can detect the presence
of ghosts only by their soft whistling, but ghosts are often visible in
dreams, when the sleeper's spirit sees them, and to diviners and
mediums, who can communicate with them. Occasionally a ghost
reveals itself to a person walking alone in the forest, an apparition

that presages misfortune. In all these cases the ghost appears as its
former owner did at the time of death. Although most people believe
that ghosts cannot assume any other shape, some assert that ghosts
may threaten future victims by appearing as birds or animals that
behave strangely.

The Mae regard ghosts as malevolent or at best neutral (never
kindly) and attribute most injuries, illnesses and deaths to them.
Either the victim has previously angered someone whose ghost now
'bites' him, or a ghost is angry with a relative of the victim and attacks
the latter in order to distress the relative. As a rule people explain
misfortunes differently only when there is good reason to blame the
clan ancestral ghosts, the sky beings, forest demons, or sorcerers.

Although a ghost may 'bite' a number of people, it should kill only
once. Then the ghost of its victim drives it off to be absorbed into the
homogeneous group of clan ghosts (ancestors). (A woman's ghost
normally remains in her husband's clan territory.) The defeated ghost
can no longer act as an individual but it adds its power to that of
the ancestral ghosts as a whole. These usually aim their malevolence
at the clan parish and not at particular members, and the clan tries
to placate them in group rituals.

A person need fear only the ghosts of certain relatives, especially
those of the father and mother and of siblings and offspring who
died unmarried. Only occasionally are misfortunes attributed to the
individual ghosts of other relatives, or of unrelated persons slain by
the present victim.

It is understandable that domestic ghosts are seen as the most
dangerous, for family relationships among the Mae are the source of
many tensions. Members of the family have to work hard together for
long periods in the gardens; they have to agree on the allocation of
onerous tasks and to decide on the disposal of pigs and other kinds
of wealth. Differences of opinion are common and give rise to disputes
within the family. But ideally, as well as in fact, only the father as
head of the group is able to vent his anger in physical violence. He also
should choose spouses for his sons and daughters, and he need not
consider their feelings in doing so. Moreover, his sons may compete
with him for control of pigs and other valuables in the family estate,
and to discipline them he may try to withhold land and bride price.
Given such conflicts it is no wonder that people regard the father's
ghost as threatening and those of the children as vengeful. Indeed,
men discussing ghost attacks often say, 'the ghost of my father's father

killed my father, and my father's ghost will kill me!'

What is puzzling is the belief that the ghosts of the mother and the siblings are malignant. In ordinary life the mother constantly tries to protect her children from the oppressive behaviour of the father, and brothers frequently support each other against him. These are themes that recur in a number of the myths and legends.

When particular cases of ghostly attack are examined, however, and the identities of the ghosts tabulated, a marked difference is apparent between the patterns of 'ideal' and 'observed' identifications.

TABLE

Stated frequencies of ghost-attacks among the Mae

	Relationship of ghost to victim					
	Father	Sibling	Mother	Child	Other	Total
Attacks	15	13	1	1	0	30
Deaths imputed to attacks	11	7	1	0	0	19

In practice the people emphasize the likelihood of being attacked, not simply by domestic ghosts, but by domestic agnatic ghosts. They assume that injury by a dead agnate is the greatest danger facing the flesh and vitality which a person gets from the mother. The ghost either destroys the victim's agnatically-acquired spirit so that his body dies, or it directly harms the body. The matrilateral relatives may then expect the injured person or his clansmen to pay compensation; they argue that the victim and his agnates are at fault for not effectively placating the particular ghost in the past.

Ordinarily, a man who kills a pig for any reason dedicates it to a potentially dangerous ghost as a form of insurance, but such offerings may prove insufficient. If the man falls ill or is seriously injured, his brothers or sons should immediately kill a pig and give it (or its spirit-double) to the ghost they think is causing the misfortune. Normally only members of the man's families of orientation and procreation and his mother's brothers and their sons attend the pig-killing. While the ghost eats the essence of the pig present in the cooking meat and the blood, the men perform simple rituals to drive away the ghost. (If a child is ill, the father or elder brother similarly acts on its behalf and may also cut off a fingertip in order to allay the ghost's anger.) The maternal kinsmen of the victim then receive half or more of the pork to take home as 'payment for his skin', and the agnates and their families eat the rest.

If the sick man does not recover, his agnates decide that they have killed too few pigs, or killed the pig in the wrong way, or selected the wrong ghost. It is usual then to resort to one of a number of divining techniques to ensure that the next pig-killing is effective. The men consult a female medium (who uses her son's ghost as a control) or a male diviner, and they kill more pigs as the specialist directs. The agnates give a large portion of each beast to the victim's maternal kinsmen. The specialist (usually but not necessarily a member of the victim's clan parish) receives pork, salt and minor valuables as payment for services.

Sometimes the men kill several pigs and try three or four kinds of divination to no avail. If the victim is socially unimportant, they do nothing more but merely wait for death to follow. The diviner need not refund his payment, for the ghost has tricked him as well as the relatives. When an important man is ill, however, his brothers not only continue to kill pigs to each ghost named by the diviners but also may persuade the men of his patrilineage to initiate a ritual to placate all the clan ancestral ghosts. Men of the sub-clan, and perhaps of parallel sub-clans, give pigs as well as lesser valuables to offer to the ghosts. They invite a highly-paid specialist, who may be of another clan, to carry out the ceremony. Pigs and game are cooked, and the specialist exhumes the clan fertility stones, rubs them with pig fat and beseeches the ghosts to release the victim.

A sick man on recovering does not make a thank-offering to the ghost for letting him go, but he gives pigs and other valuables to his maternal kinsmen.

Should the patient die, his relatives mourn briefly and publicly, then bury him in his clan territory. Close relatives who attend the mourning are expected to demonstrate their grief and to placate the ghost of the deceased by slicing their ear lobes or cutting off finger joints. If the man died in battle, his clansmen display his corpse on the clan dance ground for several days while they make dramatic speeches promising his ghost that they will soon avenge the killing.

For two or three weeks after a death, the immediate family of the deceased do not tend their pigs or gardens lest their concern with mundane affairs anger the ghost. Close agnates carry out these tasks, and other relatives provide the mourners with food, water and firewood until the latter hold a feast to mark their return to everyday life. The ghost of the deceased should now be satisfied, for a time at least, with all that his kinsmen have done.

Sometimes, however, misfortunes injure a clan parish as a whole. These may include military defeats costing many lives or leading to the loss of clan territory, a sudden rise in the death rate of children or pigs, a series of deaths of important men, a noticeable increase in the incidence of diseases such as leprosy or yaws, or a clan-wide failure of crops.

Individual families at first deal with these circumstances at the domestic level and kill pigs to placate particular ghosts. But, as the events recur and affect more and more people, clansmen look to the whole body of clan ancestral ghosts as the source of the calamity and turn for guidance to the older and important men. Eventually the latter, after consulting among themselves, summon all the clansmen to one of the clubhouses. Women are excluded. The elders announce that the ancestors are indeed angry with the clan, and the men (except young bachelors, who have no voice in such matters) then seek the reasons for the ancestors' displeasure. They usually attribute this to delinquencies such as the clan's failure to pursue a vendetta or to preserve the boundaries of the clan territory, laxity in observing the rule of clan or sub-clan exogamy, neglect of the ancestors in not performing placatory rituals often enough or, more commonly, simply to the fact that the ancestors hunger for pork and wish to force the clansmen to kill pigs for them.

When the men agree on an interpretation, they decide to undertake rituals to propitiate the ancestral ghosts, usually at the time of the next full moon. As an earnest of good faith they cook one or two pigs, which wealthy men contribute and dedicate to the ancestors, then they disperse to make preparations. The men tell neighbouring clans (especially of their own phratry) when the ritual will take place; and the elders ask the appropriate ritual expert to direct the affair. He is often a member of another clan, and his office and special knowledge are inherited within his own patrilineage.

Details of the ritual vary from clan to clan. Not only is there a major division between eastern clans, which employ stone rituals, and those to the west, which usually possess pools rather than stones (and sometimes both); but also each clan may have a ritual differing somewhat from those of its immediate neighbours. The Mae attribute these local variations to differences in the bequests of particular clan and phratry founders. Nevertheless, a basic similarity underlies all the patterns of ritual activity and belief, and an analysis of one or two forms brings out the common core of meaning.

Clan stones, or 'eggs of the sun', are of two main kinds: natural stones that resemble such things as sweet potatoes, taro corms, pandanus fruits and pigs' scapulae, and artefacts (or fragments thereof) including pestles, mortars and club-heads which represent vegetables, portions of human or porcine bodies, and the like. The Mae have no knowledge of the true functions or origins of these artefacts.

A clan as a corporate unit may possess from one to about a dozen stones, which are buried in or near the cult house, 'the house of feasting'. This stands in a wooded and densely overgrown enclosure covering about an acre. The plot, originally chosen by the clan founder (who provided the stones), belongs to the clan as a whole. No clansman may cultivate or otherwise encroach on it. Women and children may not enter it, and men do so only in connexion with ceremonies. The ancestral ghosts injure anyone who breaks these rules. Thus, the deformity of two achondroplasics I knew was attributed to supernatural punishment meted out to their parents, who were thought to have copulated near the boundary of the enclosure.

Ideally, the generalized power of the ancestors emanates continuously from the stones so that the clan land remains fertile and crops grow, sows conceive and farrow without difficulty, women bear healthy children, men act bravely in war and shrewdly in exchanges, and everyone avoids serious illness or injury. Some people believe that the stones themselves constantly move underground about the clan territory to maintain this state of affairs. But, when the ancestral ghosts are angry, they sulk and their potency withdraws into the stones. Clansmen must then persuade them with ritual offerings to become active again and to restore the normal course of life.

Sometimes two contiguous clans of a phratry share a single set of stones located in one of their territories. Each attends the other's rituals and contributes materially to the preparations. Such clans have usually developed relatively recently from the sub-clans of a parent clan, which today may be extinct. If, however, the separation occurred long before, each clan is likely to have its own stones and independent rituals. Occasionally the largest clan of a phratry possesses stones regarded as the parents of those of its fraternal clans or has additional stones representing the brother clans, while the latter have none. In this case the other clans should hold their rituals in that territory, and all of them may attend. Such an arrangement probably records the early emergence by segmentation of a phratry from a clan now defunct.

When a clan announces its intention to perform a stone ritual, its neighbours should remain at peace with it in the intervening period. For several nights before the moon is full, large parties of men of these clans hunt in the mountain forests for tree-kangaroos, possums and smaller game. Meanwhile, in the initiating clan, nobody may prepare new gardens. The women energetically harvest existing gardens to amass food, and the men gather materials to rebuild the cult house. At the same time they call in their debts to ensure that they will have enough pigs and other goods for the ritual offering and its associated exchanges.

When all is ready, the men of the clan assemble at the site of the cult house to sing and dance all night, trampling down the undergrowth. At dawn they start to renovate the tall cult house and its ancillary shelters. Kinsmen from fraternal clans may help, and in a few hours the buildings are renewed and decorated. In some clans, elders also exhume the skull of a recently dead, important man and set it in the cult house to represent the current, individual ghosts of the clan—those which have not yet merged with the ancestral ghosts in the stones.

The men return home and adorn themselves lavishly with plumes and shells to make a display of wealth that will enhance the prestige of the clan and please the ancestors. The wives have cooked large quantities of vegetable food, and the men and their families take this and commodities such as salt, shells, oil, fibre and net-bags to the main dance ground of the clan. There the armed men (including kinsmen from fraternal clans) chant boastful songs as visitors arrive from neighbouring clans. These mainly comprise the armed and decorated hunters (and their families) who carry the game they have secured. They stand in clan groups and sing vigorously in opposition to their hosts.

Men of the host clan distribute food to the visitors and exchange other goods with the hunters, who give the biggest carcasses to the men offering the most valuable commodities. The occasion has much of the noise and bustle of a fair. The goods given to the hunters, however, do not simply purchase the game; they are also a reward for maintaining peaceful relations at this time.

The hosts set aside ten or twelve of the biggest black possums for use in the ritual, and their wives take home the rest of the animals. The women and children eat some of this meat, but the men keep most of it for another distribution next day. Meanwhile the visitors and

hosts sing on the dance ground until late that night, when the outsiders return home. In some clans, throughout the day of the fair, a
young bachelor and spinster of the host clan sit on the roof of the
cult house, so that the assembled people can see them from afar and
sing to them. The couple represents all the young people of the clan—
those who will later augment the clan's resources of children and
wealth (through bride price).

Next morning the clansmen kill pigs at their houses and cook them
with the game, while their wives prepare more vegetables. They take
the food to the dance ground and sing as the visitors return. Again
they distribute vegetables to all and meat to the hunters and important
exchange partners. As the visitors eat, women and children of the
host clan sing and dance on a hillside near by, and the decorated clansmen (plus kinsmen who have helped them) accompany the ritual
expert to the cult house. They take with them the possums previously
set aside, from about five to twenty pigs, and sundry minor valuables
that comprise the expert's fee. Sometimes, as they set off, they bury a
large black possum alive in a swampy garden as a gift to the ancestors
and to make the land fertile.

At the cult house the bachelors and younger married men watch the
elders club the pigs. The expert dedicates each beast to the ancestral
ghosts and directs the men to sprinkle its blood on the door-jambs
and floor of the house so that the ghosts may consume the essence of
the pig. The clansmen separate, on a sub-clan basis, into two groups,
and each cooks half the pigs in a long trench in front of the house.
Then, while the pork cooks, the groups throw possums to each other,
back and forth over the cult house, as a subsidiary gift to the ancestors.

They cook and eat all the possums, save the largest, which they
offer to the oldest men of the clan. These elders will soon join the
ghosts, and the offering is an anticipatory placation of their potentially
dangerous spirits. Some old men refuse the meat, saying that to eat it
may hasten their deaths; others, more greedy perhaps, say that they
would risk death rather than forgo such good meat.

The expert, assisted by important men of the clan, uncovers the
stones and places them inside the cult house. As he appeals to the
clan ancestors to refrain from injuring the living, he rubs rendered
pork fat and tree oil on the stones (and also on the skull, if one is
present) and smears them with ochre. Then he throws pieces of pork
fat on a small fire in front of the stones. Some of the fat he burns
to ashes, so that the ghosts may eat the smell and thus feast with their

children. He calls the clansmen to enter the house in turn. Elders go first, then younger married men, and bachelors last. The expert holds up before each man a fragment of bespelled, cooked fat impaled on a stick and bids him inhale the steam before swallowing the piece whole. Young bachelors may only smell the fat, lest the powerful spell damage their bodies and stunt their growth.

When every clansman has thus eaten with the ancestors, the expert reburies the stones, together with layers of raw fat, leaves from important food plants and sometimes a pearl-shell or two. In this way the ancestors receive a further offering of food and wealth and are tacitly asked not to interfere with the supplies of these commodities.

The clansmen go outside to eat the pork, which is now cooked, and give several joints to the specialist together with the rest of his fee. They return to the dance ground, where singing continues until the visitors leave late at night.

The propitiatory rituals just performed are not thought to be immediately efficacious. The ancestral ghosts take time to change their minds and revitalize the clan and its land. Consequently, for a month or two afterwards, clansmen should not copulate or prepare new gardens in the clan territory. To begin these activities too soon would not only be wasted effort but would also antagonize the ancestors.

Meanwhile, the fabric of the cult house dries and, after a week or so, the elders may invite its destruction. This initiates a vigorous competition among the men of neighbouring clans to be the first to burn the house. Much ill-feeling is generated as the winning clan cheers its respresentatives and boasts of its superiority. In some clans, however, the cult house is simply left to disintegrate; nobody visits it until the next ritual is to be performed.

Among many western clans, small pools figure in ritual intended to placate ancestral ghosts. Hidden in dense forest is a pool which clan members regard as the locus of the power of the ancestors. Women and children should not approach the site, lest they fall ill, and clansmen may visit it only on ritual occasions. In some clans men believe that a huge, invisible python, representing the ancestors, dwells in the pool, which itself is invisible to outsiders. Hence, a clan victorious in war makes no attempt to utilize the pool of the defeated clan. Occasionally two fraternal clans share one pool and attend each other's ceremonies. If a clan possesses both fertility stones and pool, its members tend to regard the stone rituals as more efficacious in major calamities.

The preliminaries to pool rituals resemble those to stone rituals. The clansmen ascertain the reasons for the misfortune afflicting the parish group and inform neighbouring clans of their intention to perform placatory ceremonies. Then, while the latter hunt, they renovate the flimsy 'propitiation-house' that stands near the pool. The old men roughly paint on each of two or three small plaques of bark a human figure to represent both the clan ghosts and the living members of the clan parish. Women may not see these objects. When preparations are complete, the hunters and other members of neighbouring clans assemble on the main dance ground of the host clan and a fair ensues.

At dawn the next day the clansmen repair to the cult house, outside which they kill and cook the pigs they have contributed. The ritual experts, usually two old men of the clan, dedicate the beasts to the ancestors. They cook the pigs' heads separately and keep these as their fee. The bark plaques stand near the ovens, so that the ghosts may share the meal by absorbing the smell of the blood and cooking meat.

When the meat cooks, the experts intone spells over the pork fat and exhort the ghosts to leave the clan in peace. The mode of offering the food to the ancestors varies. The experts may burn the fat beside the pool or throw it into the pool, or they may delegate the task to two bachelors. In a few clans, the bachelors employ a more elaborate technique. They tie fat and a pig's kidney to a long stick, which they gingerly push through a small hole in an otherwise impenetrable fence standing in front of the pool. The invisible python (the group of ancestors) emerges from the pool to consume the offering.

After the clan ghosts have been fed, the clansmen eat the pork and game and then return home. For some weeks afterwards they observe a ban on copulation and preparing new gardens. The cult house and plaques are left to moulder.

The pair of bachelors who feed the ancestors may be selected in various ways. Usually they are close agnates of the bachelors who figured in the previous ritual and are now married. That is to say, the same patrilineage or sub-clan supplies the actors on each occasion, and it need not be the group to which the ritual experts belong. In a few clans, however, selection is on a random basis. Before dawn on the day of the pig-killing, clansmen bring to the cult house all the boys from about six to fourteen years old, that is, lads who have not yet entered the bachelors' association. The boys sit facing east, as the old men display the bark plaques. The clansmen watch to see which of the boys are first touched by the rays of the rising sun. Henceforth, these lads must avoid contact with women, even their own mothers, from whom they may no longer accept food. After they enter the bachelors' association, two of them replace the bachelors already acting in the pool ritual when the latter marry.

4. THE OVERT MEANING OF THE RITUALS

We have seen that Mae ghosts, whether acting individually or in concert, are not benevolently disposed to the living. At best they are neutral until some human action or omission angers them; then they become positively malicious and try to injure the offenders. Often they appear to be malevolent without reason. Above all, ghosts are not concerned to reward the good or to punish only the wicked.

Nevertheless, despite the malignity imputed to ghosts, the Mae maintain a quasi-social relationship with them in order to keep open a channel of communication and negotiation. Two factors reinforce the people's attitude. Firstly, they believe that ghosts remain members of existing social groups. Thus, long after a man's death, his ghost may intervene in the affairs of his domestic unit; then, when the ghost finally loses its individuality, it joins the corpus of ancestral ghosts whose actions affect the fortunes of the clan parish as a whole.

Secondly, the people do not ascribe the characteristics of malevolence and self-interest solely to ghostly motives. They believe that, to a lesser degree, their fellow men also behave thus, or would do so if they could. Consequently, certain social techniques known to influence the motives of the living should also be effective with ghosts. In this view we find the basic rationale underlying the offering of pigs to ghosts.

The pig-killing is not a sacrifice. The beast is not consecrated; indeed, there is nothing sacred about it. Nor is it part of a piacular offering made in atonement for personal or collective sin. It is a placatory and, to some extent, hortatory gift made in the context of compensatory bargaining that characterizes so much of Mae social intercourse. The owner dedicates the pig to a ghost, or a group of ghosts, only in the sense of reserving it as food for consumption by a particular recipient. He does not offer the beast's life as a surrogate for a human life. In fact, he cannot do so, for Mae ghosts do not feed on human spirits; cannibalism is as repugnant to them as it is to the living. They demand pork (or its immaterial double).

The donor thus relies on his knowledge that a gift of pork often heals a social breach. If it assuages the anger and moderates the actions of an ordinary antagonist, it should achieve the same success with a ghost. At any rate, the man is sure that ghosts, like people, are not to be conciliated by mere promises or good intentions.

Moreover, although the living also partake of the same pig during the ritual, their action should not be interpreted as a form of communion in which the communicants symbolically consume theriomorphic or theanthropic ancestors in order to acquire their strength or virtue. Both the ghosts and the actors simply share the beast in formal commensality. Eating together is a conventional Mae expression of the creation of an amicable social relationship or of the repair of a damaged relationship. For instance, the long series of exchanges of goods that accompany a wedding culminate in the killing of pigs. The kinsmen of the bride and of the groom both share this pork. Only then does each group view the other as affines and use affinal terms of address and reference. Similarly, two men who formally eat a particular food together may henceforth call each other by its name and regard themselves as close friends and exchange partners.

In situations where a person or group has the right to demand compensation for an injury of some kind, the offending party usually gives pork to the aggrieved as the initial step in attempting a reconciliation. Conversely, some social breaches are thought to be irreparable, so that a transfer of food between the people concerned is improper. Thus, a homicide should never take food from the agnates of his victim, nor marry into the latter's sub-clan.

These kinds of considerations help to clarify the expectations and intentions of the Mae when they kill pigs for angry ghosts. A further indication of the relatively matter-of-fact attitude underlying their bargaining with ghosts may be seen in the effects of European contact on the rituals. Already, large-scale propitiation of clan ghosts is beginning to lapse. Men are aware of this and most are unworried. In their view, the activities of the Administration and, to a lesser degree, of the Christian missions preclude the possibility of major calamities such as wholesale military defeats, epidemic illnesses, or famines following crop failures. Clans can now afford to ignore their ancestral ghosts. On the other hand, the presence of Europeans has not yet noticeably affected the frequency of individual illnesses or injuries or the intensity of domestic antagonisms, so that the family rituals for ghost placation still persist. Presumably, these will also decline in importance with the extension of medical services and the growth of personal freedom of action following increased employment opportunities and higher wages.

5. DEMONS

The Mae also assume the existence of a class of anthropomorphic demons, distinct from human beings and from ghosts, that inhabit caves and waterfalls. These creatures in a sense embody the dangers and inhospitality that the Mae, who are sedentary gardeners and inept bushmen, associate with the dense forests of the high mountains. They are not connected with particular social groups but constitute a broad category whose members are not consistently differentiated in terms of functions or individual spheres of activity. The forest and everything in it comprise their estate, so that human exploitation of sylvan flora and fauna is essentially a trespass, likely to anger the demons.

Usually they are ill-disposed towards ordinary people and are ready to kill and eat solitary travellers who approach their lairs too closely. A few, however, do not care to eat human flesh. Female demons can change themselves into all manner of natural objects and species, and some, in the guise of huge pythons, are thought to abduct males from the men's houses. Others, appearing as beautiful girls, inveigle men with promises of wealth into marrying them. Such a wife dissipates her husband's property, destroys his pigs and kills his kinsmen with sorcery, then vanishes into the forest, leaving behind a crazed pauper.

Although demons do not figure prominently in the people's every-day conversations, certain unusual circumstances are attributed to their actions. Thus, if a traveller disappears without trace in the forest or, soon after returning home, dies or goes mad, his relatives may believe he met a demon. Hunters who glimpse a strange form among the trees think they have seen a demon and for a time everyone avoids that locality.

People also believe that, if a woman leaves her baby unattended while she works in the garden, a female demon may substitute one of her own children for it. (Nobody knows whether the demon wishes to rear the stolen child or to eat it; demons are thought to copulate and bear children just as human beings do.) The replacement may remain undetected until the demon–child exhibits characteristics such as a withered limb or a crippled gait, a deformed sternum or excessive hairiness, or is obviously moronic. Nobody tries to kill the changeling, but the unhappy foster-parents neglect it and it usually dies young.

Should the changeling survive to maturity, it is discouraged from marrying lest it produce half-demon offspring. For instance, one physically attractive girl in my neighbourhood who was mentally deficient and a putative changeling had received no offers of marriage by the age of eighteen or so, even though her embarrassed father was willing to accept only a token bride price for her.

Demons often appear in stories that men tell at night in the club houses. Most of the stories simply entertain the adults, but occasionally they are phrased to point a moral for boys in the audience. Thus, the lads may hear how a demon, impressed by the virtuous or prudent behaviour of a married woman, spares her life and even gives her game and valuables to take home. For the outside observer, however, one of the most striking features of the tales is the clarity with which they reflect basic domestic tensions. Some, for instance, tell how a demon ambushes a pair of co-wives but kills only the dishonest or backbiting wife. Others recount how a little boy, after killing a huge phallus-like demon, acquires great wealth and marries his sister, mother, or some older woman, with whom he lives happily and raises a large family. But, although many Mae men are aware of the covert struggle for wealth and independence that goes on in real life between fathers and sons, they do not consciously connect this with the themes of the stories they tell.

The Mae do not include demons in their ritual activities; there are no techniques designed to control the actions of these creatures. Essentially, they exist simply as expressions of opposition. At one level, they symbolize the basic disjunction between uninhabited forest and settled clan territory, between a world of half-known dangers and one of order and security. At another level, the behaviour of demons points to structurally induced and to some extent irreconcilable antagonisms in the minimal domestic units of the Mae.

6. MAGIC

By magic I mean the recital of spells in conjunction with prescribed and stereotyped manipulations of various objects, behaviour which in certain situations is thought to be in itself an effective substitute for, or supplement to, empirical action in achieving particular aims.

The Mae do not rely greatly on magic to attain desired ends. Indeed, they assert that they have much less magic than do the Saui Enga and the Ipili near by, from whom they sometimes acquire spells. Their generally prosaic and realistic view of their difficult physical environ-

I

ment includes the assumption that success in important enterprises depends primarily on the rational application of skill and effort. There is, for instance, almost no garden magic, for, as men say, abundant crops can only be produced by hard work, which in turn makes magic redundant.

Men usually control magical spells, even those to cleanse women after menstruation, to determine the sex of unborn children and to promote the growth of infants. Most women learn from their mothers and mothers-in-law only a few miscellaneous spells, for instance, to enhance their appearance and attract husbands, to alleviate pain in childbirth, to overcome barrenness and to fatten pigs. An elderly man who respects his wife's judgement, however, may teach her his own magic to hold in trust for his young sons.

Men acquire magic through inheritance and by purchase. It is believed that each clan founder possessed, in addition to ghost-placatory rituals, a collection of spells which, when used in conjunction with the leaves of bog-iris (*Acorus calamus*), ensured his physical development and good looks, averted the danger of sexual pollution and drew pigs to his house. He bequeathed them to his sons, a process that has continued to the present day; every married man of the clan should know variants of the spells and have scions of the original irises. Moreover, the sons of the clan founder, when they were bachelors, had other spells and irises, which they used in group rituals to rid themselves of the contaminating effects of contact with women. Today, the bachelors of each sub-clan form a corporate body owning a house in the forest, where they regularly perform these rituals.

Although a man has a claim on his father's magic, he must make a payment, however small, when he receives it. Moreover, the father retains the right not only to use the magic but also to sell it again to other kinsmen who have lost their own magic. By and large, sales of these kinds of magic rarely cross clan boundaries and, when they do, the price goes up. Other sorts of magic, including those bought from non-Mae, are freely, although not extensively, sold to extra-clan relatives and to unrelated exchange partners. They may also be offered as repayment for hospitality or labour. The general view is that magic given for nothing is worth nothing, whereas magic of proved efficacy, for instance, that owned by a wealthy man, should command a higher price. However, the possibility of such sales does not necessarily mean that the magic is highly valued in itself. Men frequently buy exotic magic simply to demonstrate their own affluence, and they may never bother to use it thereafter.

The relatively limited corpus of Mae magic falls into four fields of application: protection of personal health, especially from ghostly attacks and alien sorcery; attraction of portable wealth, particularly of pigs; enhancement of personal appearance and avoidance of sexual defilement; and the injury of enemies. This classification suggests that people are most likely to perform magic in situations where their technical knowledge is insufficient to achieve a desired outcome, or where chance elements are likely to enter.

The context of health protection illustrates this clearly. Although the people here distinguish between magic (as I have defined it) and the intrinsically fallible rituals aimed at placating ghosts, in practice they may combine the two to supplement their rudimentary medical knowledge. There is a continuum comprising rituals to placate an attacking ghost, magic to drive off the ghost (albeit temporarily), magic that simultaneously repels the ghost and alleviates the victim's symptoms, magic that merely treats the illness itself, and non-magical remedies for minor disorders.

Thus, the propitiatory offering of a pig to a ghost may be accompanied by aggressive stabbing of the earth-oven with bespelled tongs. In cases of leprosy, the magician may thrust bespelled sticks into the pig's head, not only to frighten away the ghost but also to strengthen the animal's blood, which he rubs on the patient's lesions. Similarly, the specialist gives a person with an abdominal complaint bespelled foods to lessen the pain or reduce the swelling, then sprinkles bespelled water on the belly, which he massages to cure the illness and to overcome the ghost. If the ghost has released the victim, the magician deals with the illness by rubbing bespelled plant juice on the body or brushing it with bespelled twigs, by sucking the part through a piece of bespelled sugar cane, or by making the patient inhale smoke from bespelled iris leaves or swallow quantities of bespelled foods to induce vomiting. The last treatment is favoured for a person suffering from alien sorcery in which he has unwittingly eaten food magically 'contaminated' by an enemy.

Only in the field of health protection are there semi-professional magicians, analogous to diviners, mediums and fertility-stone ritual experts. The curing magician, who may be an old man or woman, usually but not always belongs to the patient's clan parish, and the patient's kinsmen pay him at the conclusion of the curing. The fee, which may include pork, salt, axes and net-bags, varies roughly with the practitioner's reputation, the severity of the illness and the elaborateness of the treatment. Should the patient fail to recover, the specialist does not refund the fee; but his reputation suffers and his practice declines.

Although some men regard as wealth-magic spells and actions intended to facilitate the trapping of game, most assert that true wealth-magic is concerned with the acquisition of pork and pigs. Thus, when a house is built, magic may be performed to attract pork to it; the householder burns pig-bones in the first fire, while he mutters spells into the smoke. Sometimes, as a men's clubhouse is erected, a wealthy occupant kills a pig and recites spells as he splashes the house-posts with blood or buries the guts under the posts; the men then eat the pork. Although the donor first 'offers' the pig to a ghost, the dedication is not part of the magical act, which is thought to be automatically effective in drawing pork to the house (as well it might, while a wealthy man lives there).

Men are more interested, however, in acquiring pigs in public exchanges and distributions, and they believe that, although an inept business man will inevitably fail in this, shrewdness alone will not guarantee success. Even the cleverest man cannot hope to control all the factors that may affect his chances of receiving pigs. Consequently, when he expects to participate in a group transaction, he may employ magic to induce his debtors to meet their obligations. Some days before the distribution he bespells one of his iris plants and places packets of the leaves in the gable of his wife's house. (A man wishing to distribute fat pigs gives the bespelled leaves to his wife to rub on the beasts or to mix with their food.)

When a cyclical ceremonial distribution of pigs is in progress, agnates who occupy one clubhouse may pool their magical resources to ensure that extra-clan exchange partners do not overlook them. The men bring their packets of iris leaves to the clubhouse and, for five days before the distribution, silently watch a circle in the courtyard. The circle is divided into segments, one for each man, and the number, size and colour of insects entering a segment indicate the pigs each is likely to receive. On the day of the distribution, the man may also daub his face with red pigment bought from Maramuni Enga and mixed with bespelled leaves and bats' bones, so that, when his exchange partners see the markings, they will be impelled to treat him generously.

Men equate a sleek skin and strong body with self-confidence and mental well-being, and they believe that close contact with women, especially in sexual intercourse, impairs these attributes. Consequently, they may employ magic to acquire the desired personal characteristics, which in turn attract women, but they must also protect themselves magically from pollution by the women. People also believe that, whereas the flesh of males is attached 'horizontally' to their frames, that of females is laid 'vertically'. Hence, women attain physical maturity (and marry) earlier than do men, who need to use magic to speed their own development.

When a boy is about six years old, his father encourages him to sleep in the men's house and to associate less with his mother and sisters, lest their presence endanger his skin. At the age of fifteen or so, he first participates in the group rituals which the bachelors of his sub-clan perform to nullify the effects of their unavoidable contacts with clanswomen, and he attends such gatherings regularly until he marries. The rituals include seclusion in isolated houses, prolonged body- and eye-washing, rubbing with bespelled iris leaves, singing of spells, observance of regulations concerning dress, diet, conversation and general behaviour, interpretation of dreams, and finally emergence of the decorated bachelors at a festival.

In addition to attending the group rituals, which occur every twelve or eighteen months, the youth privately uses spells and iris leaves (bought from an elder brother or other close agnate) to promote the growth of his hair and beard, to improve his skin and in general make him strong and handsome. Girls learn from their mothers or sisters similar spells, which they use to enhance their appearance, but they have no collective rituals.

A man marrying for the first time must not copulate with his bride for at least a month after the wedding. During this period he wears his bachelor's finery and is occupied in learning from an older married agnate (or sometimes a mother's brother) both the magic that protects him from the dangers of marital intercourse and that which nullifies the evil effects of his wife's menstruation. He usually selects as his teacher a man whose appearance testifies to the efficacy of his magic, and he pays him a customary fee of a new net-bag containing a cowrie shell and cooked pig's guts. When the groom's senior agnates think he knows the magic, they tell him to take his bride into the forest for intercourse.

On the way the couple perform a ritual in which they plant an iris and a taro in a secluded plot to ensure a long and prosperous married life. Then, as the husband prepares for copulation, he spits on his hand, rubs his belly and mentally utters a spell to prevent the loss through ejaculation of the vital juices in his skin. After the pair have visited the forest several times, they doff their wedding dress and settle down to married life. Some men say that the husband need practise his copulation magic for only a year or so; others insist that he should continue until the birth of his first child.

A menstruating woman is not merely unclean but is also positively dangerous. She should not leave her house for five days or touch food and fires belonging to others. Before emerging from menstrual seclusion she must cleanse herself magically. Unmarried girls and widows, who in theory and largely in fact do not receive men in intercourse, need only employ simple magic taught them by their mothers. The woman recites a spell and paints white crescents under her eyes (and sometimes a stripe from navel to pubic hair). But such treatment is inadequate for a married woman. On the fifth morning of her seclusion, her husband faces the rising sun and bespells a small packet of Evodia leaves and Setaria grass which he sends to her. She bites off the ends of the leaves; the remainder of the packet she may either burn, place in the house-gable to rot, or bury with her menstrual pads of moss. Then she puts kaolin under her eyes and is free to resume her normal activities.

The Mae rarely accuse each other of performing sorcery. Because they can account for most injuries, illnesses and deaths in terms of physical violence, the malice of ghosts or demons, or the will of the sky beings, they have little cognitive need of sorcery as an explanatory device. Generally they use it thus only as a last resort, for instance, when the victim is suspected of stealing, or has recently visited sorcery-using non-Mae, or (if a woman) has quarrelled with a co-wife, or (if a person of some importance) has died for no apparent reason.

When the cause of death is in doubt, the agnates of the deceased may hire a specialist to perform an autopsy. He opens the victim's chest and inspects the organs for evidence of old battle wounds (lesions, suppuration, arrow points and the like) to which death can be attributed. The agnates determine which clan is responsible and later demand homicide compensation. If, however, there is no indication that the death followed from old wounds, the expert seeks evidence of sorcery. He examines the interior of the heart and lungs for black marks. Marks in the right-hand cavities demonstrate that a living member or a ghost of the deceased's partriclan killed him with sorcery; marks on the left-hand side point to a maternal kinsman or ghost. This information is sufficient for the two groups of relatives to agree on the payment of compensation. No attempt is made to ascertain the actual identity of the sorcerer, lest the ensuing recriminations destroy the solidarity of the corporate kin groups concerned. Finally, if the expert considers the signs of sorcery to be ambiguous, he blames an unknown outsider and nothing more is done.

It is understandable that the Mae possess but a limited range of sorcery techniques (some of which are thought to be imported) and use them rarely. Their view is that sorcery is an inefficient and somewhat immoral substitute for physical violence and economic sanctions in settling inter-personal or inter-group disputes. Thus, I heard of only one instance of a group of men combining to use sorcery to injure another clan. In this case the collapse of marriage negotiations had angered the groom's patrilineage. These men induced a Saui exchange partner to bespell a frog, mutilate it and hide it in a clay bank. Afterwards, three women of the bride's patrilineage died and several people fell ill. Other men excused the behaviour of the groom's agnates by remarking that his clan was too small to make war on the bride's clan.

Men also said that in some circumstances an aggrieved person, lacking the physical strength or economic resources to overcome an opponent, might use private sorcery. This involves muttering spells while staring fixedly at the victim's shadow, pointing a bamboo tube or pierced stone at him, swallowing one's own spittle, or covertly placing menstrual blood in his food, on his body, or on his magical plants. A poor man might retaliate thus when a wealthy and influential clan leader defrauded him of a pig; an ageing wife might employ the evil eye to injure a young co-wife during childbirth, or she might introduce menstrual blood into her husband's evening meal. Nevertheless, as the Mae assert, such behaviour is rare; most people prefer to attempt physical reprisals against their adversaries, even when these are members of the same corporate descent group.

There is, however, one field of activity in which people recognize the utility of sorcery, and that is to harm unidentified trespassers and thieves. The Mae strongly disapprove of stealing and trespass within the clan and deal directly and firmly with known offenders. Although such delicts are uncommon, it is usual for men to attach 'no-trespass' signs of leaves to garden fences, partly-built houses, felled trees and the like. Some go farther and sow the perimeter of the garden with needle-pointed bamboo slivers intended to cripple intruders. Others suspend from vines pieces of worn aprons belonging to their wives, in the belief that the female emanations from the aprons will injure any man passing under them.

Nevertheless, despite his precautions, a man may lose food from his gardens. If he fails to catch the culprit, he may secretly take certain leaves to his latrine and beat them while intoning spells. The leaves fall among the faeces and rot. Should a member of his or a neigh-bouring clan parish sicken or die within the next few weeks, the garden-owner believes that person to be the thief. But, if the thefts continue, he reveals to fellow clansmen his actions in the hope that the news will reach and frighten the unknown offender. There is, however, no evidence to suggest that men often use anti-theft sorcery.

It might be expected that the attempts of Administration officers to prevent violence by imprisoning offenders would increase the frequency of sorcery practices or accusations. So far this has not occurred and, I think, is not likely to do so. It is true that inter-clan warfare has almost completely ceased; but it has been replaced by strenuous litigation in the Courts for Native Affairs and in moots convened by *luluais*. Most Mae men regard the new situation simply as another form of fighting that demands new weapons. Similarly, although people still resort readily to brawling in intra-clan and inter-personal conflicts, when they cannot do so, they take their disputes to court rather than employ sorcery.

7. SUMMARY CONCLUSIONS

Neither the religious dogmas nor the ritual activities of the Mae are highly elaborated. Although there is no sharp disjunction between these and other kinds of belief and behaviour, they do not effloresce to the extent of impinging on all sectors of the culture, as, for instance, do the totemic philosophy and rituals of the Australian Aborigines.[3] Mae religion exhibits no great depths of intellectual subtlety or heights of emotional fervour. Rather, it reflects a sort of stolid and joyless realism, a prosaic concern with *quid pro quo* that in itself may well inhibit further development in these directions. This, at any rate, partly accounts for the relatively minor role ascribed to magic in Mae culture.

We may say then that only a comparatively narrow range of ele-ments or traits goes to make up Mae religion, and in this respect it resembles other religions in the New Guinea Highlands.[4] Indeed, many of the elements themselves exist almost unchanged in these religions. What seems to be peculiarly Mae, however, is the degree of internal coherence in the arrangement of the components; they may be few but they form a relatively self-consistent system. For instance, not only are there few loose ends in the cosmological accounts of the elders, but the collective rituals also connect neatly with the cosmology. This apparent orderliness is largely a function of the isomorphism of the structures of the lineage and the religious systems. A definite hierarchical order runs through both.

Moreover, the religious and the lineage systems reinforce each other, both directly and indirectly. I have shown elsewhere that the relative scarcity of arable land among the Mae is a significant determinant of the rigidity of their lineage structure, and that the people emphasize the importance of the continuity of solidary descent groups which can assert clear titles to the highly valued land.[5] The popular religion is well designed to support these ends. On the one hand, rituals regularly reaffirm the cohesion and continuity of the patrilineal group; on the other, the dogma in itself implies a title to land by relating living members of the group to a founding ancestor who is believed to have first selected that locality for settlement.

NOTES

[1] This paper is based on field work carried out among the Enga in 1955-57, 1960 and 1962, at first as a W. M. Strong Research Fellow under the auspices of the Department of Anthropology in the University of Sydney and later as lecturer in that Department. I thank the Research Committee of the University of Sydney for its financial assistance.

[2] Reference to the following will supplement my introductory remarks: Bus (1951); Elkin (1953); Goodenough (1953); Meggitt (1956; 1957a; 1957b; 1957c; 1958a; 1958b; 1958c; 1962a; 1962b; 1964; 1965).

[3] See, for instance, M. J. Meggitt (1962c).

[4] See, as well as the papers in this symposium, Lutzbetak (1956); Read (1952a); Reay (1959); Ryan (1961) and Vicedom and Tischner (1943-48).

[5] In Meggitt (1965).

R. N. H. BULMER

The Kyaka of the Western Highlands[1]

THE Kyaka people of the New Guinea Highlands speak a dialect of Enga and are related to the Mae, whose religion is also described in this symposium. This essay, as well as giving an account of Kyaka religion, compares it with Mae religion and suggests how differences between the two may be related to differences in social structure.

The Kyaka number about 10,000 and live on the north slopes of the Mount Hagen Range between the Baiyer, Lai and Ku rivers. To the east and south their neighbours are Metlpa-speaking peoples described by Vicedom and Tischner.[2] Most Kyaka and Metlpa groups whose settlement areas are adjacent intermarry and have extensive social contacts, although their languages are mutually unintelligible. North of the Kyaka, beyond the Lai River, live the Saui Enga but, until effective European control was established, contact between Kyaka and Saui was restricted. West of the Kyaka, and in direct contact with border clans, dwell the Laiapu Enga. Kyaka themselves consider Laiapu also to be Kyaka, and in fact there is little difference between Kyaka and Laiapu clans on either side of the Ku River.[3] However, the Kyaka themselves are not culturally homogeneous; the four main river gorges which intersect their territory are minor cultural boundaries, and every clan parish differs in cultural details from some of its neighbours, the general axis of differentiation being east-west. Thus, over all, the Kyaka do contrast significantly in culture and dialect with Laiapu and Mae Enga.[4]

In broad outline Kyaka and Mae are alike in economy, social organization and religion. They are horticulturalists with sweet potato as the staple crop, while pig-raising has considerable economic, social and religious importance. The persisting political groups in both societies are local parishes whose male members are usually recruited by patrifiliation and consider themselves agnatic descendants of a single founding ancestor. These localized descent groups, which are normally exogamous, are internally segmented and themselves generally form segments of ideologically patrilineal groups of wider span. The settlement pattern of both societies is one of dispersed homesteads, each normally associated with an elementary family, a polygynous compound family, or a three-generation patrilateral expanded family. Ceremonial grounds form the focus of corporate activities for clan parishes and for settlement groups within the parish.

In the religious sphere there is also much in common. In both societies ghosts of the recent dead are of great significance, having power to injure and kill their living kin, constantly interfering in everyday life, and requiring propitiation. Clan fertility cults, concerned with collective prosperity and health, and invoking more distant ancestors, are also important. Anthropomorphic nature demons provide residual explanations for certain kinds of misfortune. Forms of divination and magic show many common features.

However, there are also significant contrasts. Kyaka cosmology appears less systematic and coherent than that of Mae; it is impossible to show the detailed isomorphism of supernatural society and human descent group structure which has been demonstrated for the Mae. Kyaka ghosts, though often minatory and punitive, have also a more amiable side, acting on occasion as well-intentioned helpers and guardians of their living wards. Clan fertility cults seem to have been less standardized and less important than among the Mae; they were being incorporated into the cult of the Goddess, introduced from Metlpa groups at the time when Christian evangelization commenced. Nature-demons are differently categorized and have different relationships to ghosts and other spirit-beings from their Mae counterparts. Although Kyaka magic is much the same as central Enga, there are differences of emphasis, and sorcery is of greater significance to Kyaka than it is to Enga groups living farther west.

1. ETHNOGRAPHIC BACKGROUND[5]

(a) History

At present adequate historical records of the peoples of the New Guinea Highlands can be established only for a period of about two generations before the arrival of Europeans in the 1930s. However, it is worth noting the Mae tradition that human ancestors of their descent groups have always dwelt in their present homeland, being descended from spirit-beings from the sky. The Kyaka, in contrast, believe their country was colonized by human ancestors who came from areas to the west or south-west, and they do not connect these ancestors, the eponymous founders of their maximal descent groups, with spirit-beings in any systematic way.

(b) Ecology

Kyaka territory differs from that of Mae in several respects:

(i) spanning a wider altitudinal range it is ecologically far more diverse;

(ii) much of the cultivated zone, which lies between 6,000 and 3,500 feet above sea-level, appears more fertile than Mae territory, producing crops of sweet potato in shorter growing periods, permitting a larger range of subsidiary crops and producing spectacular spontaneous growth of bush fallow;

(iii) topographically it is less regular than the valley system occupied by central Enga;

(iv) overall population density is lower, about 65 per square mile (as against Mae 120 per square mile). Although Kyaka territory includes large areas of unoccupied forest and grassland, some parish territories in the cultivated zone have densities of about 200 per square mile, but this is still a lower figure than that for the most heavily populated Mae areas.

(c) Social organization

Kyaka descent and local groupings, domestic groups and forms of leadership differ from central Enga patterns in ways which are consistent with ecological differences between the two peoples and which bear directly on contrasts in the two religious systems.

Kyaka descent groups are more heterogeneous in size and in their levels of segmentation, and are on the whole smaller, than those of central Enga. Kyaka clan parishes range in size from 40 to 540 persons, with a mean of about 200. Mae clan parishes range from about 100 to 1,000, with a mean of about 350. Seven or eight Kyaka clans are maximal descent groups. Forty-one clans are segments of eleven maximal descent groups, whose compounded clan parishes range from 300 to 1,350 in size, with a mean of about 780. Mae clans are all segments of phratries, which range in strength from 920 to 5,400 with a mean figure of 2,290. Mae phratries are never exogamous and clans are sometimes not, though ideally they should be. All Kyaka maximal descent groups are exogamous, whether they are clans or the combinations of clans I term 'great-clans'.

Larger Kyaka clans are segmented into named subsidiary descent groups or sub-clans, and the larger of these are segmented into named sub-sub-clans. These differ from their Mae counterparts. Firstly, they seldom possess well-defined tracts of land within clan territories, and their members are seldom restricted to one settlement area. Secondly, they lack the genealogical structure which is a feature of Mae descent groups. Although in a few Kyaka minimal named descent groups all members can be placed on a single genealogy, in most groups there is a number of men, sometimes a majority, who believe themselves to be descended from the eponymous ancestor but who cannot demonstrate their genealogical connexion to him. Thirdly, except in the calculation of exogamic ties, the exclusive corporate functions of clan segments among Kyaka cannot be readily defined in any way which fits all, or even most, cases, as is possible for Mae.

The less orderly arrangement of Kyaka descent groups may be related to the topographic and ecological diversity of the Kyaka domain, which does not lend itself to the establishment of stable local groups with approximately equal land resources and numerical strengths in balanced opposition. Although, over all, land is not short, population pressures have built up in territories between 5,500 and 4,000 feet, and there is a complex recent history of population movement and expansion and contraction of clan territories.

This pattern of movement has created frequent opportunities for men to acquire rights in garden land in diverse ways, so that although in theory paternal inheritance is the strongest claim which can be exercised, in practice they are seldom restricted to plots inherited from lineal agnatic ancestors. Clan territorial boundaries formerly expanded and contracted with the fortunes of war or through simple annexation of land. Subsequently pigs and valuables were sometimes handed over in attempts to legitimize the *de facto* situation. At the same time, men who moved on to land in this way frequently asserted a claim to it by descent from the previous owners through a mother or other recent ancestress. Within clan territory it is possible for a man to acquire land rights by gift or purchase from men other than his closest agnates. The small minority of co-resident affines are freely permitted to use land, and their sons' and grandsons' rights to inherit these plots are rarely questioned.

Kyaka men depend on their agnates, particularly near agnates resident in the same parish territory, in many important respects, notably for assistance in marriage and exchange transactions, and are obliged to collaborate with them in religious activities. But they often reside at considerable distances from close agnates, seldom require to cite genealogies for more than two or three generations to establish claims to land, and frequently cite recent non-agnatic descent, or recent histories of conquest, gift or purchase, to justify present holdings. Mae men appear to be much more closely tied by land interests both to close agnates and to named descent groups within the clan which have clearly defined corporate estates.

Leadership in both Kyaka and Mae society is achieved rather than ascribed. There is, however, evidence of incipient stratification among Kyaka along the lines of the Metlpa[6] which is not present among the Mae. At the same time Kyaka leadership reflects the lower degree of corporate solidarity of segments within the clan and the greater stress on affinal and cognatic relationships in establishing personal status in the society. Kyaka 'big men', unlike those of the Mae, emerge as leaders of factions within the clan as much as of segments within the clan. This fact, as well as the significance which affinal alliances have for establishing a Kyaka leader's status, is reflected in the organization of clan fertility cults, or at least in the Goddess cult adopted by eastern Kyaka.

2. THE TRADITIONAL RELIGION

(a) Kyaka cosmology

Traditional Kyaka cosmology includes the following categories of spirit-beings, here listed in approximate order of significance in their influence on the affairs of living men: ghosts of the recent dead (*semangko*), nature demons (*kilyakai*), the Fertility Goddess (*Enda Semangko*), ancestral ghosts (*semangko*) who are generally equated with forest spirits (*epalirai*), sky beings (*yakirai*), Komba Ralingki, the 'stranger' ghost whose bone is the object of a fertility cult performed by one Kyaka great-clan, a female forest spirit (*Yama Enda*), cannibal ogres (*kewanambo*), and minor nature spirits or semi-supernatural beings, including tree spirits, echoes and snails. Certain birds and animals are believed to have special properties and their killing, handling and consumption either are restricted or involve restrictions on persons performing these actions. Thus cassowaries, dogs, the *kyakapi* python and the *raleya* lizard are thought to be inimical to garden crops and should not be cooked in garden areas, while people who have eaten these creatures should not enter gardens for two or three days. The Black Chat (*Saxicola caprata*), a common garden bird, is not eaten because it is an omen bird and can bring harm to men. Other creatures which are associated with the ghosts and accordingly avoided are mentioned briefly below.

Kyaka also claim to practise several kinds of sorcery (*mauli*), which they group conceptually with material techniques of poisoning; and they believe in a mild form of witchcraft (*yama*).[7] They also have many techniques (*pipu*) for divining, curing sickness, promoting the health and fertility of pigs and bringing luck, which we may lump together as 'white magic'.

No creation myth has been recorded for the Kyaka and no account of how the universe came into being, or of how mankind and animals and nature demons came to inhabit it. Myths or folk tales and traditional histories describe remarkable events in the long-distant past, when animals spoke to, turned into, or interbred with human beings, and men turned into animals; when living persons died and became powerful ghosts whose relics now form the focus of fertility cults.

Although sky beings figure in Kyaka cosmology, I have no evidence for belief in a world of sky beings, mirroring human society, such as has been reported for both Mae and Metlpa,[8] nor for any special mythological or religious significance ascribed to the sun and moon. Some informants, while specifically denying local beliefs of this kind, said that they had heard that Enga groups farther west had stories of this sort. Moreover, the term *rai*, which is cognate with both Enga and Metlpa terms for sky beings, is used by Kyaka not only for sky beings (in its compound form *yakirai*), but most frequently for the spirits of the mountain forest, who are generally believed to be ancestral ghosts. The Kyaka concept of luck (*embone*) is not related to a belief in destiny ultimately determined by the sun and sky beings, as is the case in Mae cosmology. Of a man who is phenomenally lucky, it may be said that he is under the protection of some powerful and zealous ghost; but ghosts of the recent dead and to a lesser extent ancestral ghosts are significant influences on all aspects of a person's life.

Kyaka mythology does not, then, provide a coherent explanation of the universe. Instead, it provides *ad hoc* and somewhat perfunctory explanations of the origins and character of particular human groups and of the cults which they perform. One may assume that the irregularity of Kyaka descent group structure would defeat any attempt to project an isomorphic pattern on the supernatural plane; all that can be done is for particular Kyaka groups to have *ad hoc* mythological traditions to account for their own provenance and special characteristics. To some extent these traditions are related to quasi-totemic observances and to details of group cults.

(b) Ghosts and ancestors

The most important beings and agencies in the traditional cosmology are the ghosts of the recent dead. Kyaka do not distinguish terminologically between these and more distant ancestors; both are *semangko*, a term applied to any spiritual being believed at some time to have had human existence. The main categories of *semangko*, as they emerge in relation to human activities, are:

(i) ghosts of the recent dead, who are extremely important to their living near kin;

(ii) collective ghosts, both ancestral and recent, of descent groups, whose members may collectively propitiate them;

(iii) individual named ancestral ghosts of descent groups, generally their founding ancestors, with whom fertility stones are sometimes associated;

(iv) collective ghosts of previous owners, recent or long dead, of garden plots, whether or not related to the present occupier, who makes sacrifices to them;

(v) individual named ghosts, often of unknown groups and times, associated with some forms of magic, divination and sorcery;

(vi) powerful spirit-beings who, although not ancestors, are believed to have had human existence—the *Enda Semangko* (Woman Spirit or Goddess), Komba Ralingki, the 'stranger', whose bone is the object of a fertility cult, and *Yama Enda* (Sickness Woman, a forest spirit).

Kyaka believe that when a person dies his or her soul (*imwambu*), which may also leave the body during sleep, becomes a ghost. Shadows and reflections are also *imwambu*. Some informants say that shadow and soul are the same, but most say that, although animals and objects have shadows, only humans, dogs and possibly pigs have souls. Those who attribute souls to pigs use this in their rationale of pig sacrifices, explaining that the soul goes as a ghost-pig to the ghost of the human kinsman.

✗ Beliefs about the nature of ghostly existence are unstandardized, but it is agreed that the ghostly condition is unenviable. Ghosts haunt trees and burial grounds, and their normal diet is human excrement. They can manifest themselves either as human apparitions or in the shape of certain reptiles, insects, animals and birds, though some say that these creatures are merely emissaries or portents of the ghosts. They may also be met in dreams.

✗ A ghost can help and harm his surviving near kin. He can protect them from danger, help them in war (by lending strength to a man's weapon arm), foster their fertility and that of their pigs. He can also inflict sickness upon them and kill them. Although any deaths may be attributed to ghosts, either through their direct action or through their failure to protect living kin from other agencies, in practice the ghosts are held responsible for only about half of all deaths (see Appendix). Ghosts can inflict blindness, leprosy, yaws and internal swellings, and can make people mad. They can also hurl people into trees, where they are found hanging helpless, their eyes and ears full of excrement; I am assured that people have been found in this state.

Several informants said that ghosts made children, and one that a child was a reincarnated ancestral ghost; but I have no evidence that a person's soul (*imwambu*) is thought to be acquired specifically from patrilineal ancestors, as has been reported for the Mae. Kyaka beliefs concerning physical aspects of procreation differ somewhat from those of central Enga. Kyaka hold that both male fluid, from many acts of intercourse, and female fluid are required to form the foetus, but do not differentiate the two terminologically (*ipwengki*). Growth of the foetus then results from the transfer of menstrual blood through the umbilicus. They do not attribute any one element in the child's body—flesh or bones—to either parent exclusively. This lack of conceptual opposition between maternally acquired flesh and paternally acquired bone or spirit is consistent with the Kyaka view that, other things being equal, both father's kin and mother's kin have an equal claim to the child and an equal interest in him. It is only through payment of the mother's bride wealth and, equally important, their nurturing of the child, that the father's group establish their superior claims to him. It is also on the basis of continual association and development of individual, personal claims in life that recent patrilateral ghosts assume their predominant importance. It is significant that at

K

the feast held after a child's birth, when the father makes gifts to the wife's kin, pigs are sacrificed to the ghosts of both parental groups.

Funerary practices also illustrate this point. At the wake preceding a burial the dead person's maternal kin (or the agnates of a married woman) used formerly to tear down thatch from the bereaved family's dwellings and slash down banana palms around their homes. The explanation of these actions was that the maternal kin of affines were displaying their anger with the agnates (or the husband of the dead woman and his group) for failing to protect their member; their neglect by causing ghostly wrath made them responsible for the death. Compensation of pigs and valuables made to maternal kin or affines at the mortuary feast is also explained by Kyaka in these terms.

How a ghost behaves towards the surviving family and close kin depends in part on the character he had in life; thus, poor and malicious people become particularly malicious ghosts. More significant determinants are the treatment the ghost received from his relatives during life and by way of pig sacrifices since death, and the treatment his living kin accord each other, since a ghost may protect the interests of family members to whom he is particularly attached. Thus, I have heard stories of old men threatening to punish neglectful sons when they became ghosts, and I was told that theft from a fellow clansman, adultery with his wife, or failure to settle a debt to him might cause the offended person's ghost to kill the offender.

There are many cases reported of ghosts, especially paternal ghosts, punishing their sons with sickness, death, or the loss of a child for failing to sacrifice promised pigs to them and using them instead in other transactions. Moreover, if serious sickness occurs, people are likely to remember any recent family quarrel and assume this to be its origin. Not only has each person a guardian ghost who is kindly and protects his or her interests[9], but ghosts also have a general interest in family morality among their surviving kin. Most informants say that anger provokes the ghosts to punish, though many now say it is God who is punishing, while others say that anger itself can cause sickness and death.

In short, ghosts do not necessarily behave more morally than the living, being subject to the same kinds of personal motives, and are in no sense the originators of Kyaka morality. At the same time they are the guardians of a very important part of this morality, having powers of punishment beyond those of the living and also having knowledge of offences hidden from living members of society who might otherwise take action about them.

Although some individuals have personal ghostly guardians, in general ghosts are more feared than loved. However, some deaths are explained not as ghostly punishment but as evidence of affection. Thus, elderly widows or widowers may be taken by their spouses' ghosts who are sorry for their lonely existence, and a female ghost may be particularly dangerous in that she may try to take her young children. For this reason, it is dangerous to say aloud the name of a recently dead person, lest his attention be drawn and he kill someone or 'touch' the speaker with sickness.

Two kinds of data indicate which categories of ghosts are thought to be particularly dangerous. One is the customary precautions Kyaka take, or say they take, to avoid ghostly attention; the other is the incidence of specific occasions when ghosts are deemed to have caused sickness or death.

It is of interest that special precautions are taken mainly against female ghosts, and in the period immediately following their deaths. These customs clearly reflect the Kyaka anticipation of retaliatory hostility from women who, like women in other Highlands societies, are jurally mere pawns in the transactions between groups of men and suffer the social disadvantages inherent in a system of patri-virilocal residence. They also reflect the ambiguous social status of women who are members by birth of one group and by marriage and procreation of another. There could be no point to such observances after a man's death; most men are unambiguously affiliated to one group only and their ghosts, although having power to kill within that group, are unlikely to do so wantonly, since they must depend for sacrifices on their near kinsmen.

In contrast with the degree of malice precautionary observances impute to recently dead female ghosts, actual cases of death and sickness are most frequently attributed to male ghosts, particularly the father's ghost. Paternal authority is a salient feature of the Kyaka family, at least till the sons have established their own families and their own sets of exchange partners. Although relations between fathers and sons normally appear cordial, open conflicts occur between fathers and adolescent or young adult sons over allocation of garden land and arrangement of marriages and exchanges, and implicit conflict is evident between sons of any age and elderly fathers whom they should respect and support. The special duty of a son to sacrifice frequently to his father's ghost, the jealousy shown by paternal ghosts in demanding sacrifices, and the punishments they inflict for offences committed while they were alive reflect and reinforce the obligations and tensions of the filial relationship.

The role of the mother in inculcating standards of personal conduct, particularly of daughters who are constantly in her company until they marry, is also reflected in her ghostly activities, illustrated by cases cited of punishment as much as thirty years later for childhood thefts. However, there is no evidence of a mother's ghost showing jealousy about the size and frequency of sacrifices made to her, except shortly after death. Female ghosts do, in fact, receive offerings on most occasions when pigs are cooked, but ghostly women are as unlikely to demand sacrifices continually as are living women to demand pigs from their children.

Ghosts are also important to their grandchildren. The death or serious sickness of a child is almost always interpreted as punishment of one of its parents inflicted by a grandparental ghost. At the same time, three informants who discussed guardian ghosts with me cited grandmothers in this role.

Thus, ghosts of people who have married and had children are thought to be primarily concerned with their own offspring and descendants, although they may also interest themselves in the affairs of other kin and settle old scores with them. Although it is said that all ghosts have power to cause sickness and to kill, I have little information on ghosts of childless people and of children. They are certainly of significance to their parents and siblings, and the ghosts of childless women are thought to be particularly malevolent.

(c) Sacrifice

I use 'sacrifice' in its wide conventional sense of any offering to a spirit-being. Although the pigs presented to the ghosts of the recent dead are not thought of by Kyaka as surrogates for human life, this is possibly a legitimate interpretation of pig-offerings to descent group ancestors and other spirit-beings.

Except in the case of wild pigs and stolen or sick beasts[10] every pig-killing and -cooking is also a sacrifice to the ghosts; they are addressed by the owner of the pig or a senior close kinsman in a dedicatory prayer (loma silyu) as he holds the tethering rope before the pig is clubbed. The carcass is singed and the ghosts are believed to consume the aroma of the singeing (rindam). Until recently each burial ground had on it a small round hut, containing an oven-pit in which heads and certain joints of sacrificial pigs were cooked. Many homestead clusters included such a 'ghost house' (*semangko anda*). Pigs cooked in these huts were dedicated to male ghosts only, and the pork could be eaten only by males. Other pigs cooked in ovens in the open were dedicated to male and female ghosts and their flesh could be eaten by both men and women.

The occasions on which pigs are cooked and presented to ghosts of the recent dead fall into three categories. Firstly, there are the feasts associated with life crises and other social occasions: mortuary feasts, marriages, presentations to affines following the birth of children, Moka exchange ceremonies. Secondly, there are the special propitiatory offerings made to avert crises. Kyaka make these unwillingly, since the killing of pigs at unexpected times disrupts plans for their use, and when possible a man will merely promise pigs to an angry ghost, waiting to make the sacrifice until the next regular occasion for a feast. However, if the ghost will not brook delay the pigs must be cooked. Thirdly, there are the clan fertility cults, which focus on the collectivity of ancestors and on other spiritual beings but in the course of which offerings are also made to recent ghosts.

Pigs are individually owned and contributed for sacrifice, although a father normally makes the dedicatory prayer for his sons and dependants. However, no man sacrifices alone. The minimal group to collaborate in sacrificial cooking consists of brothers and their sons and fraternal nephews, who share responsibilities towards their deceased parents and siblings, although not all contribute pigs on any particular occasion. All the domestic dependants of the man holding the feast are also likely to attend, together with married sisters and daughters and their children and, possibly, husbands. Often one or two clansmen of the feast-holder who are also related to him through his and their mothers or grandmothers and on this basis are exchange partners and close friends help with the cooking and perhaps contribute a pig.

On any important occasions, such as a marriage or mortuary feast, other clansmen, particularly men of the same sub-clan and men of the same and neighbouring settlement groups within the parish, assemble after the meat has been cooked and receive a share. On certain of these occasions those affines and cognates who are also exchange partners of the feast-holder also attend or send representatives to collect pork. The mortuary feast, held some months or even a year after the death, is the first substantial offering of pigs to the new ghost, though if it has been long delayed small sacrifices may have been made earlier. Until it has been made, the ghost's close agnates cannot make bride-wealth gifts or public ceremonial exchanges, and the deceased's widows cannot remarry. Pigs received in wergild payments are used in mortuary sacrifices to the slain person. The clansman of the deceased who marries his widow must sacrifice a pig to the dead husband, while the flesh is eaten by the latter's near agnates.

The mortuary feast for an unimportant person is a small-scale affair and is often postponed to be held at a feast for others recently dead. In contrast, the mortuary feast for an important man is likely to involve his whole clan. The deceased's immediate kin sacrifice to him at their own ground, but other sacrificial groups within the sub-clan or clan also kill pigs at their own grounds and bring cooked pork to the dead man's ground for distribution. Clansmen express respect for the dead man by co-ordinating their sacrifices in this way.

Co-ordination of sacrifices by a number of expanded family groups within the clan occurs on other occasions. When one family is cooking pigs for a marriage feast, the families of other men who have con-tributed to the bride wealth may simultaneously cook pigs, which are sacrifices to their own ghosts, but the pork of which is contributed to the total supplied by the groom's kin. Similarly, in the course of ceremonial exchanges there are occasions on which a number of groups sacrifice independently, each at its own cooking place, but in a synchronized fashion, with the bulk of the cooked pork assembled at one place for formal distribution.

According to informants, a special form of sacrifice to the *semangko* was adopted when the group had killed a man in war. Each clansman present contributed a pig which was killed and cooked.[11] But apart from this occasion when, it seems, both recent ghosts and the collect-ivity of ancestors were invoked, mass cooking of pigs at one locality for the ghosts of the recent dead never took place. Collective sacrifices, as distinct from co-ordinated sacrifices, are only made to the Goddess or Male Spirit, and the collective ancestors of the descent group, not specifically to recent ghosts.

(d) Divination

✝ When death, serious sickness or misfortune, such as the unexplained loss of a pig, occurs, a number of divining techniques can be used to ascertain whether a ghost or other agency is at work, which ghost it is, what angers the ghost, and what the ghost demands as inducement to desist. The two most important means of divination are the arrow test (*walika pipu*) and the spirit medium seance (*ropaka*). Many mature men know how to work the arrow test, and experts may be consulted by members of their own and other clans.

The diviner bespells an unbarbed arrow (*walika*). The spell invokes a long-dead ancestor who has no significance outside this context. The diviner jabs the arrow slowly and deliberately into the ground and withdraws it. He recites the names of ghosts of the patient's family and with each thrust asks if a particular ghost is causing the sickness. If the arrow is easily removed, the answer is negative; if it is held firm in the ground or jerked in the diviner's hands, it is positive. The diviner then asks, in questions which can be answered yes or no, what has angered the ghost and what pig sacrifice is required to appease his anger. The oracle sometimes indicates that it is useless to sacrifice, since the ghost is determined to kill the sick person. The diviner will be given pork for his services when pigs are sacrificed. Unless the sickness is extremely serious the pigs may not be sacrificed immediately but the ghost is promised that they will be given later.

The arrow test is normally used for cases of sickness when there is reason to suppose that a ghost is responsible. The spirit medium is consulted for a wider variety of misfortunes, some trivial such as the loss of a small object, some serious as in attempting to discover the responsibility for a death. The medium is, among the eastern Kyaka, always a woman, whose ghostly controls or familiars (*ropaka*) are deceased near agnates. Seances are held in a darkened house, attended by household members, clients and casual visitors. In the darkness the medium lapses into an apparent sleep or trance, and the control speaks through her mouth. Members of the audience ask questions and the ghost replies in whistles. Kyaka intonation patterns are distinctive and short whistled sentences are in context unambiguous.

The medium, who may or may not receive payment, can achieve a degree of social prominence and influence far beyond normal female expectation in this society. There are one or two mediums in most of the larger clan parishes. Their positions cannot, however, be considered as parish offices, as their clients come not only from their husbands' and their own clans but may include persons from other groups, provided that amicable relations exist between them and the medium and her family.

These divining techniques can be used in the case of sickness, but there are others to ascertain the cause of a death. Kyaka do not practise autopsies but they take account of the corpse's appearance in trying to establish responsibility for death. Thus, swelling of the stomach is assumed to indicate poisoning. If it is believed that ghosts and family quarrels are responsible, a corpse may be greased and decorated, one side by a paternal and the other by a maternal kinsman, and according to which side spoils first it will be known which kin are responsible. Oracles may also be consulted to test the truth of assertions as to human responsibility. If a group is accused of sorcery (or poisoning), mediators suggest that vegetables be cooked in an earth oven and then examined. If they are still raw when removed, the accusation is true.

There are also divining techniques, of which the use of a stone pendulum is most common, which are frequently employed to determine whether livestock has strayed or been stolen, or whether a journey is to be safe and prosperous. Some informants say that ghosts manipulate the pendulum, others that it moves of its own accord.

(e) Ancestors and descent group cults

Since individual ghosts normally have influence only over people who were important to them in life, their importance persists only while they have surviving close kin. Kyaka say that a ghost only has the power to kill one of his kinsfolk, after which he becomes impotent.

Ghosts who have ceased to interfere directly and personally in everyday life continue their existence in the forests, certain areas being associated with the ghosts of particular maximal descent groups (clans or great-clans). Game killed in the forest may be sacrificed there to the forest ghosts (epali rai) who have permitted or helped in its capture. The forest ghosts, however, smite trespassers on their (and their clan's or great-clan's) preserves. Specific ghosts, both recent and ancestral, are also associated with garden plots which they cultivated during their lifetime. When a man clears a new garden he cooks possums and rats at the edge of it for these ghosts, whether or not they are his own direct ancestors. The ghosts are concerned with the fertility of the garden and its protection from animal pests. Some men possess on their land rock shelters where it is traditional to cook the larger game. Such cooking is conceived as sacrificial, addressed to ghosts of recent and distant ancestors who have previously cooked at that spot.

Although ancestral ghosts are deemed collectively to guard the fortunes of their descendants, ghosts of distant ancestors, even those who are supposed to have founded the groups which are named after them, seem to be much less important to the Kyaka than ghosts of the recent dead.

Some, possibly all, Kyaka groups possessed fertility stones associated with the ancestors in general or with named founders of clans or their segments. They included prehistoric mortars, pestles and figurines, and rounded stones from watercourses.[12] These stones were in the custody of individual men, but sacrifices at which they were decorated with ochre and smeared with the blood and grease of pigs conferred benefits both on individual cult participants and their families and on whole descent groups.

There were several traditional cult places where numbers of stones of power were supposed to have originated. These sites (imbwünda) are said to have been the resting places of Komba Ralingki, a man who travelled across Kyaka territory and died near Kamensipa, where one of his bones is preserved. He was, according to informants, a large fair-skinned man, and present belief is that he was a European, for his bone is supposed to have been discovered wrapped in a blanket or bag of European cloth. He is credited with the introduction of cane much used in building and fencing, of a favoured kind of sugar cane and, some say, of certain kinds of bananas and taro. He is not cited as an ancestor of any present-day descent group.

It is said that previously sacrifices were made at all imbwünda sites; but some of them have not been used within living memory, while in the last decade only that at Kamensipa is still a place of cult activity.

The cult at Kamensipa, known as the Kewa Kuli ('Stranger bone') or Akali Semangko ('Man Spirit'), is the only recent or contemporary Kyaka cult performed by members of a whole great-clan. According to the participants this is because the founding ancestor of the group discovered the shrine and the bone. Direct participation is strictly limited by the rule of patrilineal succession; only men whose fathers participated have access to the cult ground, though other clansmen cook pigs outside the shrine and take part in the pork distribution and other public activities. The two priests of the cult, the only men actually to handle the bone, succeed to their office from their fathers. In contrast, in the newly introduced Goddess cult, all clansmen participate, while cult leaders are the men of greatest general importance who have taken the initiative in organizing its activities.

The main cult house is a circular structure, twenty feet in diameter with wall and doors more than eight feet tall. It is unlike either cult or dwelling houses made by Kyaka or Metlpa but is like the cult houses of the central Enga. A curious feature is a special latrine pit which participants must use during the night-long feasts at which tremendous quantities of food are consumed. It is said that when the pit is filled with excrement the death of one of the participants is imminent.

Both game and pigs are sacrificed to the *Kewa Kuli*. All axes and knives are left outside the cult ground, and the game is cooked in the open fire and not cut in any way. Bananas are also cooked and participants must grab the meat and fruit from the flames. If a man fails or is burnt in the process, it is a sign that he will shortly die.

Although the priests often sacrificed game to the bone, large feasts at which pigs were killed occurred only when the cult houses were rebuilt, which was not often, since hardwood was used in their construction.

(f) The Goddess cult

This is the *Kor Nganap* cult described by Vicedom for the central Metlpa.[13] Although Vicedom says that the Metlpa adopted the cult from Enga, Kyaka believe it is of Metlpa origin. They call it *Enda Semangko* ('Woman Spirit'), *Kor Enda* (*kor* is Metlpa for ghost or spirit) or *Enda Kondapala*. The cult is introduced from clan to clan through the initiation of 'big men' who are instructed in its procedures by affines and other exchange partners who are cult leaders in clans already participating.

When the Baptist Mission started work in the Baiyer Valley in 1949 the cult was new among the Kyaka. By 1958 only two clans near the Metlpa border had completed the cycle of ceremonies, which takes at least five or six years. Some others had begun the cycle but none of these have performed the final rites. People say that, because of the mission, they will not do so, though one leader suggested that a secularized *Enda Semangko*, with no spells or prayers, might be held without antagonizing the mission. Many Kyaka have attended Metlpa festivals.

Like the cults it replaces, the Goddess cult centres on stone artefacts and natural stones.[14] As in the Metlpa *Kor Nganap* one stone embodies or represents (it is unclear which) the Goddess.[15] However, whereas among the Metlpa the other stones represent individual members of the cult group (living and deceased, male and female), this is not the case with the Kyaka. Although all the Kyaka stones are believed to have special power, some are inherited and are associated with either individual ancestors or the ancestors in general, others are discovered accidentally or following dreams, others are purchased and others may be stolen.

The main culminating festival requires preparations over a period of a year or more. The cult ground is extended and partitioned into private enclosures, each containing houses. Only participants in the cult and their male relatives can enter the first enclosure, which a high wall separates from a large public dancing ground. Only cult participants can enter the second enclosure, where they cook pigs and spend periods of seclusion in a special house. In the third enclosure is a house containing the stones, which can only be entered by the cult leaders.

Participants are subject to dietary and sexual restrictions, as described by Vicedom.[16] When vegetable foods are assembled for the final feast and water is drawn from special pools, women, children and strangers may not see the collecting parties, whose members blow whistles to warn people to keep indoors. An unauthorized onlooker may be killed by the Goddess. During the culmination of the festival, for several days most of the males of the clan performing the cult spend the nights in the cult houses and on the cult grounds, where they chant and practise the earth-trembling, shuffling dance of the cult.

The hundreds of pigs cooked in the final feast are slaughtered at family cooking sites near the homesteads. About half the meat is cooked there as a sacrifice to the ghosts of the recent dead and consumed locally by women and children as well as men, while the remainder is carried raw to the cult ground. There the undecorated males form two columns on the dancing ground. The first represents the 'man house' or males, the other the 'woman house' or females. The performers divide along, approximately, sub-clan lines and later dance publicly in these divisions. Each group also has its own position inside the cult house but, like Vicedom,[17] I am not clear what this symbolizes. As the men and boys form up in column, each person has a heavy net-bag of raw pork on his back and bends forward under sides of meat on his shoulders. In solemn silence the two columns, one after the other, proceed the length of the dancing ground and into the door of the private enclosure.

The meat is cooked overnight on open fires and next day about half is distributed to exchange partners, who sit with their descent groups along the sides of the public ground. This meat, and the remainder distributed on the following final day of the festival, cannot be eaten by females, except women past childbearing age.

On the final day the dancers, now magnificently decorated and each carrying a mounted pearl-shell,[18] proceed thrice round the private enclosure and then circle the public dancing ground three times. There is no singing, simply the earth-trembling, rapid stamping of feet. It is an impressive performance. The dancers return to the cult enclosures and reappear on a platform constructed along the end wall and one side of the public ground. They are joined by one or two wives of the most important men present. The remainder of the cooked pork is cut up and distributed to the assembled crowd of male guests, each of whom holds up a spear for lumps of meat and fat to be impaled on it. There is great excitement and much jostling and shouting and competition to get as many pieces of pork on one's spear as possible. This performance, which ends the cycle, is greatly enjoyed in a most uninhibited way, very different from the solemn manner in which the meat is carried into the cult enclosure, the first distribution of cooked meat made, and the dancing performed.

The stones are now hidden and the Goddess moves on to another group. However, she is not exclusively associated with a single group for the duration of the cycle; several clans can have concurrent cycles, though their final festivals are not synchronized.

Several points may be noted about the *Enda Semangko* cult. One is the emphatic exclusion of women, except during the final pork distribution when wives of one or two important men may assist their husbands. Informants said that the cult is conceived as a marriage between the men of the clan concerned and the Goddess.[19] One added that should a woman obscenely insult a man who had participated in the cult, the Goddess would punish her. Similarly, Kyaka said that special huts used to seclude menstruating and parturient women had recently been introduced, following Metlpa practice, because the Goddess would kill a menstruating woman who polluted a male participant in the cult.[20] Thus, Kyaka men believe one function of the cult is to protect them from their women and to keep these in their place. The other functions, as Kyaka see them, are those listed by Vicedom for the Metlpa, to promote the health of the clan and the fertility of women and pigs, and to bring success in warfare and the Moka exchange festivals.[21]

So far as the Moka is concerned there is actually some conflict between the cult and the institution it is supposed to benefit. Although the *Enda Semangko* cult can be readily co-ordinated with the Metlpa Moka, in which each clan chooses its own time to make its main exchange festival, it is more difficult to fit in with the progress of the Enga (Kyaka) Moka in which all clans have to co-ordinate their exchange festivals in one cycle every three or four years.[22]

I have little information on the theology of this cult. My surmise is that this is much less consistent and important among Kyaka than, according to Vicedom, among Metlpa. The Kyaka are not concerned with theology or, indeed, any form of systematic cosmology to anything like the extent which Vicedom reports of the Metlpa. However, the status of the Goddess as a bride, 'married' to the clan and thus an affine and not an ancestress, is consistent with the Metlpa myth which describes her as a sexless virgin sister of women who themselves acquired full sexual characteristics and became the ancestresses of Metlpa descent groups.[23]

Two main points concerning the social and political significance of this cult may be made: firstly, it co-ordinates the activity of more people, both within the clan and outside it, than any other religious activity of the eastern Kyaka, and indeed than any other traditional institution with the exception of the Moka; and secondly, the influential men introducing the cult can do this in such a way as to enhance further their own personal influence and power. The Goddess is an affine not to one group but, in sequence, to all participating in the cult; her cult links descent groups which are, in fact, already in affinal relationships to each other. It is also organized by men who use their own affinal ties to establish the cult and, to a great extent, to become prominent in other spheres of activity.

(g) The Sandalu

When the Goddess cult was spreading among the eastern Kyaka, another cult performed on a clan basis was being taken up by the western Kyaka. This was the *Sandalu* initiation cult, the local version of the central Enga *Sanggai*.[24] It involved the seclusion and purification of boys and unmarried young men, who had to remain chaste until they graduated from the cult. Only then could they wear the Enga wig and associate with women.[25] The objectives of the cult were to foster the health, strength and prosperity of the individual participants, to strengthen the clan in war and ceremonial exchange, and to weaken its enemies.

The cult had spread as far as the Simbwe River when the Europeans arrived. Clans between the Simbwe and the Lanim were preparing to take it up but have not done so, for the extensive occupation of youths in mission and government activities makes the organization of the cult difficult. Hence, my own information on the *Sandalu* is limited. However, the Reverend E. Kelly has kindly permitted me to consult an unpublished manuscript which includes a very interesting account of the cult, and I summarize this here.[26]

The cult is performed at approximately three-year intervals by youths and unmarried young men guided by a bachelor who has passed the age at which most men marry.[27] The sacred substance *sandalu* is a black liquid kept in twenty containers, each about one foot long. Ten of these, called *Puimi*, are known as 'the woman', and the other ten *Puiwa*, are 'the man'. *Puimi* is distinguished from *Puiwa* by an excrescence which grows on its surface. Each ten is done up in a separate bundle and between cult performances hidden in the muddy bed of a stream.

At the outset of the cult cycle the participants build a long house in the forest. They return home, gather sweet potato, sugar cane and bananas, and spend the night in a men's house to rehearse the special *Sandalu* chants. Early in the morning they go to the forest and dam a small stream to obtain a strong jet of water, under which they wash their eyes till blood appears. This cleanses them from the effects of having seen women and also makes the eyes keen to see game.

The bachelor who leads the cult and two young men, who alone will handle the *Sandalu* containers, bring these at dusk to the house and place them outside the doorway, one on each side. The other men and boys meanwhile prepare and cook food. *Puimi* and *Puiwa*, the spirits of the liquid, are greeted in song, and food is ceremoniously distributed and consumed by all present. An uncomfortably hot fire is made along the centre of the house, and the participants sit facing each other across it.

Throughout the night the participants sing the *Sandalu* chants in order to come into contact with the spirits.[28] Contact is achieved in a number of ways. A spirit may grab a participant's wrist and drag him, shuddering and groaning, from the house. Outside, the youth may rush around all night in a frenzy, climbing trees and approaching precipices, or he may return and pelt his companions with stones, in which case they retaliate. However, the main mode of contact with the supernatural is established through the dreams of those who doze in the cult-house. These dreams are interpreted as indications that war should be made, that the time is ripe for ceremonial exchanges, or that particular men who appear in them will shortly die.

The deaths of enemy leaders can be deliberately sought by the participants, who chant and call the leaders' names, saying 'So-and-so, come and die for us', and then listening for rustling outside. The man's imminent death is confirmed if a member dreams that the victim's hair is being dragged by ghosts of the participants' own clan.

The ceremonies last for four nights. During the day girls from other clans who are interested in the youths sing and dance outside the house. The youths reply with insulting songs and tell them to go away because they are busy with their *Sandalu*; but betrothed men, pleased by this attention, may hand their fiancées brands from the fire as tokens.

On the final day the liquid is transferred into new vessels which are buried in the stream bed. Preparations are made for the public dance next day, when the participants, who have eaten the special *sanggaiya* herb and rubbed their skins with pig's grease, make a dramatic entry through a screen constructed where the track from the cult house meets a main thoroughfare. At the dance songs referring to the dreams and other activities of the cult are sung. The men who have actually handled the *Sandalu* appear exhausted and shudder violently, and spectators regard them with awe. Girls rush at the line of singers, seize their ornaments and drag the young men away.

Each youth is likely to participate in three *Sandalu* ceremonials before he marries and becomes ineligible.

(h) Other supernatural beings

The Kyaka have no traditional beliefs in a creator deity. Nor do they personify the sun and the moon or the forces of nature, except the rainbow (*pwiya*), which is believed to be a great serpent in the forest. With the exception of the sky beings, the non-human spirit-beings are only of local significance.

The most important are the *kilyakai*, nature demons who live in and around streams. These small and ugly creatures are entirely malicious. They steal and injure pigs, shoot with arrows men who enter their water-side preserves, so as to cause malaria, and steal babies from net-bags left unattended, substituting their own horrid offspring who grow into half-wits, deaf-mutes and other monstrosities. Boils are also attributed to *kilyakai*. Some informants said that *kilyakai* could kill men, but I heard of only one actual death attributed to them.

The *kilyakai* provide a useful explanation for misfortune alternative to ghostly wrath; no one need feel guilty if attacked by such a creature. There are magical remedies for exorcising *kilyakai* and curing the complaints they have caused.

Sky beings (*yakirai*) are believed to be responsible for storms and thunder and lightning, and to kill men, if the ghosts remove their protection. They are not conceived as ghosts or ancestors. In the community in which I gathered most of my information younger informants knew nothing of the *yakirai*. Older informants could tell me something about them and thought them dangerous, but still maintained that it was the ghosts themselves who directly brought about most deaths and sicknesses. However, the Reverend K. Osborne tells me that informants whom he has consulted, drawn mainly, I understand, from clans on the Metlpa border, stated that these beings, together with the *kilyakai* and *epalirai*, cause most deaths, the role of the ghosts being merely to protect their kin from these evil beings, or actively to summon them to bring harm.

Less important in the Kyaka cosmology are puck-like tree spirits (*ningkyapen*), echo spirits (*palinda*), and snails (*kyanggaroli, yama*), whose bite is believed to cause serious sickness. With these creatures it is difficult to know where the natural ends and the supernatural begins; whereas they are the 'brothers' of *kilyakai*, their own 'brothers' include other insects and small animals of curious appearance but with no special powers to affect human beings.

Cannibal ogres (*kewanambo*) figure in Kyaka folklore but are not met in everyday life, though Europeans were once placed in this category.[29] In the folk tales, male ogres often masquerade as old women and lure children to their homes; but there are also female *kewanambo* who have fire burning in their sexual organs.

Eastern Kyaka also believe in the *Yama Enda* (Sickness Woman), a female spirit of the forest who appears to lone men as a beautiful woman, and seduces and kills them. She is generally thought to be a Metlpa spirit, with special power over forest game.

(i) Sorcery and magic

Kyaka frequently use magic to cure sickness caused by nature demons or human sorcery, to make pigs grow fat and prevent them from straying, to bring luck on journeys and in exchanges, to win lovers, and to hold the affection of husbands. Most magic consists of spells with associated rites known jointly as *pipu* or *nimungka*. Divining techniques, except that by a spirit medium, also fall under this heading. Most *pipu* also involve paraphernalia, such as leaves and stones and twigs and painted arrows in techniques to banish water demons, coleas juice and pork fat on skewers to cure 'poisoning', ashes rubbed on pigs to make them grow fat, special powders and leaves in love magic, and special stones greased and rubbed on the skin to bring luck.

All adult Kyaka know some of these techniques, but some specialize in medicinal magic and receive small payments. These *pipu lengki* are usually also diviners or spirit mediums.

Certain sicknesses, notably those involving stomach disorders, are normally attributed to sorcery or poisoning (*mauli*) rather than to ghosts or water demons. Sudden deaths, especially of important people, are also likely to be attributed to *mauli*. There are four main sorcery techniques. One consists of adding substances to the victim's food, another of placing substances where the victim will come into contact with them, while the last two involve the waving and the throwing of stones at the intended victim.[30]

The sorcery stones which are waved are highly valued; they are small prehistoric figurines or club-heads or natural stones of curious shape. Before use a pig is sacrificed and the stone smeared with its blood and grease, and invocations (*nimungka*) made over it. The sorcerer mounts the stone on a stick or quill and, from a place of concealment, waves it in the direction of his victim. If he waves vigorously the victim will die in a few hours, if more slowly he will sicken and die in a matter of days. Kyaka distinguish this sorcery, which is believed to be highly lethal, from that in which stones are thrown towards the victim to cause slow sickness involving lumps, swellings, aches and lassitude.

Informants have privately acknowledged ownership of poisons and sorcery stones which are waved, and one boasted of the successful use of his stone by affines. Christian converts have sold me stones and poison.[31] Men do not advertise their possession of these materials but it is widely known that certain people have them, and important men sometimes enjoy considerable reputations as sorcerers. In contrast, I have no evidence that stone-throwing sorcery ever actually takes place, although belief in it is general and some informants said that it had become more prevalent since Europeans had prevented settlement of disputes by physical force.

Kyaka assume that poisoning and sorcery are used only on unrelated members of different clans, and never on clansmen. In other words,

L

they are used against people on whom one might otherwise make war, and wars have started following dysentery epidemics and other cases of actual or presumed poisoning or sorcery. Important men, or their near relatives, are most likely not only to use sorcery or poisoning but also to be its victims.

Pollution by menstruating women (also *mauli*), either through food or direct contact, can kill a man, though medicinal *pipu* may counteract its effects. It is alleged that women, out of personal malice or on behalf of male kin, sometimes seduce and deliberately destroy men in this way.

Kyaka also believe in a mild form of witchcraft (*yama*) which anyone can operate on anyone, close kin or stranger. When an envious person sees another with food but is not offered any, he may voluntarily or involuntarily swallow his saliva and cause sickness to the other. Informants say that children can kill each other in this way, but that this procedure could not kill an adult.

(j) Kemali

The important concept of *kemali* is best translated as 'supernatural danger', and the word normally occurs with the verb 'to strike' or 'to kill'. *Kemali* is associated with deaths, corpses, human bones, burial grounds, with those reptiles and other creatures which are portents or manifestations of ghosts, with the Goddess cult and its stones, and with sorcery stones. *Kemali* is a word never used lightly, for, as Kyaka say, it kills. Yet, in practice, I never heard a death explained simply in these terms; it is the ghost or sorcery or *epali rai* who is cited. *Kemali* is rather a reminder that special precautions have to be taken, that ghosts and the Goddess must be respected and given their due, and that failure in one's obligation to these beings will lead to disaster.

3. THE TRADITIONAL RELIGION: CONCLUSION

It is apparent that Kyaka cosmology is not systematic or highly structured. It consists of an *ad hoc* collection of beliefs and practices relating to the problems the society faces, both those shared with all other human communities (death, sickness, human malice and guilt, human prosperity and fertility) and to key aspects of the particular social structure, especially to family and clan morality, to clan solidarity and to the competitive system of leadership. The benign nature of the Kyaka habitat may partly explain their lack of concern with the forces of nature and the absence among them of the elaborate forms of garden magic prominent in many parts of Melanesia.

It is significant that Kyaka nature demons (*kilyakai*) are specifically associated with watercourses, which are the most hazardous feature of the natural environment and take a frequent toll of human life, and with the lowlying bush and garden areas on river banks, where malarial and other infections are commonly encountered. The forest, in contrast, is thought by Kyaka only to be dangerous to persons unfamiliar with it. It is appropriate that forest spirits are not *kilyakai* but *epali rai*, ancestral ghosts, who on the whole protect the interests of the legitimate owners of the bush and menace intruders.

The territorial instability of Kyaka descent groups may partly explain the relative unimportance of their ancestor cults as compared with many societies organized in segmentary unilineal descent groups. Groups which have occupied new territory and have relinquished lands held within remembered history cannot maintain cults associated with traditional shrines. The diversity of size and of levels of segmentation of Kyaka descent groups, as compared with the Mae and some other Highlands peoples, may also account in part for the lack of overall structuring in their cosmology.

Differences in the ghost cults of the Kyaka and the Mae, and in particular the Kyaka belief that ghosts are sometimes amiably disposed and helpful, must, one would suppose, reflect differences in the pressures and claims exerted by living kin in the two societies. The limited evidence suggests that the 'helpful' Kyaka ghost is likely to be that of a grandparent. Since this accords with Radcliffe-Brown's classic analysis of the relations normally prevailing between alternate generations, it is perhaps more of a problem to understand why the Mae do not expect grandparental ghosts to be well-intentioned than to explain why the Kyaka do so. But this difference may also be related to differences in modal personality which appear to exist between the two peoples, and to the overall contrast in the religious systems. Mae Enga religion provides a bleak, pessimistic view of the universe, whereas the Kyaka system provides a somewhat more optimistic and reassuring outlook.

The significance of sorcery and poisoning to the Kyaka, as compared with their negligible importance to the Mae, may be related in the first place to Kyaka contact with Metlpa, among whom sorcery is also a significant practice.[32] It may also possibly reflect greater difficulties experienced by the Kyaka than by the Mae in settling scores by open warfare and bloodshed. The relationship between sorcery and social prominence in Kyaka society has been noted, and differences between Mae and Kyaka leadership and social stratification may also be relevant here. However, it would also seem, from evidence from other ethnographic areas, that sorcery and witchcraft do, in general, only flourish where the religious system in the narrow sense does not account for all of a man's fortunes and misfortunes and does not provide modes of action appropriate to stresses occurring in all important categories of social relationships. It may thus be argued that there is a logical consistency between sorcery and the restricted competences of the Kyaka ghost and ancestor cults, whereas the more coherent and universally competent Mae ancestral cult leaves little place for this.

4. CHRISTIAN EVANGELIZATION

The lack of systematic order in traditional Kyaka cosmology has undoubtedly made syncretism with Christian doctrines very much easier than it might otherwise have been. Since 1949 the 10,000 Kyaka have been subject to the evangelical attentions of a single, energetic and materially well-equipped Protestant body, the Australian Baptist New Guinea Mission, operating on a scale unusual in the New Guinea field. Between ten and twenty European missionaries, doing evangelical, medical and educational work, divided between two stations, have been present for the last ten years. Nearly all have spoken some Kyaka and several have learned the language very well. Between 1956-61 about 2,000 adult Kyaka became members of the Baptist Church, which now has its own local native pastors and literate secretaries.

Those who have become Christians have given up almost all their traditional practices relating to the supernatural, and even the unbaptized have given up many of the outward forms of the old religion. Thus the ghost houses for sacrifices had disappeared by 1955, and few Kyaka today will admit openly that when they kill pigs they make dedicatory prayers to the ghosts, though many still do so in private and others, it is said, 'think' the prayers. The Goddess cult is in abeyance. The incidence of magical and divining techniques has greatly increased, and many former diviners, mediums and magicians are now leading Christians.

Probably all Kyaka, whether church members or pagans, 'believe' in the Christian God (Anatu), Jesus Christ and Satan, in the sense that they do not dispute their existence, and that they accept the Christian story of the creation of the universe and of man, which fills what was previously a blank in their cosmology.[33] However, I am also convinced that no Kyaka for this reason no longer believes in the existence or powers of the ghosts and other beings in the traditional cosmology. Christians still believe in these, but think that Jesus Christ has greater power; pagans believe in Jesus Christ but think that the ghosts may still be more immediately influential in their everyday affairs.

In the new cosmology the previous functions of the ghosts are now shared with God and Satan. Where the ghosts punished family immorality, God now does so; where the ghosts were, and still are, merely being malicious, God offers protection, while the ghosts are 'doing Satan's work'. A common present-day title for the ghosts of people who died before becoming Christians is 'Satan People' (*Satana Wambu*).

There are, of course, difficulties. Many Christians realize that Christian morality is wider than the old family and clan morality, but Christians, like pagans, still explain deaths in terms of supernatural anger for offences between kinsfolk. However, I have not yet heard of deaths explained in terms of God's anger punishing unrelated members of the Christian community for offences against each other.

APPENDIX
Ætiologies of 33 deaths[1]

Ascribed cause of death	Men	Women	Children	Totals
Ghosts of recent dead	4	5[2]	7[3]	16
Forest ghosts (*epali rai*)	2	—	—	2
Water demons (*kilyakai*)	1	—	—	1
God (for making fun of mission)	1	—	—	1
Sorcery or poisoning	4[4]	—	—	4
Female forest demon (*yama enda*)	1	—	—	1
Menstrual poisoning by wife	1	—	—	1
'Natural causes'				7
Old age	1	2	—	
Childbirth	—	2	—	
'Mere sickness'	2[5]	—	—	
Totals:	17	9	7	33

[1] This is not a random sample of cases, but a tabulation of all deaths which informants were prepared to discuss with me. Only toward the end of my second field trip was I able to get extended information about ghost-killings, though information on more spectacular forms of death was freely offered from the first. My main informants on recent deaths were five teenage boys of Roepo Wapisuk clan whom I interviewed independently in three groups. Their explanations tallied in most instances: where I have two, and in one case three,

explanations for the same death, I have included in this table the one with the most circumstantial detail supplied.

[2] Including one woman who was killed to punish her husband and another killed to punish her brother.

[3] All cases of children being killed were said to be punishments by the ghosts not of the children themselves but of their parents.

[4] Two of these were very important leaders and two were young men of important families, with powerful fathers and brothers.

[5] Both unimportant men.

NOTES

[1] I carried out thirteen months field work among the Kyaka in 1955-56 as a Research Scholar of the Australian National University, and four months in 1959 as part of an Auckland University project supported by the American Philosophical Society, the Wenner-Gren Foundation and the Carnegie Social Science Research Fund of New Zealand. I am grateful to all the institutions which assisted my work. I am also grateful to the staff of the Australian Baptist New Guinea Mission for hospitality, for ethnographic and other information freely given, and for comments on an earlier draft of this paper.

My information on Kyaka religion is deficient in some respects, partly because of the phase of European contact during which I worked and particularly of the impact of Christian mission activity among the Kyaka. I witnessed little traditional cult activity, and inquiry among practising pagans was difficult. A second difficulty was linguistic. It was impossible to get a competent interpreter who was also a member of the community with which I lived, and only toward the end of my second period of field work could I speak Kyaka well enough to get information on the supernatural directly from those informants who knew me well and trusted me.

It is impossible in this paper to document and qualify every statement made. I have tried to use my data with caution but must stress that on many points my information rests on few observations or informants' statements. I intend therefore to prepare a mimeographed supporting document 'Notes on Kyaka religion', which will list informants, give references to manuscript field notes and tapes, and indicate such qualifications to my statements as cannot be included in the present account. Copies of these notes will be placed in the libraries of Auckland University, the Australian National University, and the Royal Anthropological Institute, London, and will also be available to other institutions and students with special interests in the New Guinea Highlands.

[2] Vicedom and Tischner (1943-48).

[3] Meggitt (1958c: pp. 256-63).

[4] Wurm (1961: p. 22).

[5] Kyaka ecology, social organization and putative history are dealt with at length in Bulmer (1961), those of the Mae Enga in Meggitt (1962a; 1965).

[6] Vicedom and Tischner (1943-48 II: part I *passim*).

[7] *Yama* is lexically a tricky word, probably best treated as a number of related homonyms all concerned with sickness induced in any uncanny way: 'witch-craft', 'some kinds of sorcery', 'sickness', 'covetous envy', 'snail'.

[8] Vicedom and Tischner (1943-48 II: pp. 308 ff.).

[9] I learned this only at the end of my field work. Of the three adolescent boys I questioned on the point, two cited their maternal grandmothers' ghosts and the third his paternal grandmother's.

[10] Wild pigs are probably sacrificed to forest spirits; however, there were none in the forest tracts accessible to clans with which I worked. Some informants

said sick pigs were still sacrificed. Possibly the kind of sickness is relevant here. Very sick animals are cooked away from the homesteads so that the smell of the cooking will not infect other pigs with the disease.

[11] cf. Vicedom and Tischner (1943-48 II: p. 170).

[12] Bulmer and Bulmer (1962: p. 195).

[13] Vicedom and Tischner (1943-48 II: pp. 423 ff.).

[14] Bulmer and Bulmer (1962: p. 196).

[15] Vicedom and Tischner (1943-48 II: p. 431).

[16] Vicedom and Tischner (1943-48 II: p. 448).

[17] Vicedom and Tischner (1943-48 II: pp. 437 ff.). Probably the 'woman house' dancers are representing the ancestors of the group through females. In ceremonial exchanges the 'woman house' refers to maternal cognates and affines.

[18] Vicedom and Tischner (1943-48 II: pp. 447-8).

[19] Crouch (1955: *passim*).

[20] By late 1959 these menstruation huts had largely disappeared. Informants said that, having heard the mission's teaching, they no longer feared the Goddess.

[21] Vicedom and Tischner (1943-48 II: p. 430).

[22] Bulmer (1960); Bus (1951); Elkin (1953).

[23] Vicedom and Tischner (1943-48 III: pp. 25 ff.).

[24] Goodenough (1953: pp. 41-3); Meggitt (1965).

[25] Men of Kyaka clans who have not taken up the *Sandalu* also wear wigs for ceremonies, but do not don them for the first time on any particular formal occasion.

[26] Kelly (n.d.).

[27] One man told me it was timed to take place before the Moka exchange festivals, which occur at intervals of three years or more; Bulmer (1960: p. 7).

[28] It is not certain whether these 'spirits' are *Puimi* and *Puiwa* or whether they are the ghosts of the clan; I suspect that both are included.

[29] *Kewanambo* have large tusks. That Europeans lacked these puzzled the Kyaka at first, but when an early missionary was observed to remove his false teeth, the problem was solved.

[30] cf. Bulmer and Bulmer (1962: pp. 197-9).

[31] Mr G. Whitten, of the John Curtin School of Medical Research, Australian National University, kindly examined one phial of 'poison' and tested it on laboratory mice. He found it innocuous, but said that it was organic material which at an earlier stage of decomposition might well have been toxic.

[32] Vicedom and Tischner (1943-48 II: *passim*).

[33] My pagan friend Luluai Sipunyi surprised me by explaining the occurrence of putative artefacts of fossil wood at great depths below present land surfaces as evidence of 'Noah's clan, from the time when God destroyed all'.

C. A. VALENTINE

The Lakalai of New Britain[1]

THE Lakalai are a linguistic and cultural group numbering approximately 3,000. They occupy the Hoskins Peninsula on the central north coast of New Britain. They make up roughly three-quarters of the inhabitants of the West Nakanai Census Subdivision and thus constitute the majority of the people commonly referred to as the West Nakanai. Lakalai is the westernmost of five dialects of the Nakanai language, a Melanesian tongue. Speakers of the other four Nakanai dialects inhabit the coast and parts of the adjacent hinterland eastward to the Toriu River near the base of the Gazelle Peninsula, which is some 100 miles from the Lakalai area. Two small linguistic groups among these western neighbours make up most of the remainder of the West Nakanai population.

Contemporary Lakalai religious life is in considerable part a product of culture contact and acculturation. Christianity and cargo movements have made as important contributions to modern Lakalai culture as have local, traditional religious beliefs and practices. It has been more than half a century since the indigenous religion functioned entirely untouched by extra-Melanesian influences. The traditional religious system of the Lakalai thus cannot be studied in isolation. What is presently available for research and analysis is a component sub-system, derived from traditional indigenous sources but existing within the more inclusive contemporary religious life of the modern Lakalai. All available information points toward the conclusion, however, that the historical process leading to present Lakalai religious patterns has been characterized more by the acceptance and creation of added new elements than by the loss or destruction of traditional beliefs and customs. The description set forth here, therefore, refers to a relatively self-contained component of contemporary Lakalai religious life which probably reflects with substantial fidelity the nature of the precontact religious system. Recent changes in Lakalai religion have been summarized elsewhere, and a more extensive account of the full modern religious system is in preparation.[2]

The present account is focused upon the beliefs which the Lakalai hold and the behaviour in which they engage with respect to traditional spirit-beings. Comparable patterns relating to the spirit entities of local Christianity and cargo movements are too elaborate and complex a blend of old and new orientations for satisfactory treatment in the available space. The major traditional ceremonial activities of Lakalai society have been described in some detail in previous publications.[3] Moreover, as will be made clear below, the connexions between these rituals and the spirits are often nominal or peripheral rather than central to the rites themselves. The large body of Lakalai magic which has no direct connexion with spirit-beings is reserved for future description. For these reasons and in the interests of presenting a reasonably full account of the central aspects of traditional Lakalai religion in the space available, the account of ritual and magic which appears here is far from complete.

1. THE TRADITIONAL WORLD

(a) The setting

The Lakalai habitat is a narrow coastal plain bounded on the south by mountains of volcanic structure. These peaks include one, Mt Pago, which has erupted violently within living memory. The Lakalai plain is flanked by two sizeable rivers, the Kapeuru to the east and the Dage to the west. Most of this littoral is covered with second-growth bush, and virgin rain forest clothes the mountain slopes. Seventeen of the twenty Lakalai villages are at sea-level, many of them built right on the beach. The whole West Nakanai coastline is approximately fifty miles in length. Inland from the villages lie the gardens which are the chief mainstay of the Lakalai economy. Farther south are the un-inhabited jungles which supply the Lakalai with products of the chase and forest resources, but which are also part of the domain of spirit-beings. Only along the flanking valleys of the Dage and Kapeuru do the Lakalai have human neighbours to the south, and in both cases these are peoples who have cultural and linguistic affiliations with New Britain's south coast. The Bismarck Sea affords salt-water resources which are systematically exploited, constitutes a major traditional avenue of travel and trade outside the Lakalai homeland, and is also the dwelling place of important spirit-beings.

The central feature of Lakalai social structure is the matrilineal sib (*maratatila*).[4] The Lakalai sib is a named, corporate, land-holding kin group. Its membership is not residentially localized in a particular community or district, and it may own land in several parts of the Lakalai area. More than sixty sibs are known in the contemporary society. With members residing in various Lakalai villages and with traditionally equivalent kin groups among all neighbouring peoples, the sib constitutes the chief traditional unit of both safety and obligation for the individual. It establishes his place not only in the human world but also in the wider universe, linking him permanently by social and supernatural ties alike to other men and to the spirit world.

Each sib is distinguished by a set of special associations which constitute links with the world of spirit-beings. First, each kin group has its sacred mountain, headland, island, or other height (*olu*). Secondly, each has a sacred stream, pool or other body of fresh water (*lalu*). In the third place, certain food animals or plants are tabooed for each sib as prey or food and known as *lelea* (perhaps from *lea* or *ilea* 'illness'—sickness being one of the penalties for infractions of these taboos). Finally, the kin group is associated with a number of items (*rivu*) which play some part in people's lives, such as objects of material culture, edible substances, useful plants and animals, rituals, and heavenly bodies. Thus the Kevemumuki, the most important of all the contemporary Lakalai sibs, have as their *olu* the volcano Mt Pago, and a spring on its slopes known as Kalea is their *lalu*. The *lelea* or tabooed foods of the Kevemumuki are chicken, sea turtle, a variety of lizard, a species of edible fish, and a variety of coconut with a yellowish husk. Their *rivu* are the sun, fire, and taro, which is the principal staple of the Lakalai diet.

The *olu* or sacred height is the principal permanent dwelling place for the dead of each sib. The leaders or 'big men' (*ururu*) of these ghostly communities are also sib members, and at least some of them are gods, not mere spirits of the dead. Thus when Kevemumuki men and women die, they go to live in a great village on the top of Mt Pago, and their leader is Sumua, the greatest god of the Lakalai. The tabooed animals and plants máy take the form of spirit-beings which are likely to dwell at either the *olu* or the *lalu* of their sib. There are myths, involving various non-human beings, which account for the connexion between sibs and their associated cultural objects. These *rivu* also are frequently controlled in various ways by spirit-beings of the associated sib. Spirit roosters inhabit the slopes of Pago and also appear in other places, such as a reef where a myth relates that they helped Kevemumuki men to catch many fish. Sumua is credited with the creation of taro and he controls the growth of this most important plant in the gardens of men. Another myth tells how Sumua created fire and gave it to people through a man of the Kevemumuki. Taro and fire are therefore said to 'belong to' the Kevemumuki, but there is no indication either that they are taboo to any sib or that their use is restricted to any particular kin group. The same is true of the items called *rivu* by other sibs.

While the Lakalai universe becomes richly meaningful in terms of the varied beings which inhabit it, there is little in the way of formal or abstract cosmogony or cosmology. Despite persistent inquiry, no definitely traditional accounts of the origin of the world were obtained, though local versions of the Christian creation and myths connected with the cargo ideology are well known. According to one mythological fragment, the first man came forth from a plant, and in another traditional story all people are descended from the union of the first woman and a wasp. All other narratives of ultimate human origins are associated with religious traditions which are new to the Lakalai. The origin of death is narrated in a form which is familiar from other parts of Melanesia.[5] When men were immortal, a child was frightened by the sight of her grandmother who had renewed her youth by washing away her old skin. To please her grandchild the old woman put the skin back on and became familiar again. Thenceforward men could no longer live on and on by changing their skins, and death thus came into the world. In the context of Lakalai culture, this is an isolated myth.

A few constellations of stars are said to resemble human beings in certain stances or situations, but no further implications are forthcoming. It is said that thunder is the voices of the spirits of the clouds crying out when they are rent by lightning, but this too seems to have no further ramifications. Clouds are closer to the ground than the sky; the stars are farther up than the sun and moon; the weather is good or bad depending on whether the sun sets over smooth or jagged horizons—but all these beliefs are stated in a matter-of-fact manner which seems devoid of further imaginative or symbolic implications. A fragment of myth in which the sun and moon are personified and a sky world populated by manlike spirit-beings will be dealt with below.

(b) Human beings

In spite of their manifold connexions and multiple interrelations with spirit-beings of various kinds, humans constitute a distinct category in Lakalai thought and belief. The basic term for a living man is *tahalo*, for a woman *tavile*. Since many spirit-beings take anthropomorphic forms and most if not all of them may assume human shape on occasion, modified terminology is sometimes needed to make the necessary distinctions. A living human male may thus be designated *tahalo sesele* ('true man') or *tahalo lo-luma*, which means literally 'man of the house' with the implied meaning 'man of the village'. The latter phrase is used in contradistinction to one of the ways of designating any anthropomorphic spirit-being, *tahalo lo-rivo* or 'man of the bush'. Identical modifiers are likewise applied to the term for female (*tavile*). Anthropomorphic spirit-beings in general are also termed *egite lo-rivo*, which means 'they of the bush'. These designations reflect the Lakalai assumption that the normal domain of mankind is made up of the villages, their environs, the gardens, and other cleared areas. Forested tracts and particularly the virgin jungle and higher reaches of the mountains, on the other hand, constitute the natural realm of spirit-beings. These are of course not mutually isolated domains, for the nomal inhabitants of each frequently invade the other.

Traditional ideas about the nature of human beings are typical of Lakalai belief in that the presence of distinct and apparently clear named concepts does not rule out inconsistency, ambiguity or a degree of confusion. Three soul-like entities are prominent in Lakalai thinking. The individual human being is represented by one of each. First, the *halulu*, usually best translated as 'shade', is generally conceived of as the shadow, reflection, mirror image, and by extension in the modern context, the photographic representation of the individual. It is usually said to disappear at death. However, Hees's informants equated the *halulu* with the ghost or spirit of the dead,[6] and since this term has been used by missionaries as a translation of 'soul' it is now sometimes said that the shade goes to Heaven.

A normally invisible spirit 'double of the living person, called the *kalulu*, is the second traditional entity. It is this double that leaves the individual in sleep and unconsciousness, goes forth and witnesses or participates in the events experienced as dreams. It may be captured by spirit-beings which cause illness, and it is permanently separated from the individual's remains at death. There is considerable confusion between the two terms, *halulu* and *kalulu*, perhaps partly because of their close phonetic similarity. Nevertheless, the majority of contemporary informants clearly state that it is the spirit-double or *kalulu* which survives the death of the individual. Both soul-like bodies are generally said to be insubstantial in composition, though the independent adventures of the *kalulu* often seem to imply a corporeal nature.[7]

The third Lakalai concept is represented by the term *hitu*, which can generally be translated in the present context as 'ghost', 'soul of the dead', or 'spirit of the dead'. A minority of informants represent the *hitu* as an entity which is inherent but unseen in the living human being as well as appearing after death. In terms of this conceptualization, all three soul-like entities are part of the living person. The most generally expressed opinion, however, derives the *hitu* from the *kalulu*. The ghost may thus be said to constitute the form which the living spirit double takes after death, or the ghost may be seen as developing out of the *kalulu* after the individual has died. In Melanesian Pidgin, as spoken by the Lakalai, all three soul-like entities are designated by the term *teven* (probably from the English devil) or the phrase *teven blong man* ('soul of a man').

(c) Spirit-beings

All spirit-beings share certain characteristics which differentiate them from other classes of beings, particularly living men. Though there are various genetic connexions between certain spirit forms and humankind, no spirit is a living, normally born offspring of two human parents. All spirit-beings are in some degree or at some time distinguishable in appearance from living men and women. Even some of those which most successfully impersonate particular human beings are always ideally detectable by such small signs as unusually long eyelashes. The poignancy, threatening quality, or other emotionally toned significance of both mythological and contemporary encounters with spirit-beings often hinges on their close resemblance to humans. However, there is usually either a detection of the difference which avoids harm or an implication that untoward results *could* have been avoided if the human being involved had been more attentive or had heeded available warning signs.

Certain capabilities which are widely shared by spirit-beings are quite outside ordinary human potentialities. Many spirit forms can change their shape, make themselves invisible, move over great distances in a moment's time, fly through the air, enter the body of a living person, capture human souls, cause environmental upheavals and catastrophes, and survive bodily injuries, including dismemberment, which would kill a man. It is symptomatic of man's kinship with the spirit-beings that he can approach some of these feats through the independent action of living souls in sleep, the special powers conferred by magical procedures, or the presence and aid of a spirit. Man is still set apart from the spirit world, however, by the fact that none of these abilities is fully his and none can be exercised to its full extent without superhuman aid. Thus a man's soul may travel great distances while he is asleep; it may fly to the dwelling places of ghosts and other spirits if he knows the procedure for sleeping with properly charmed ginger in his bamboo pillow; or he even may be suddenly transported bodily over great spaces if he is in the company and under the guidance of the god Sumua. Many magical formulae may be employed to enhance human abilities: fighting magic strengthens a man's spear arm or prevents his enemies from reacting to the sight of him; sorcery causes illness or death at a distance; love charms induce uncontrollable desire. There are even procedures for controlling ghosts which then perform various helpful deeds for the magician. Otherwise the special powers of spirit-beings are beyond human capabilities.

The incompatibility of humankind and the spirit-beings is perhaps most clearly evident in the various stories which tell of attempted adjustments by beings from one realm to life in the other domain. There are numerous tales of living men who marry spirit women of various categories, sometimes bringing them to their human communities but more often going to dwell with the spirits. Spirit-beings also capture living human women to be their wives. Only in a few mythological cases do such tales of exile work out happily. Otherwise the captive becomes homesick, one of the parties to the arrangement becomes offended, or some other misunderstanding arises. Then the exile returns to his or her previous home. Thus the domain of men and the spirit world interpenetrate very frequently, but few indeed are the individuals who can cross the line between them permanently, except through death.

The behaviour of spirit-beings is unlike that of humankind in many ways, though here again manlike traits are also to be found in abundance. One key to behavioural differences is that spirit-beings are less predictable than men. There is no time when one can be sure that a spirit will not appear and no place where it is certain that one will not be met with, though the daylight hours and the village area are safest. Innocent looking people, animals, or objects may all turn out to be spirits on closer inspection or when it is too late to avoid them. While all the many named spirit forms have more or less definite behavioural characteristics traditionally assigned to them, these characteristics cannot always be relied upon. One may offend a spirit-being quite unintentionally or unknowingly. The possibilities of expectable behaviour are often so varied as to provide little ground for confident prediction. A man who unexpectedly meets a ghost or a god, for instance, may be seriously threatened, greatly benefited, or simply ignored.

Another general behavioural trait of spirit-beings is that they tend to go to much greater extremes than living men in their reactions and responses. The benefits bestowed by spirits are often far beyond human capacities, whether they be protection in dangerous situations, gifts of great material wealth, or aid in prosecuting some difficult enter-prise. The threatening and punishing behaviour of spirit-beings is similarly extreme by human standards. Some giant bush spirits are malevolent without apparent cause and kill off or drive away whole villages of men. A man who unwittingly eats the fruit of a forest tree which belongs to a spirit-being is likely to be killed by its owner, while a human owner would be content with a moderate illness through sorcery as revenge even if the culprit had deliberately stolen the fruit. The aggressiveness of some spirit-beings, both against men and against other denizens of the spirit world, extends to eating their victims, though the living Lakalai have never been known as cannibals.

The beings of the traditional spirit world are seldom abstract or formless in character. The descriptions which follow will give some idea of how much concreteness can be combined with inconsistency and ambiguity in verbal characterizations derived from the oral literature, reports of experiences, and discussions with informants. A similar concreteness is also manifest in other forms of expression. A few spirit forms are dramatically portrayed with quite theatrical effects by masked performers. Wood carvings representing ghosts in particular were made traditionally and continue to be employed as decorative props in some of the larger and more spectacular ceremonies. More-over, coloured drawings and paintings of the majority of spirit forms were made spontaneously for anthropologists in the field. Many of these are strikingly representational images which achieve a high degree of differentiation among the various types. These graphic portrayals are often perfectly recognizable to individuals other than the artists.

As will become clear below, the traditional Lakalai spirit world can be seen as an elaborate pantheon ordered in terms of quite specific named concepts. At the same time, however, spirit-beings are often referred to simply by the more general terms available in both Lakalai and Pidgin. Listeners frequently do not request any greater specificity. Many types of spirit-beings are capable of metamorphosis into other types, and several forms specialize in impersonating living humans. Moreover, in contemporary encounters people are sometimes vague or unsure as to precisely which variety of spirit-being they have met. The Lakalai recognize that there are alternative interpretations for events and experiences which they connect with the spirit world. Yet they do not necessarily insist on clarification by choosing a single explanation and eliminating others. Logical consistency, clearcut symbolic categories, and systematic assignment of experience to particular classes of phenomena can all be found in this system of belief and behaviour, but they represent only one side of traditional Lakalai religion. With all the cognitive orderliness that characterizes this system, there is also a pervasive quality of ambiguity and ambivalence.

(d) Spirits of the dead

The most general Lakalai term for spirits of the dead is *hitu* (plural *hituhitu*). Not only is this a standard designation for all the ghosts of the recently dead, as already noted, but it is regularly applied to the spirits of remote ancestors as well. Beyond this, however, the same word is also used to designate certain anthropomorphic spirit-beings which have never been human and are not closely connected with men (see (g) *Manlike spirits of the bush* below). When specific reference to ghosts and/or ancestral spirits is intended, therefore, the phrase *hitu-la-tahalo* ('spirit of a man') may be used. In Lakalai Pidgin, *tambaran* is the equivalent of *hitu* in each of the senses just noted, and the generic Pidgin phrase for spirits of the dead is *tambaran blong man*.

The dichotomy between material and non-material orders is no more applicable to spirits of the dead than to the traditional soul-like entities. Some accounts of both recent and ancestral ghosts indicate an incorporeal nature, but numerous exploits by spirits of the dead imply a substantial bodily form. While they gain the power of metamorphosis in the afterlife, ghosts retain the basic form and identity of their former living existence. They can thus often be recognized as individuals when met by the living. Persons who die in childhood may grow to maturity in the spirit world, though they do not seem to grow old. Neither ghosts nor ancestral spirits are said to die either of illness or of old age. There is no expressed belief in reincarnation.

Yet spirits of the dead are not immortal in a strict sense. Genealogical depth is quite shallow, individual ancestors usually being forgotten after three generations. Though no explicit belief was recorded that their existence then comes to an end, their individual entities are no longer among the spirit-beings with which the living interact. Furthermore, spirits of the dead may be killed by violence, at the hands of either other spirit-beings or living men. Myths relate the killing and eating of ancestral spirits belonging to one sib by deceased members of another.[8] According to a common mythological theme, spirits of the dead struggling through the night with human adversaries turn into trees or birds with the coming of the dawn, and they are then vulnerable to destruction by their erstwhile victims.

In former times, bodies of the dead were buried in the earth floor of the dwelling to keep the deceased near his kin. The head remained above ground for a time. Then the corpse was completely buried in the same grave, with the body placed in such a position that its head faced the sacred height of the dead man's sib. Close relatives were secluded in deep mourning within the house, wore special items of costume, and observed food and grooming taboos for periods of up to two months. Today combined government and mission influence has led to the establishment of village cemeteries, and burial in the dwelling is no longer practised.

While the soul may be seen at distant points soon after death, the ghost is also said to linger near the corpse for some time. The ghost may haunt its former dwelling, the village, or particular persons for varying periods ranging up to several years. Some accounts imply that spirits of the dead may wander freely for an extended time after death. According to one common tradition, when the people of any hamlet die, they repair to an invisible counterpart of the living community in the near-by bush where they live a life that parallels their former existence. Another belief holds that the dead of each sib go to the sacred river of their kin group and assume the form of nipa palms growing on its banks. A log floating against the current in a sacred stream is interpreted as carrying the invisible ghost of a newly dead sib member journeying to his resting place. Other cases of spirits of the dead residing at the *lalu* include contemporary accounts of

M

ancestors inhabiting the hot springs at Pokili at the eastern end of Lakalai territory and an earlier story of Holuholu ancestors living in houses that could be seen under the water of the spring known as Bolubolu. One of the most recent interpretations is that ghosts lurk about the village cemeteries for at least a brief period.[9]

In what is by far the dominant traditional belief, however, the *hitu* goes to the *olu* of its sib soon after death. Here on the sacred height the ghost is welcomed into a village inhabited by all the recent and ancestral dead of the sib, and in this permanent home the spirit has a life essentially like that of the living in precontact Lakalai communities. Such is the pattern described by contemporary informants. Exceptions to it appear in two earlier accounts given by Hees.[10] In one of these, Gararua ghosts try to return to their living communities before finally settling in the village of the dead. The other exceptional account is that of the Holuholu spirits of the dead who kill and eat the ghosts of other sibs as noted earlier. These ghostly communities are ordinarily invisible to men, though the spirits of the Kevemumuki on top of Mt Pago can sometimes be discerned in the smoke rising from the volcano. Hunters on the slopes of this and other mountains sometimes hear the barking of dogs or the crowing of cocks which belong to the villages of the dead.

Ghosts are by no means confined to these dwelling places of theirs, and their numerous contacts with human beings nearly always take place elsewhere. Since it is universally assumed that ghosts may be dangerous, these contacts are always more or less feared by men. Nevertheless, it is recognized that interactions with the dead are often rewarding to the living, not only because specific benefits may be bestowed but also because ghosts generally continue to honour their traditional duties and obligations to surviving kinsmen and sibmates. In one traditional tale a man is lost and presumed drowned near a reef which is associated with his sib. Sometime later, his mourning kinsmen are overjoyed when he returns richly decorated and laden with wealth, relating that his dead sibmates kept him with them under water, rejoiced in his visit, and heaped him with presents when it was time for him to return.[11]

Spirits of the dead are occasionally given credit for the origin of cultural items of great value to people in general. A myth tells how an ancestral ghost of the Mamapa sib was responsible for the origin of the coconut palm, thus making the coconut a *rivu* of that sib. (This is a local version of the widespread narrative according to which face-like markings on the surface of a nut reveal how the original palm grew out of a buried human head.) Even ghostly actions prompted by seemingly generous motives are not necessarily beneficial to the living, however. A common theme of Lakalai folklore involves a deceased grandmother who observes how a surviving grandchild is being treated by its family and decides that her descendant is not being properly cared for. She then steals the soul of the child and takes it to her ghost village to care for it, whereupon the child sickens and dies unless its soul can be rescued by magical means. Ghosts also sometimes remain attached to surviving lovers or fall in love with living people.

Cases of more protracted interaction with humans voluntarily entered into by spirits of the dead are generally benevolent in character. Several contemporary informants remember cases of the following sort. The ghost first returns to the house in which mourning relatives are secluded, often to do them some favour. Then it comes repeatedly, performs many services, and becomes widely known. The spirit always remains in a dark corner where it cannot be seen, but its hands and arms may be felt. It may begin by communicating through whistles and rustlings in the thatch, though it soon speaks more or less freely with whoever is present. Superhuman services performed by these ghosts include announcements of distant deaths, warnings of approaching enemies, communication of other news from afar, detecting and undoing the work of sorcerers, and bestowing gifts of food or other forms of wealth. Perhaps the most notable of them was a girl who died shortly after birth, grew into an adolescent in the course of her regular appearances, and continued her visits over a number of years until both her parents died of old age.[12]

Of all contacts with the living which are initiated by the dead, however, those which are most frequently described involve behaviour on the part of ghosts or ancestral spirits which is aggressive and threatening in the extreme. The commonest result of an encounter with a ghost is a physical attack which a mortal being has great difficulty surviving. Sometimes these attacks are motivated by slights to the memory of the dead or unsettled scores left over from their living existence. More often, however, the accounts imply no other motive than a lust for human blood. Single spirits or even groups of ghosts are described as setting upon humans whenever they meet them, with no indication of any special relationship to the victim, who evidently often does not know the specific identity of his attackers.

Many tales recount epic struggles between men and bloodthirsty ghosts or ancestral spirits. Human heroes may survive by great strength, by superior guile, or by holding out until the coming of the dawn changes the spirits into other forms, but the outcome is seldom assured. Elaborate narratives sometimes involve repeated escape and recapture.

In spite of the dangers which may be involved, there are a number of specific contexts in which humans summon or otherwise initiate contact with the dead. One of these is the magical technique by which men or women fly to the dwelling places of ghosts and ancestors. The magical key to this procedure is sleeping on properly charmed ginger. It is usually in order to rescue souls captured by ghosts or other spirit-beings that these flights are undertaken. According to contemporary practitioners, the soul rescuer may persuade or trick the ghostly captors into giving up the lost soul, but he often has to struggle with them and flee for his life with the recaptured soul. If he is successful, the illness caused by the loss of the soul will disappear. In the course of these encounters the magician learns of the affairs of spirit-beings, and he may carry messages between the living and the dead.

While this procedure involves invading the realm of the ghosts and ancestral spirits, other important magical practice summons them temporarily into the human domain. This is a form of divination employed to identify the killer of a recently dead person. The ghost is summoned, together with deceased sibmates, into the dwelling which he occupied during life. The diviner thrusts a charmed stick into the house and intones the names of suspected culprits in turn. When the name of the murderer is spoken, the spirits pull the whole staff suddenly into the house, thus exposing the diviner to the great danger of being pulled inside with it. The whole procedure, like that of rescuing souls, is regarded as highly hazardous for the practitioner.

In other situations spirits of the dead can be summoned more easily and safely, principally because they involve a relationship with a ghost that was a close relative or good friend in life. Spells involving the name of the ghost to be called are recited as ginger is chewed. The ginger is next spat on to an object, and the spirit then comes and resides invisibly in this object. The invisible ghost is thus induced to inhabit a bracelet, a knife, or a piece of ceremonial paraphernalia for an indefinite period. The owner of the object keeps it with him whenever he is engaged in an activity for which he needs the aid of his helping spirit. The activities in which such helping spirits are most commonly used are hunting, with the ghost catching the game or guarding it in the forest, and love magic, in which the ghost invisibly inspires a specified woman with irresistible longings for his master. Souls of the dead are brought in a similar way to inhabit the decorated wristbands (*mileki*) with which young men are ritually invested for use in major ceremonial performances. In this case, the ghost remains in the object permanently, acts as a protecting spirit for each successive owner of the wristband, and enforces the taboos which surround the wearing of it. One further type of invocation of ghosts through spells is practised by magicians to control the weather for important ceremonial occasions. The soul of a deceased kinsman is directed to inhabit a special bundle and drive away rain clouds during the course of the ceremony.

Spirits of the dead are further connected with the two major forms of large group ceremony traditionally practised and still carried on by the Lakalai. The most elaborate and impressive of these are the memorial festivals dedicated to important men two years or more after their deaths. An early stage in the lengthy preparations for one of these festivals is marked by the exhumation of the body and the removal of the humerus. When it has been publicly announced that preparations are under way, the arm bone is elaborately decorated and hung up for a few days in a men's house. The ghost of the deceased individual is said to reside in the bone during this period, and all noise and disturbances are prohibited in the neighbourhood of the men's house where it hangs. At the much later holding of the memorial festivities proper, three days of feasting and dancing take place with the participation of performers and guests from a number of communities. In the most spectacular of the performances, lavishly costumed and painted men are carried on platforms above the heads of a singing and dancing throng in the centre of the hamlet. One of these performers carries the decorated bone of the man to whose memory the whole festival is dedicated. The others manipulate carved and painted wooden figures or tricky props of other sorts involving sleight of hand for the mystification of onlookers. The spirits of dead kinsmen are called to stay in these objects during the performance. A platform performer may also carry out rites of love magic, and the ghost that has been summoned insures that the desired woman will be attracted to the performer.

Following the end of the festival, the bone of the dead man was traditionally made into a spear point and blooded against an enemy.

(Today exhumation is no longer practised, a cassowary leg bone is used as a substitute for the human humerus, and the blooding of the spear has been abandoned with the prohibition of warfare.) The entire ceremony is a highly complex affair, only the briefest outline of which is presented here. The general atmosphere during the climactic stage of feasting and dancing is one of intense excitement and exuberant merrymaking. The attention of all is focused on the excitement and satisfactions of the activities themselves. The presence of selected ghosts at various stages seems almost incidental to the main activities of the feasts and dances. There is no hint of any more serious or threatening involvement of spirits in the festivities.

The other major ritual activity is carried out each year by a masked society known as the *valuku* (Pidgin *tubuan*), which is also the general term for the masks themselves. Membership in the society was traditionally limited to mature men but is now open to all males from adolescence onward. Over a period of two or three months the men construct a series of increasingly elaborate painted and decorated bark cloth masks. Each type of mask is shown publicly in a succession of regular order, either by single individuals or by groups of costumed figures. Some of these figures attack the onlooking populace in a playfully aggressive manner, concentrating on women and children. Others dramatize complex scenes such as a battle between two groups of warriors or a funeral. The most elaborate masks are simply paraded through the villages to be admired by all. The processes of making and donning the masks are strictly taboo to the uninitiated. The fiction is maintained rather lightly that the costumes hide the identities of their wearers, but in fact almost any masked man is widely recognized by his gait, peculiarities of his exposed feet, and other circumstances. Only the youngest children are actually deceived by the disguises.

The activities of the *valuku* are thus a series of theatrical performances. They are nevertheless connected with the spirit world and particularly with ghosts in a way which gives them a sacred character. This aspect of the ritual cycle emerges from the two chief traditional conceptions of its origin. One of these conceptions is associated with the Gararua sib, the other with the Kevemumuki. According to the Gararua tradition, the *valuku* was created by Gararua ancestral spirits, remains closely connected with them, and is therefore a *rivu* of this group. It is also said that the ceremonial cycle is initiated each year by a signal from Gararua spirits of the dead residing at the Dage River, which is the sacred stream of this sib. In the Kevemumuki story, the masks and instructions for their use were brought to men long ago by ancestral spirits of this sib from Mt Pago acting on the command of the Kevemumuki god Sumua. Sumua decreed that the *valuku* must be taboo to women and children, and that the masked performances should be enacted by his command each year among human kind and ghosts alike. According to one widespread interpretation, even though the masks do not represent spirit-beings in any but a purely theatrical sense, each mask does have a *halulu* or shadow-soul of its own. It is believed that these shades come from the Dage River each year, attach themselves to the masks as they are constructed, and return to the river when the masks are destroyed at the end of the seasonal cycle.

New mask designs continue to be introduced from time to time. While some of these are created by unaided human invention, many are inspired by ghosts. The spirits of the dead involved in recent and contemporary inspirations are not limited to Kevemumuki or Gararua ghosts but belong to many sibs. The dead in their hamlets of the bush and their communities on sacred heights perform the masked rituals at the same time as men. During this season there are many ways in which they come into contact with the living who thus acquire new mask patterns from them. A ghost may come seeking a relative or some other person who can pass a design on to his kinsmen. Representatives of the dead and the living may come upon each other by accident in the bush. Men may meet ghosts bearing masks in their dreams, either by chance or through the use of charmed ginger. Women may acquire mask designs in some of these ways as well as men, but in all known cases they turn over their acquisitions to male kinsmen since men alone may make them and perform in them. These encounters are not ordinarily dangerous to the human beings involved.[13]

For the most part, the spirits of the dead which take the forms and manifest the behaviour described so far are called simply *hituhitu* and are not divided into named types. A variety of more specific categories of ghosts and ancestors is also recognized, denoted by special names in most cases, and differentiated in terms of both appearance and behaviour in each case. Eleven of these types have been recorded with some confidence. Only one of these specialized forms has already been mentioned. This is the spirit of a dead kinsman summoned magically to live in an object and aid its owner; it is called *tatabu*. The same term is also applied to other forms, one of which is a walking skeleton which goes abroad as the soul of a dying individual.

The names of some of these spirit forms are translatable or have obvious derivations. Thus the *balepa* (from a word meaning 'wrapped bundle') is a corpse which flies over the villages wrapped in a burial mat. The *tarogolo* (from a verb meaning 'to change form') impersonates the living and kills human victims by various horrible methods including intercourse made lethal by obsidian blades in the genitals of the spirit. Only two types are limited to one sex. One of these is the bleeding women who have died in childbirth and are known as *pigobara* (*pigo*, 'to give birth'; *bara*, 'badly'). The other is the leader of the ghosts distinguished by his gigantic testicles and called *putu-perereko* (*putu*, 'scrotum'). The names of other special types have no known translations and appear to be simple class denominations. The *visu* flies at night, shines with a great light, and gouges out people's eyes with long fingernails. The *savei*, which also lights up, and the *tausogolo* are wild, shy forms inhabiting the forest and seldom seen close at hand. Under certain conditions at least, the ghost of any individual not excluded from a category by reason of sex may assume any of these forms. Traditional stories and memory accounts that tell of individual ghosts appearing in more than one shape indicate that taking on the characteristics of a particular category is not necessarily permanent.

The majority of the specialized spirits of the dead are more or less threatening to human beings. Only the *tatabu* summoned to aid a living relative or friend is invariably benevolent. Others like the wrapped corpse which merely signals a distant death or the wilder forms that may be glimpsed in the bush, are not seriously frightening. The night-flying *visu* and the shape-shifting *tarogolo*, on the other hand, may inflict injury or death in peculiarly terrifying forms. Both the *visu* and the *putuperereko* with his company of lesser ghosts are sometimes man-eaters. The ghost of a woman who has died in childbirth embodies special hazards for male victims. Menstrual fluids and other forms of female genital blood are considered poisonous to men, capable of weakening them generally, neutralizing any magic which they perform, making them easy victims in warfare, and causing them illness. The newly dead *pigobara* blames her suffering and demise on human males in general, and towards them she is therefore one of the most savage of all the ghostly forms. One of her favourite modes of attack is to hurl her poisonous fluids into the eyes of men.

THE LAKALAI OF NEW BRITAIN

The *pigobara*, the *visu* with its knife-like nails, the deceptive *tarogolo*, and the anthropomorphic ghost leader are all frequently met with in Lakalai folklore. Their horrible deeds against men are recounted at length, and those few who triumph over them are heroes whose exploits are well known, even though the heroes themselves are often anonymous. Contemporary informants remember recent encounters with the shrouded *balepa*, the *visu*, the *tarogolo*, and the women dead in childbirth. During my visits in 1954 and 1956, in and around one village alone more than one *visu* appeared in the air, several persons encountered either the wild *tausogolo* or the *savei*, and all three forms of *tatabu* were in evidence. In the same community and during the same periods, various additional episodes were recorded of encounters with ordinary ghosts not classifiable within these special categories. Thus, despite the fact that ghosts are often said to have manifested themselves less often since the establishment of the Christian missions, these spirits of the dead do continue to appear with considerable frequency among the living.

(e) Animal spirits and related beings

The Lakalai word *taua* designates a large and various class of spirits many of which are especially associated with human kin groups and particular localities, and all of which may have an important effect on human fortunes. Despite some instances of overlapping and ambiguous uses of the term, the *taua* are essentially distinct from the ghosts that have already been described and from the gods, bush spirits, and other forms which will be noted below. They are generally said to have existed always and to have come from unknown non-human origins. While they may and often do take on human form in particular circumstances, their ordinary shape is almost never manlike. In the local form of Melanesian Pidgin all kinds of *taua* are known as *masalai*.

In the form in which they are most frequently encountered by man, the majority of *taua* are indistinguishable from ordinary animals and plants unless they reveal their true nature by exercising their power of metamorphosis. Many are more or less monstrous in their ordinary shape, having gigantic proportions, being coloured with bright hues unlike ordinary animals, or combining parts of a number of different animals and/or plants. A few ordinarily have the appearance of large stones or boulders. Only two recorded forms approach anthropomorphism in their usual appearance. One of these is the *vavato* which has a double manlike body. The other is a human skeleton which lives far up the Kapeuru River. Both dwell outside Lakalai territory and are primarily associated with neighbouring peoples.

Any seemingly ordinary animal, and many apparently normal plants or stones, may turn out to be *taua*. All the animals and plants (*lelea*) which are taboo to any of the sibs have *masalai* counterparts, and these account for most of the seemingly normal denizens of the forest which turn out to be spirits. However, some species which are not recorded as taboo to any sib are also found to be *taua* on occasion.[14] All plants and animals of monstrous or fantastic form are *taua* spirits. Many of these monsters are also said to 'belong to' particular sibs, and like the more ordinary looking ones they are addressed as sibmates by men of the appropriate kin groups. No concept of human descent from *taua* animals appears in traditional stories or is mentioned by any informant, however, and any such concept is denied by all who are questioned on it. Other monsters classified as *taua* were not known by informants to be affiliated with any sib.

Most, though not all, *masalai* are known to inhabit specific locations on land or in the sea. Most of the sib-affiliated *taua* definitely reside in such places, and these locales are usually at or near either the sacred height (*olu*) or the sacred water (*lalu*) of their respective sibs. All the more monstrous spirits of this class represented in our data dwell in such special habitats. At the same time, however, *taua* for which no sib connexion has been recorded, including stones, also inhabit specific locales. In all cases, these areas become known as 'taua places' which are dangerous and ordinarily avoided by men. *Masalai* places other than the sacred areas of sibs include sections of forest, springs and pools in the brush, holes and caves, steep valleys, and other unusual landscape features. By virtue of their sacred connexion with particular groups of men, most *taua* are symbolic of kin group unity and constitute sib totems. The others appear to be non-totemic, largely zoomorphic local spirits of land and sea.[15]

A special category consists of disease-bearing spirits called *taua-la-ilea* ('*taua* of sickness'). These usually appear as gigantic, multi-coloured, four-footed animals like dogs or pigs, though they are also said to take human form. There is such a spirit which is afflicted with and spreads abroad each of a large variety of illnesses. They may appear in groups, coughing and groaning as they come, bringing epidemics to human villages. One function ascribed to the masked *valuku* performances described above is to frighten away these creatures, and other similar measures are also taken against them. The disease *taua* are said not to be connected with any sib, and no special locale is known for them.

While the general belief that *taua* spirits as a class have existed since before there were men is unambiguous in itself, there are also some exceptions to this rule. An occasional informant insisted that ghosts might turn into *taua*, perhaps permanently. A few myths relate spirit origins which are connected with human beings. In one of these a pair of human brothers belonging to the Ugeuge sib discover for the first time the eggs of the wild bushfowl (megapode), which are plentiful in the thermal area near the Kapeuru River known as Pokili, and which constitute an important source of protein in the Lakalai diet. After explaining their secret and distributing the first eggs among men, the brothers retired to Mt Liu-a Hatotolu (meaning literally 'to take away eggs') on the edge of Pokili. There they were transformed into *taua* in the form of cassowaries which are still said to bring the eggs down from the mountain and place them in the warm earth of the thermal area where they can be collected by men. Thus this mountain became the sacred height of the Ugeuge, the cassowary became one of their *taua* spirits as well as a *lelea*, and the eggs are a cultural item (*rivu*) especially associated with the same group.

In general, *taua* spirits are neither progenitors of men nor mythical creators, nor with the exception just noted are they associated with culture heroes. A legend recorded by Hees relates the affairs of the first human couple, whose origin is not stated, and a wasp.[16] The woman has intercourse with the wasp and bears many children from whom all human beings are descended. The insect is not identified as a *taua*, however, being called simply *vivu* ('wasp'), and none of the characters in the story is explicitly associated with any sib. A single case of creating an item generally useful to men was an impersonal, perhaps unintentional, gift not connected with any particular kin group as far as we know. A *masalai* bat made the first breadfruit tree appear, it too being a *taua*. Other bats ate its fruit, and from their droppings ordinary breadfruit trees grew everywhere. *Taua* spirits are not said to have given men any other cultural items, and no special ritual is devoted or addressed to them as such.

The majority of encounters with *taua* are fraught with danger for human beings, and they are generally feared. When a person becomes ill after having been at or near a *masalai* place, it is possible that one of these spirits has given him a sickness or stolen his soul. In the latter case, a soul rescuer will fly to the habitat of the spirits by the same technique which is employed against soul-capturing ghosts. Earth-quakes and violent storms are caused by *taua* whose areas have been disrespectfully trespassed upon. Human victims are often taken un-awares because the spirits are indistinguishable from ordinary animals, but this is seldom taken into account by the vengeful *taua*. A woman catches and eats a fish which speaks to her from inside her stomach, reveals her error to her and then kills her. The special locales and peculiar sensitivities of these spirit creatures are often discovered by hard experience. Everyone knows that whistling offends the *taua* cassowaries and other spirits of Pokili because an egg collector who once violated this taboo was led into the bush by the spirits, became temporarily insane, and later developed a serious case of elephantiasis of the legs. One such victim was living in the village of Koimumu in 1956. When men ignore indications that they are dealing with a *taua* and in the exceptional cases in which the associated taboos are defied, vengeance may be particularly terrible. Within recent years an enthusiastic Lakalai Christian leader became agonizingly ill after explicitly defying traditional belief and eating wood grubs from a well-known *masalai* place. In 1954 he died in a hospital outside the Lakalai area (diagnosis: cancer of the stomach) and was mourned as a victim of the spirit grubs.

Relations between men and *taua* totems are patterned in terms of the sib structure. The spirits remain dangerous in this context, but here their important benevolent aspects come to the fore as well. The chief sanction against disrespectful behaviour toward the *lelea* species of one's own sib and particularly against violations of the associated food taboos is punishment by the appropriate *taua*. This may come in the form of physical attack, induced illness, or soul stealing, any one of which often leads to death. If the transgressor is not immediately killed, his death will be lingering and painful whenever it does come. The victim may be eaten by an animal which says to him, 'You ate me first', or a tree whose taboo he has violated may fall upon him and crush him. Even if the animal or plant against which the offence was committed was not a spirit itself, the corresponding *taua* will soon appear or administer the punishment invisibly.

Those who conscientiously observe the taboos of their kin group have nothing to fear from totemic spirits. Beyond this, the *taua* of a person's sib will often aid him in important ways if he has been respect-ful of the relevant prohibitions. *Taua* birds and animals appear in order to guide lost human sibmates, and *masalai* trees may prevent ordinary trees from falling on their sibmates. A canoe carrying men of the Buhalihali sib and other passengers was recently caught in a stormy sea to the west of the Lakalai area. When the canoe went down and all other hands were lost, the men of the Buhalihali were said to have been picked up and carried safely to shore by cassowaries which are *taua* of their kin group. These spirits sometimes also protect their human sibmates against the depredations of other spirit forms. No magical, ritual, or other technical procedures for summoning *taua* or invoking their aid were recorded in the field.

It is widely believed that the *taua* appear less often than formerly and that their strength has been reduced by virtue of the work carried on by the mission churches. Lakalai Catholics believe that some of the *masalai* have been exorcised from their special habitats by mission priests, and Methodists assert that because these spirits are now under the authority of the Christian God they only punish those who are sinners in the eyes of the Church. Sib-associated food taboos have now been broken by some individuals, and some young men may be found who do not know the *lelea* of their kin groups.[17] Nevertheless, for the majority of the Lakalai, *taua* of all the various types remain entirely real, are still often met with, and continue to enforce the rules which are associated with them.

(f) Superior spirits and gods

A variety of beings in traditional Lakalai belief are superior spirits in one sense or another. About most of them, however, rather little information could be gleaned from contemporary informants. A mythical anthropomorphic being is named both Haro ('sun') and Tauahili ('man of Hailili sib'); his wife is named Taio ('moon'). Myths about them make it clear that they are concretely identified with these two heavenly bodies. Moreover, Tauahili is sometimes said to be not only the founder of his sib but the progenitor of all mankind, or even the creator of the world. These personages are not well known, however, and there is reason to believe that the more creative roles ascribed to Tauahili may owe much either to Christian belief, to the cargo doctrine, or to both.

Before coming to earth, Tauahili and Taio lived in a mythical sky world known as Gimigaigai. Various other manlike spirits inhabited the same region. Among these was a being, named Pasiko in some stories about him, who first brought fire to men on earth. Gimigaigai is generally pictured as a somewhat miraculous region where people with superhuman powers dwell. Also appearing there and elsewhere in a series of very popular stories are a number of half-human, half-animal characters who may transform themselves from one state into the other. These include Pakasa Uru ('Big Wallaby') who is usually portrayed as a trickster and buffoon in comic tales, but who also is credited with giving their present form to certain animals. Another is Tulagola ('dog', 'orphan') who often plays a kind of Cinderella role in getting the better of Big Wallaby in the humorous stories. He is also presented as the creator of the first slit-gong and discoverer of the first hand drum, the two most important instruments in Lakalai music and dancing. Another fragment of belief, known rather widely but little elaborated, refers to a group of superior beings known as 'children of the sun' (*gulikiliki-la-mata-la-haro*). They are represented as small in stature, light skinned, and possessed of great strength. It is said that long ago they came to the Lakalai area—in some versions from the east, in others from the west—easily overwhelmed the taller human beings in battle, and disappeared again. None of these beings has any contact with living men, and none figures in any ritual. They are all regarded as belonging to the remote past.

Among the most powerful beings in the spirit world with which the living have to deal are the leaders or 'big men' (*ururu*) of the villages which the dead of each sib inhabit. Unlike their human counterparts, they appear to hold their positions permanently. Several of them are mentioned in mythology, but in most cases there is little reason to regard them as more than leading ancestral ghosts. The major exception is Sumua, the one being in contemporary or remembered belief who seems unquestionably classifiable as a god. Some of the traditions about him and the way informants sometimes speak of him seem to imply that there are or were other beings of comparable nature and status, but no other specific example can be established without doubt. The beings who most closely approach this position are certain close kinsmen and sibmates of Sumua, but for the most part they remain rather shadowy figures in traditional mythology and contemporary belief.

No word has been found in the Lakalai language which corresponds to 'god', nor indeed is Sumua classified in any really distinctive category of spirits. It is emphasized in stories of his origin that he is neither a human being nor just a ghost. He is most often called *tahalo lo-rivo*, 'man of the bush', a designation which as we have seen may be applied to any essentially anthropomorphic spirit. He is also sometimes referred to as *tahalo-la-taua*, in Pidgin *man masalai*, both meaning something like '*taua*-man'. He is never pictured as primarily zoomorphic, however, and his character is definitely quite different from that of the *taua* spirits already described. This usage appears to refer to his connexion with *taua* in some versions of his history. He is often called *tama-le-Gaike*, which is a standard teknonymous usage meaning 'father of Gaike'.[18]

Each of several stories portrays Sumua's origin somewhat differently, but they all agree that he was born to a woman of the Kevemumuki sib under unusual circumstances. According to one version, his mother died in pregnancy and gave birth as a ghost at the Mt Pago *olu* of her sib. In another story, his mother had a miscarriage in the gardens, the foetus was thrown into the bush, and Sumua came forth from it and repaired to the place of the Kevemumuki dead on top of Mt Pago. In a third account the Kevemumuki woman was married to a *taua* cassowary (sometimes in human form) who belonged to the Buhali-hali sib and lived on the slopes of its *olu*, Mt Oto. There Sumua was born to this pair, and his mother gave him temporarily into the care of other *taua* spirits at a near-by *masalai* water. When he grew up, his father sent him to Pago, which is considered his rightful home by virtue of his sib membership. There he became the big man of his *olu* and the head of all the Kevemumuki.

All this is usually said to have taken place long ago, and Sumua is subsequently credited with a number of important creations and gifts to mankind. The major human possessions represented in various myths as having originated with Sumua on Pago are taro, sweet potatoes, pigs, chickens, fire, the *valuku* ceremonies, and a special dish which combines taro, manioc, or sago with Canarium almonds (*ulalu*). It will be remembered that both taro and fire are *rivu* or specially associated items of the Kevemumuki group and that the chicken is one of their tabooed foods (*lelea*). There are alternative stories of the origin of fire, but in one the manlike spirit Pasiko, referred to earlier in the present section, is a sibmate of Sumua, who obtains the fire from him and distributes it among men with his consent. Sumua instructed men in the use of many of his creations, and he continued to enforce these instructions.

The most important of these gifts to humanity and the one most surrounded by special sanctions is taro. This tuber is both the major staple of the local diet and the food which is preferred by men above all others; no matter what else they have, without taro the Lakalai say they are hungry. By virture of its association with Sumua it is, in effect, a sacred food. Properly respectful treatment of it requires that the tuber be peeled by scraping but never cut into deeply, that it not be squeezed through small spaces or openings, and that children never play with it. The first time the highly prized dish of *ulalu* is made each year, the woman who makes it should hold up a loaf and say, 'Sumua, your *ulalu*', before anyone eats it.

Sumua's usual form is described as that of a very tall and exceptionally handsome man. His physical nature is said to be definitely corporeal. At the same time, however, he has the ability to transform himself into the likeness of any being, to possess a person or animal, and to make himself invisible. From his distant home at the summit of Pago he can see and hear perfectly events in the human villages. He has great powers over nature, being accompanied by wind, rain, thunder and lightning when he travels rapidly over great distances, and causing volcanic eruptions or floods at will. He is immortal and seldom or never defeated. He thus comes as close to possessing omniscience and omnipotence as any being in the traditional Lakalai spirit world. According to one informant, Sumua's father sent him among men to watch over them and see how they were living. The father is supposed to have sent word that all men should be especially respectful or worshipful toward his son.[19]

Sumua's reactions and motivations are portrayed as being much like those of men. In general, he behaves rather like an heroic version of a big man in a human community. Actions which bring about both beneficial and dangerous effects for humans are characteristic of him. He remains a member of the Kevemumuki, but he is known and acknowledged by all men. He does not always favour his sibmates over other human beings, and the effects of his behaviour are felt very generally. When a person is ill, the god may inform his kinsmen that his soul has already reached Pago and there is no hope for recovery. He sometimes appears to people and exposes a sorcerer who is making them ill. It is said that in former times he was often in the villages of men disguised as a human being. Many stories are told of his accosting women to have intercourse with them or to take them to Pago as his wives. Women who have intercourse with him may go mad or bleed to death, but others seem to be married to him without dire results, since he accumulated no less than ten human wives. Numerous battles erupted with human villages as a result of the god's woman-stealing. It is said that more than once he killed off whole communities single-handed.

There are several methods of communication between the deity and mankind. Most simply, he may appear in the flesh and speak to anyone. On occasion he makes contact by methods also employed by ghosts: whistling, tapping on the thatch of a house, or speaking as an invisible presence. He is the only spirit-being known to have communicated directly with men through chosen human mediums. These mediums were usually Kevemumuki men, Sumua's sibmates. He might either possess them or speak from afar through their lips. Some of them were also men who had been taken bodily by Sumua to the *olu* on Pago where they were treated well, in one case given a wife, and sent home with valuable gifts. The medium would typically sit surrounded by a silent audience in the village, relaying the words of the god in a normal voice, but trembling as he spoke. There does not seem to have been any more abnormal behaviour on the part of the medium or any further ritualization of the procedure.

Mediums were usually important men, but their position does not appear to have been specifically formalized. If a reply to the god was needed, the medium would stand and give it aloud from the village. Practitioners of the soul-rescuing technique described earlier might also fly to Pago and converse with Sumua there. Ordinary men often addressed him more informally, calling on him by name while in the forest, for example, and asking that he send game. The deity could not be summoned in any of the ways that spirits of the dead are called to do service for men. As will be seen, the only effective human approach to Sumua was one of supplication rather than compulsion.

The most important powers which this god has exercised over human fortunes have been his control over the food supply and over the volcanic energy of Mt Pago. He has the ability to cause famine or plenty by controlling the growth of taro. This is done chiefly through his power over the spirit entities called either *kalulu-la-mavo* ('soul-double of the taro') or *halulu-la-mavo* ('shade of the taro'). Unless Sumua sends these soul-like spirits from Pago to inhabit the vegetables at each planting, the crop will not grow. He may withhold the souls of the taro or allow the ghosts to use them all in their gardens whenever he is displeased with human beings. The usual cause for such action is violation of the rules for treating the tuber which Sumua established when he gave the plant to men.

More drastic than any other action, however, is an eruption of Pago.

N

Early in the present century the volcano erupted repeatedly and with devastating effect.[20] During a considerable part of this period, Lakalai gardens were laid waste under a covering of volcanic dust and made completely useless, while forest fires raged in the bush. Apparently no villages were destroyed, but the disaster forced most of the Lakalai population to move first to less affected parts of the Hoskins Peninsula and later into near-by sago swamps or the territories of neighbouring peoples. During the course of these events, Sumua announced through several mediums in different villages that he was responsible for the disaster. He explained that the rules for handling taro had been repeatedly violated, that the people had been generally disrespectful toward him and the other spirits of Pago, and that men had killed too many of their fellows by sorcery. The eruptions were punishment for all this and would not cease until humans mended their ways. A long series of communications back and forth, including trips by mediums to the Pago *olu*, followed. The people pleaded for mercy, stressing their pitiful state and promising no more offensive behaviour in the future, much as a sick man would plead with a sorcerer to release him from the effects of magic. They also deposited quantities of traditional wealth in the forest as offerings to Sumua and his spirit kinsmen.

The god communicated further through his mediums. He commanded the people to acknowledge his power, which they did. He said that he would rule over them and they must worship him, never being disrespectful or disobedient. He admonished them to live rightly, work well, order their communities properly and care well for their food supplies. The moralistic tone of these last admonishments and the accompanying demands for worship contrast rather strikingly with the rest of traditional Lakalai religion, which shows few or no comparable elements. They imply an incipient transformation of the medium into a prophet and a further development of the sib god into a universal tribal deity. To be sure, more usual attitudes are also ascribed to Sumua, some versions emphasizing his pique at being defied and one mentioning that the murder of a Kevemumuki man was among the motives for his action. Some accounts of the eruptions, including an early one recorded by Hees,[21] also describe them simply as results of building a large fire in Sumua's men's house without mentioning any motivation or considerations of punishment at all.

Finally, the activity of the volcano subsided. Sumua communicated with the people through his mediums no more; the Lakalai were

gradually able to move back to their home villages; and the disaster
became no more than a vivid memory. From that time onward,
Sumua seems to have lost much of the importance which he had,
for it is said that he appeared and intervened in human lives less often.
He is seen as having been in more direct competition with the mission
churches than perhaps any other traditional being. He is compared with
the Christian God, and relations with him are sometimes identified
with church worship. Now it is said that because of the power of the
missions he no longer appears. Nevertheless, the belief is widespread
that he continues to live invisibly on top of Mt Pago and that he is
still aware of all that transpires among men.

It is possible that Sumua is the last of many older deities the rest of
whom have been entirely forgotten. It seems more likely, however,
that at least some of his unusual characteristics represent relatively
recent innovations. It may even be that before the eruptions just
described he was merely the 'big man' of the Kevemumuki dead and
hence only one of many leading ghosts.[22] Certainly it would appear
that his importance was greatly enhanced by the events of the disaster.
None of the several informants to whom the question was put could
say with certainty that they remembered the medium or prophet
pattern as existing before that period, though this may be at least
partly a function of the time that has elapsed since then. The very
fact that Sumua has no certain counterpart or peer elsewhere in the
traditional spirit world suggests that he may be a recent comer to that
world. Although resident European missionaries were not at work
among the Lakalai until 1922, it is nevertheless possible that indirect
Christian influence may have had some effect on the moulding of
Sumua's image. Much earlier than the establishment of mission stations
in the area, native men had brought back some Christian ideas and
practices after periods of plantation labour in thoroughly missionized
areas.

The more universal and morally oriented aspects of Sumua's
message, his insistent demands for worship, and the more prophet-like
role of his intermediaries were reported chiefly by the one surviving
medium and another contemporary informant who is deeply committed to the cargo ideology. Though no one disputed Sumua's
reality or the essentials of his career, some informants scoffed at the
pretensions to former greatness and questioned the veracity of the old
man who had been a medium. So it is possible that those aspects of
the god which seem most unusual have been elaborated in the mean-

time during a period of intense mission work and preoccupation with cargo themes, many of which are Christian in origin. Nevertheless, the Sumua mythology is firmly rooted in traditional conceptions. It seems probable that much of what is new in the pattern was an indigenous Lakalai response to conditions of extreme stress. Then as those conditions became mitigated and disappeared, and when intensive contact with Europeans, developing immediately thereafter, concentrated attention on other problems, the greatest god of the Lakalai seems to have slipped back toward relative obscurity once more.[23]

(g) Manlike spirits of the bush

The last major category of non-human beings with which people have to deal is a group of manlike demons. These are more or less monstrous but still anthropomorphic creatures. They are generally gigantic, dwarfed, or deformed in shape and more or less brutish in behaviour. Most of them are regarded as loathsome in appearance. In spite of their bodily resemblance to men and women, they are not connected by any ties of origin or kinship with human beings. These bush spirits have no association with sibs or other kin groups, and it is generally said that they existed before mankind. Though sometimes called simply *hitu*, they were probably differentiated from the ghosts by the designation *hitu-la-hoi* ('spirit of the bush'), and the corresponding Pidgin usage is *tambaran blong bus*. With one important exception to be noted below, the lives of bush spirits are decidedly distinct from those of other anthropomorphic spirits. They live in hollow trees or other natural shelters in the wilderness rather than structured communities, and their locations have no relation to the sacred grounds of human sibs. They are said to live largely without material culture or social customs and some of them are specifically described as speaking no language. They may have great physical strength and the ability to become invisible. In temperament they range from harmless elfish pranksters to stupid but dangerous man-eating ogres. They are often easily fooled or outwitted by men, however, and their general behaviour often stamps them as subhuman rather than superhuman.

These rather oafish creatures are not celebrated in mythology as creators or doers of heroic deeds. Though one type is dramatically portrayed as a fierce and frantic evil spirit in the *valuku* ceremonies, they have no other place in ritual. The more dangerous forms are greatly feared. Few benefits ever come to men from contact with them. There are no magical or other formalized means of summoning them. Nearly every encounter with a *hitu-la-hoi* is either accidental or brought about by the intent, usually more or less malicious, of the spirit. Otherwise inexplicable commotions in the forest are often explained as the unseen doings of the shyer forms. Numerous men have had the experience of being molested, chased, or captured temporarily by various types of bush spirits. Mythology also includes many episodes of contact with them, some involving protracted struggles but almost invariably resulting in an ultimate human triumph. These wild creatures are believed to occur in a wide variety of specific forms. The characteristics of eighteen types have been clearly established.

As was the case with the specific forms of ghost outlined earlier, among the bush spirits some of the type names have more or less clear derivations. For example, two forms of mischievous long-haired dwarf, known as *pii* and *tuu* respectively, are said to be named for their vocal cries. The *suguala* (*sugu-a*, 'to push forward, extend') is a prankster which shoots one extremely long leg out across paths to trip people. The *viri* (*viri-a*, 'to twist') is a stunted being distinguished by twisted limbs which it owes to an arthritis-like illness. A form which eavesdrops on the plans of the living and then lures its victims by impersonating a friend or loved one is called the *lolomaholi* (*lolo-a*, 'to hear, overhear'). The *matea* lights up at night but seldom injures men. The *buata* and a number of similar monsters are giant ogres or ogresses equipped with great tusks and renowned as man-eaters.

Several of the dwarfed forms are the least offensive or frightening of the bush spirits. Both the *pii* and another pygmy type called the *patuki* constitute exceptions to the general rule that men do not seek contact with such beings. There are several stories of people capturing these little spirits, taming them, training them to be useful workers, keeping them as playmates for human children, and sometimes becoming quite fond of them. It is one more instance of the incompatibility of human and spirit natures that these captivities always seem to end with the dwarfs escaping to the bush once more. They are usually thought to be offended or shamed in some way by their treatment at the hands of men. The continuing vitality of this tradition is indicated by the fact that strenuous efforts were made to catch a *patuki* in one Lakalai village in 1956 and considerable interest was aroused by reports that a *pii* had been captured by a neighbouring Nakanai group to the east.

The bush spirits are among the few forms often pictured as humorous in nature. There is something at least a little comical in either the pranks or the stupidity of all but the most dangerous forms. Apart from Big Wallaby and some of his companions among the superior spirits considered earlier, some of the diminutive *hituhitu-la-hoi* and the oddly deformed *suguala* are perhaps the only consistent pranksters in this spirit world. Affinities with various other orders of spirits may be seen among the bush forms. Like some of the animal monsters discussed earlier, the *viri* is a disease-bearer which symbolizes in its own condition the affliction that it carries, though it is otherwise quite distinct from the *taua* demons of sickness.

The major echoes from other corners of the spirit world relate to ghosts, however. A form called *kukubara* is specifically described as resembling a corpse, which is also said of many spirits of the dead, and the *matea* is sometimes confused with the ghostly type known as *visu* because of the habit of lighting up at night which they share. The shape-shifting and dangerous impersonations of the *lolomaholi* are quite analogous to the behaviour of the *tarogolo* form taken by spirits of the dead. There is, in fact, a general tendency to confuse bush spirits with ghosts, and once again there seems to be little countervailing demand for precision or exact differentiation. Some specific named forms are assigned to one category by certain informants and to the opposite class by others. This occurs particularly with *buata* and the other gigantic man-eating forms which resemble it.

The *buata* is an unusual bush spirit in other respects as well. While more often than not it is said to live like the other bush spirits, some traditional narratives, including two collected by Hees,[24] portray the existence of the *buata* quite differently. In these tales the spirit lives in a house, has a family, cultivates a garden, possesses a traditional inventory of material culture, and generally leads a life not unlike that of men in many respects. Occasionally the *buata* appears in the same mythical events as Big Wallaby, whose status is also somewhat unclear as we have seen. Whatever the setting, however, and whoever the other characters, the *buata*'s bush spirit nature usually comes out in the fact that he is outwitted and overcome by his adversaries whether they be spirits or men.[25]

It should not be assumed that the powers of the *buata* and the other cannibal giants are taken lightly. Though these ogres are usually vanquished in the end, long and arduous struggles against them abound in the traditional folklore. It is a common element of these stories that whole human communities are killed off or forced to flee before the monster. Then two brothers emerge from hiding or return from exile, and, after a more or less protracted series of encounters, at last heroically slay the evil spirit. Nor should it be concluded that bush spirits are no longer important in contemporary Lakalai life. They continue to appear from time to time, and their existence seems to have been as little affected by the rise of new religious preoccupations as that of any traditional class of beings.

2. CONCLUSIONS

The nature and interrelations of significant beings in the traditional Lakalai world may be briefly recapitulated in the following form.

Lakalai Designation	Pidgin Designation	Translation
I. *tahalo*	*man*	anthropomorph: being of basically manlike form
A. *tahalo lo-luma*	*man blong ples*	anthropomorph of the house, of the village
tahalo sesele	*man tru*	true man; human being
B. *tahalo lo-rivo*	*man blong bus*	manlike spirit, man of the bush
1. *tahalo-lo-rivo*	*man blong bus*	god or superior manlike spirit, man of the bush
tahalo-la-taua	*man masalai*	*taua* man, *masalai* man
2. *hitu*	*tambaran (teven)*	autonomous spirit in human form
(a) *hitu-la-tahalo*	*tambaran (teven) blong man*	ghost, spirit of the dead
(b) *hitu-la-hoi*	*tambaran (teven) blong bus*	spirit of the bush, manlike demon, bush spirit
II. *taua*	*masalai*	theriomorph, animal spirit, spirit of basically animal or other non-manlike form
		A. totemic animal demon: tutelary spirit of a sib
		B. non-totemic animal demon: not sib-affiliated

Such an outline of course suggests a more systematic and formalized belief system than has actually been found among the Lakalai, as the preceding description shows. Nevertheless, the overall pattern of even such a relatively loose system can be illustrated by this device.

It can be seen that anthropomorphism and other manlike qualities are in some degree common to all these beings. Human form and the ability to speak are crucial attributes of even the animal spirits, since it is chiefly when they manifest these attributes that their true nature becomes apparent. Different degrees of kinship with mankind characterize the various spirit classes. All but the bush spirits are somehow associated with human social organization through the sib structure. Some of the beings have human or partially human origins. Yet even those which are most closely related to mankind are also quite distinct from men. The least anthropomorphic category, that of the animal spirits, is quite closely tied to the social structure, while another group among those most manlike in form, the bush spirits, has least to do with human society as such. In these and the many other ways which have been touched upon, the domain of man and the realm of the spirits are both distinct and at the same time interrelated.

In spite of distinctions in nature and conceptual boundaries, the world of man is thus also a world of spirits. Human beings are frequently in direct or indirect contact with non-human beings, and there is always the possibility that they may encounter such creatures at any time. There are both formalized and informal ways of dealing with the spirits. Man is neither a helpless pawn of superior powers nor a free agent who is confident that he can manipulate all the extra-human forces of his world. People employ compulsion, supplication, propitiation, avoidance, or direct combat in their relations with spirits whenever one of these approaches seems appropriate. There is a goodly proportion of both hazards and benefits which result from these relations. Many choices and alternatives exist in this as in other aspects of Lakalai life. From another point of view these can be seen as ambiguities, inconsistencies, or even contradictions, but the Lakalai do not appear to be concerned about them in this sense.

The traditional Lakalai world is perhaps above all a richly imaginative one. The multitude and variety of beings, the complexity and flexibility of relations among them and between them and man, the wealth of literature, pageantry and ceremonial connected with them, all make this an exciting world to live in. The excitements involved are both positively and negatively toned, but the Lakalai are not very often overwhelmingly oppressed by the dangers of their traditional world or excessively uplifted by its rewards. They are normally able to concentrate on limited goals and pursue them with flexibility. This same adaptability is manifest again when they are able to revise their understanding of the world and take new forms of action when circumstances require this, as apparently happened during the volcanic eruptions. The experience of living in such a meaningful world, and the background of such flexible ways for dealing with it, have apparently stood the Lakalai in good stead during the two generations of momentous recent changes which they have witnessed. During this period, their universe has widened many times, and on the whole they have welcomed this without losing their grip on the realities of their traditional world of spirits and men.

NOTES

[1] Field work which provided most of the data reported here was carried out in 1954 and 1956 under sponsorship of the University of Pennsylvania and the University Museum, the American Philosophical Society, the Tri-Institutional Pacific Program, the U.S. Educational Foundation in Australia, and the Australian National University. Co-workers in the field who helped me gain an understanding of Lakalai religion include Ward Goodenough, Ann Chowning and Edith Zeller. I am particularly indebted to Dr Chowning for the use of many mythological texts which she collected. General information on the methods employed in the Lakalai field research has been set forth in other writings (Chowning and Goodenough 1965-66/71; Valentine n.d. a; 1958). Field data on which this essay is based include fifteen interviews with informants immediately or shortly after experiences which they perceived as contacts with spirit-beings, nearly thirty accounts by informants of past events similarly interpreted, over sixty more generalized discussions of spirit-beings with informants, more than a hundred and fifteen myths and legends (a third recorded in Lakalai, the remainder in Pidgin English), and a hundred and fifty drawings and paintings representing spirit-beings and/or events of traditional mythology. In addition to these materials collected in 1954 and 1956, twenty-one Lakalai narratives recorded forty years earlier by Hees (1915-16) were also used.

[2] Valentine (1960; 1963a; 1963b); Valentine (1959).

[3] Goodenough (1955); Valentine (1961).

[4] To avoid the ambiguity associated with the term 'clan', the usage of Lowie (1920: p. 105), Murdock (1949: p. 47), and Chowning and Goodenough (1965-66/71) is followed here in employing the term 'sib' to indicate a unilinear descent group in which actual genealogical links with a common ancestor are not traceable.

[In effect, the terms 'sib' and 'clan' may be treated as synonymous in this symposium. Editors' Note.]

[5] cf., e.g., Malinowski (1948: pp. 103-4).

[6] Hees (1915-16: p. 53).

[7] The distinction between the material and the non-material or between bodily and spiritual essence is absent or unimportant in Lakalai thinking. There is no term in the native language which corresponds exactly to 'the body' as a whole and in contradistinction to any of the soul-like entities. The closest approach to such a concept is represented by the phrase *la-vovo-gu toumi*, 'my whole skin'. This is not because of any lack of interest in or knowledge of human anatomy, since the language includes well over two hundred words for internal and external body parts, and there is an elaborate lore about the functions and relations to illness.

[8] Hees (1915-16: pp. 53-4).

[9] For the Holuholu narrative see Hees, *loc. cit.* Other newer versions of the fate of the dead are also widely and simultaneously held today but lie outside the scope of the present description. These include Christian beliefs in Heaven and Hell and the cargo cult doctrine that the ancestors live and manufacture cargo in the land of the dead, variously known as Paradise, Rome, Canberra or America.

[10] Hees (1915-16: pp. 56-8).

[11] This narrative implies that the reef is the permanent resting place for the dead of the sib concerned, thus indicating what is probably still another exception to the dominant pattern of the *olu* as the home of ghosts and ancestors.

[12] While these visits are generally described as spontaneous on the part of the ghost and surprising to the survivors, there is also a magical method for communicating through the corpse a desire that the spirit should return.

[13] For a more extended treatment of the *valuku* see Valentine (1961). The Pidgin term *tubuan* (*tumbuan*) is probably derived from the identical Tolai (Gunantuna) word which refers to one type of masked figure on the Gazelle Peninsula (Parkinson 1907: pp. 570 ff.; Brown 1910: pp. 60-72). The generally similar *tumbuan* of the Sepik area is described by Mead (1934a; 1940).

[14] Unfortunately our data are not sufficiently complete to be certain whether these may represent the taboo foods of sibs for which the *lelea* were not determined.

[15] The historical process leading to this somewhat anomalous situation can only be surmised. One possibility is that former sibs no longer in existence may have been forgotten while their totemic monsters and locales are still remembered. Another possibility is that the sacred association between animal spirits and human sibs may be a relatively recent connexion which may have associated the sibs with pre-existing spirits of the land, perhaps through diffusion from some neighbouring people. There is other evidence that the Lakalai have long been hospitable to cultural influences, including items of belief, from alien societies.

[16] Hees (1915-16: pp. 60-1).

[17] It is possible that these developments may presage a major breakdown of traditional patterns, not only in religion but also with respect to social structure, in the not too distant future. The abolition of warfare, shifting of authority from older to younger men, and incipient changes in land tenure are probably all contributing to the weakening of the sib system. Since so many other aspects of the indigenous religious system have persisted so strongly in combination with both Christianity and cargo movements, however, it is certainly much too early to predict the demise of the *taua*.

[18] Gaike is also called *tama-le-Sumua*. Chowning and Goodenough (1965-66/71) have suggested that this somewhat confusing usage probably results from a traditional pattern of obligatory sequences. Informants could give no further information as to the nature of the being called Gaike.

[19] This account was given by an informant very heavily committed to the cargo doctrine. It is quite possible that his version was influenced by local forms of Christian ideas.

[20] According to a personal communication from Fr Joseph Stamm of the Mission of the Sacred Heart, who was the first European Catholic missionary to settle among the Lakalai, this more or less continuous volcanic activity was observed by Europeans from 1900 to 1918.

[21] Hees (1915-16: pp. 562-4).

[22] This is suggested by Chowning and Goodenough (1965-66/71).

[23] In terms of the theoretical formulations of Wallace (1956), the emergent Sumua cult seems to have been a small-scale 'revitalization movement'.

[24] Hees (1915-16: pp. 865-7, 874-5).

[25] In certain tales the term is used in a way which may indicate that it is a proper name or nickname for individual spirits—Buata. It may be that the word simply means 'man-eater', though there are also alternative terms which mean this literally (*ali-tahalo* or *ali-la-tahola*). If the word *buata* does have this more general meaning, it is possible that it may be applied to either bush spirits or ghosts which distinguish themselves by their appetite for human flesh. Another possible source of confusion here, and one which may be relevant in other instances as well, is an occasional tendency in Lakalai mythology to use standard plots interchangeably with different characters.

P. LAWRENCE

The Ngaing of the Rai Coast[1]

T HE Ngaing are a linguistic group of between eight and nine
hundred people near Saidor on the Rai Coast. They live mainly
on the sub-coast between the Nankina and Mot rivers, although they
have two settlements west of the Mot—Maibang and Kilang. Towards
the coast, their territory is bounded by the narrow plain (at most
about four miles deep) and low foothills inhabited by the Sengam,
Gira, Som and Neko; and inland, by a line running from Aiyawang to
Langani. In the hinterland there are two little known groups: the
M'na on the east bank of the Mot and the N'dau on the west.[2]

In this essay I attempt to give a general account of Ngaing religion.
It must be remembered, however, that in the native vernacular there
is no single word corresponding to this term. Religion, as a special
part of the culture, is something which we must abstract for ourselves,
looking at the people's total way of life and emphasizing the aspects
of it most resembling those connoted by the term 'religion' in our
own.

The Ngaing implicitly regard their cosmos or world order as a
logically integrated system. It consists of the land area known to them,
which is inhabited, in their view, not only by human beings and
animals but also by deities, totems and spirits of the dead. For our
present purposes, we must consider three aspects of the cosmos:
the physical environment and economic resources; the social structure
(actual relationships between human beings); and what we should call
religion (the people's beliefs about, and putative interaction with,
deities, totems and spirits of the dead). I shall describe, first and very
briefly, the physical environment and social structure, and second and
in greater detail, religion. I shall then discuss the part played by religion
in the natives' economic and social life, and its importance for understanding their epistemological system. The study is limited by two
factors: cultural heterogeneity and the effects of European contact.

First, the Rai Coast terrain allows a high degree of local variation in dialect, custom and belief. In the space available, such idiosyncrasies must be treated as of only secondary importance. Although they are not ignored entirely, the primary concern is with the fundamental homogeneity underlying all Ngaing religion. Even so, some of the available material has had to be omitted.

Second, Ngaing religion has been modified by Administration and mission influence. The people were brought under political influence by the Germans by 1914 and full control by the Australians by 1936. This led to the complete suppression of warfare, cannibalism and associated religious ceremonies. After 1923 the Rai Coast was subjected to pressure from the missions. Although the first arrivals, the Lutherans, quickly won over the beach peoples, the Ngaing (except in the inland Sibog region) resisted conversion for ten years. But after 1933 they formally adopted the Roman Catholic Mission (Society of the Divine Word), which had recently moved into the area. The Catholics seem to have acted with extreme caution and tolerance. Yet the effects of their work, and of the Japanese invasion and its aftermath, left their mark. By 1945 many of the younger generation knew little about traditional mythology and ritual.

During 1948, however, the Ngaing revolted against the Catholic Mission and made a determined effort to revive their religion.[3] This was five years before my first visit to the field. Thus, although some aspects were inevitably irrecoverable, I was able, by first-hand observation and from second-hand accounts given by reliable informants,[4] to record the people's most important religious beliefs and practices, and analyse the intellectual assumptions underlying them.

1. THE PHYSICAL ENVIRONMENT AND SOCIAL STRUCTURE

Ngaing territory is a series of sharp ridges which reach down from the Finisterres towards the sea, like the fingers of an outstretched hand, flattening out on the coastal plain. Between these ridges are deep gorges and swift-flowing rivers. Movement in the area is relatively easy along the ridges, which are trade routes linking the Ngaing to the peoples of the beach and Madang. The Ngaing exchange their betel-nut, wooden bowls and bark cloth for salt, fish, clay pots, Siasi beads and other marine or overseas products.[5] Movement across the ridges, however, is very difficult. This probably accounts for the development of the wooden slit-gong not only as a musical instrument but also as an efficient means of communication. Each adult male has his personal call-sign, and elaborate messages can be sent over long distances in a short time.

The people's staple crops are taro, yams, bananas, sugar cane, sweet potatoes and various types of indigenous green vegetables. The most important is taro, of which there are two main kinds—the 'red' (*kapa*) and the 'white' (*kak*).[6] 'Red' taro is grown in the central uplands of Ngaing territory. It is regarded as superior to 'white' taro, which is planted in the area near the coast and the hinterland of Sibog (inland Nankina region). Pigs, dogs and fowls are domesticated in the settlements. There are various types of game—wild pig, marsupials and birds—in the bush and grasslands. In the rivers there are fish and crustaceans.

Ngaing social structure is based on double unilineal descent. Four groups must be considered: the bush group (*masowa* or *mijowa*); the patriclan (*ya*); the patrilineage; and the totemic matriclan (*sapud* or *supud*). Each is described in turn.

Ngaing territory is divided into about twenty named bush areas. The inhabitants of each are a political unit and are here referred to collectively as a *bush group*. They maintain peaceful relations with each other, and combine for offence and defence. Except in two cases to be discussed later, they have a common war god. Bush groups are allied or linked in either of two ways: first, by formal trade relationships, which create permanent alliances between those inhabiting the same ridge; and second, by marriages between even hostile bush groups. In the past, these two factors governed traditional warfare. Fighting had to cut across the trade routes but its severity was often mitigated by interpersonal affinal and kinship ties.

Each bush group consists of a number of smaller named groups (*ya*). Each of these contains several unnamed patrilineages of shallow depth (from three to five generations). The *ya* can be described as a pseudo-patriclan. Although individual membership is determined primarily by patrilineal descent, the component patrilineages themselves do not claim a further putative common ancestor. But in other ways they have the corporate identity of a patriclan.

The distinguishing characteristics of the patriclan are as follows: It is the basic unit of local organization. In the past, it formed either a settlement on its own or part of a settlement within its bush area. Nowadays these smaller settlements have come together as composite villages.[7] The patriclan is strictly exogamous. It has exclusive rights to a tract of land for cultivation and hunting, and to certain ritual property.

There are two kinds of ritual property: esoteric formulae; and that used in the main ceremonies honouring the dead. Esoteric formulae are of little significance in the present context. They are usually fairly uniform over wide areas, although occasionally a patriclan may claim rights to minor variations in the performance of a particular spell. Their content is described later on. Ritual property used for honouring the spirits of the dead, however, is extremely important for the social structure. In each settlement there is a central cult house (*tōta*), around which the dwelling houses are grouped. Each patriclan has sole rights over either the whole cult house (in a single patriclan settlement) or a section of it (in a multiclan settlement). It may decorate the end walls, or end wall of its section, with its own carved ornaments (*buyang* or *tōra*) and erect its own special bamboo poles (*silasila*) through the roof. It has its own slit-gong, gourd trumpets (*kanggut*) and sacred melodies (*niguling-totō*), from the gong beats of which its members take their personal call-signs. Finally, it has its own sacred pool (*musurukteng* or *waiteng*), where its trumpets are washed and the spirits of its dead members invoked on ceremonial occasions.

Cutting across the patrilineal structure are a number of named totemic matriclans. The matriclan is a true clan, for its component matrilineages (again from three to five generations deep) recognize a common totemic ancestress (*sapud* or *supud*)—a bird, animal, plant or other object.

The matriclan has little common property and cannot be defined in terms of group activity. In most cases, it has no joint possession other than its totem. (The only exceptions to this rule are the two bush groups Sor and Paramus, whose members do not claim war gods in their own areas but associate each of their totems with a war god of one of the neighbouring bush groups. They regard rights to these deities as part of matriclan inheritance.) Moreover, those belonging to a matriclan never assemble for any specific task. Because residence after marriage is normally viri-patrilocal and a woman is the sole transmitter of the totem, they are always dispersed, often in different bush groups. The members of both patriclan and patrilineage are differentiated in terms of totemic allegiance.

Common recognition of the totem, however, imposes certain rules of behaviour. The matriclan is exogamous: a marriage between two of its members is said to result in death. A man should never maltreat or kill not only his own totem[8] but also other members of his matriclan, even if they belong to otherwise hostile bush groups. If a person knows that his totem[9] or one of his matriclan members has been killed, he must protect himself from evil by putting ginger to his nose. When someone has been killed, not only the members of his patriclan and bush group but also his matriclansmen elsewhere must be compensated. These dispersed totemic links are important in three ways. They guarantee a man protection when he is away from home. He may always call on individual matriclansmen for help in important activities. Finally, totemic relationships augment affinal and kinship ties which, as mentioned, used to limit violence in warfare.

Apart from food production, the most important events in social life are a series of ceremonial exchanges associated with marriage, birth, initiation and burial. A man must marry a true or classificatory cross-cousin—the daughter of a mother's brother who should be husband of a father's sister. Likewise, his male cross-cousins must marry his true or classificatory sisters. Marriage payments take the form of exchanges of pigs, food and valuables (mainly dogs' teeth and Siasi beads) between the husband's patriclan and that of his affines (i.e., his mother's brothers and cross-cousins). These exchanges occur at least three times during the first six years of marriage.

The children of the marriage have important exchange relationships with their mother's brothers and father's sisters. A boy is initiated by his mother's brothers and the event is celebrated by an exchange between their respective patriclans. When a man dies, his initiatory services are reciprocated by his sisters' sons, who prepare his corpse for burial and later dispose of his bones. Thereafter there is an exchange between them and the sons of the dead man. Girls have similar relationships with their mothers-in-law and other fathers' sisters, who perform certain duties for them when they marry. The first marriage exchange is partly in recognition of this. When a woman dies, her daughters-in-law and other brothers' daughters reciprocate by preparing her corpse for burial. This is also the occasion for an exchange.

These exchanges are important for both social structure and religion. They periodically bring together many of a person's kinsmen. The close parallel between a man's relationships with his mother's brothers and a woman's with her father's sisters, in reciprocal services and prestation, stresses a dominant theme in Ngaing life: the recognition of near equality between the sexes. The exchanges are also invariably associated with ritual honouring the spirits of the dead, which is described later on.

It is in the context of the above structural form and important activities that leadership must be considered. There is no single political authority over the whole of Ngaing society but within each patriclan there are several important men (*eik tandabi* or *eik utiring*). These men are neither hereditary nor elected officials, nor do they have any true judicial authority. They achieve their positions by their own prowess—in warfare, agriculture, the organization of exchanges and so on—and by their monopoly of sacred knowledge. This also is discussed later on.

2. RELIGION

As stated, Ngaing religion can be defined as the people's beliefs about, and putative interaction with, the extra-human beings thought to inhabit the physical environment—deities, totems and spirits of the dead. I shall describe it from two points of view: first, beliefs which explain the origin of the traditional cosmos and the nature of life after death; and second, ritual which is assumed to establish contact between man and these extra-human beings.

(a) Deities and totems: the creation of the cosmos

The beings said to be responsible for the origin of the cosmos are the deities (*tut*[16]) and totems (*sapud* or *supud*). As the totems are ordinary animals, birds and plants existing in the visible world, no further description of their nature is necessary.

The nature of the deities, however, must receive some attention. Except in one case, which appears below, they are highly personalized. They are believed either always to have existed as deities or to have been originally men and women who became deities under special circumstances. They are conceived to be the same as human beings in one sense, having similar physical attributes and emotions, but different in another, having infinitely superior powers. Although normally human in form, they can turn into birds, animals, fish or insects at will; and they can travel long distances and do things far beyond human capabilities. Yet they live on the earth with men, generally in their own special sanctuaries within striking distance of human settlements.

The Ngaing believe that their cosmos came into being in two stages: the emergence of the basic physical environment followed by that of human beings and their culture. For the first stage, when asked how their world began, the people reply: 'Parambik put (*riring*) everything'. By this they mean that Parambik 'put' the earth, bush, mountains, rivers, wild animals, birds and plants (including the totems), and the war gods in the bush areas. They make no mention of sun, moon or stars. Parambik is described as a god (*tut*) but, unlike the other deities, is said to be very remote. He is all-pervasive and has no fixed sanctuary. Even his name is merely the general word for myth. Although held responsible for the primary elements of the Ngaing cosmos, he is not thought to take further interest in it and no ritual is performed in association with him.[11]

For the second stage—the emergence of human beings and their culture—there are many explanatory myths (*parambik*). One set tells how men and women came into the world as the result of totemic births or transformations. Birds, animals and so on either brought forth human offspring or turned into human beings, and so founded the matriclans. Normally, all members (both male and female) of a matriclan know their own totemic myth, which is subject to no taboos. Children may learn it from either their mothers or any older matrilineal kinsmen.

Another set of myths tells how, more or less at the same time as the appearance of human beings, the deities created the important parts of the material culture. Bows and arrows were invented by the war gods of Gabumi and Saing, who passed on their knowledge to their followers and to war gods elsewhere. Slit-gongs, wooden bowls and hand drums were created when two brothers felled a tree, which took wing and flew to another part of the country. When it fell to earth, different sections of it were used for making the abovementioned artefacts. It also scattered seeds of the trees from which they are made nowadays. The two brothers who felled the tree are regarded as the joint deities of the slit-gong. In the Aiyawang, Sindama and Sibog region—and also among the M'na and N'dau—myths describe how local deities discovered the art of making dogs' teeth and Siasi beads, which they send to human beings via the spirits of the dead. Again, in the inland region below the cloud belt, which often blots out the higher peaks of the Finisterres, there are elaborate myths explaining the origin of techniques for controlling the weather. In the area nearer the coast, however, there are no myths for the creation of valuables and those associated with weather control are little emphasized.

The most prominent myths are those for taro and other staple crops, pigs and the Male Cult ceremonies, and the bullroarer. The Ngaing have two taro myths. In the first, a woman called Meanderi invented taro, sugar cane, and other vital foodstuffs at Asang (west of Ngaing territory). These she secreted under her skin. In the guise of a hideous old crone she journeyed east through what is now the 'red' taro belt—to Maibang, Kilang, Sereng, Saing, Gabumi, Aiyawang, Sindama and Sibog—intending to give her plants to the people of the inland Nankina region. But she was insulted there and returned in the direction from which she had come. To those along her route who had shown her kindness she gave her best crops, especially 'red' taro, and all knowledge necessary for growing them. But the inland people who had insulted her and those near the coast, who lay off her route, (at Amun, Sor and Paramus) received only the inferior 'white' taro.[12] Eventually Meanderi became a taro goddess and settled with the inhabitants of Wabing near Maibang, where she has her sanctuary today.

In the second myth, a man was transported to a cloud world above the earth, where he discovered 'red' taro and other important crops. He married a daughter of the cloud people and later returned to earth with his wife, child and the crops he had learnt to cultivate. He settled near Gabumi, where he passed on his knowledge to ordinary men and women, and where he and his wife are regarded as alternative joint taro deities. There are separate but similar myths for yams.

Pigs and the ceremonies of the Male Cult were invented by the deity Yabuling, whose sanctuary also is near Gabumi. Initially he created pigs and hence, by implication, the pig exchange. He then created the gourd trumpets used in the worship of the spirits of the dead. The women were the first to get hold of these trumpets and play them in a cult house, but they and their children defiled them with menstrual blood and excreta. They were supplanted by the men, who washed the trumpets and cleaned out the cult house. The men's music was infinitely superior. Thus men have exclusive rights over the trumpets, although adult women, because of the circumstances described, are allowed to know that they exist and that music is produced from them.[13] Women, however, may never see the trumpets.

There are at least two myths explaining the origin of the bullroarer. In the inland, it is said that Gab'me of Yakierak (N'dau) is its creator deity. He first placed a bullroarer in the net-bag of an old woman. She tried various methods of whirling it but they all failed. Then her grandson was taught the secret by Gab'me in a dream. Hence women may see the bullroarer as a piece of black palm, without its rope attached, but may never see it whirled. In the coastal area, there is a different myth based on a different local deity.

The above deities are believed to have their sanctuaries in various places on the Rai Coast but their distribution has no great social or political significance. Except in the cases of Sor and Paramus, war gods are regarded as belonging exclusively to the inhabitants of the bush areas in which they reside, and are inherited patrilineally. Otherwise allegiance to deities does not correlate rigidly with group membership. Some myths and deities are common to all Ngaing—such as the Parambik creation myth, the first taro myth, and those for the slit-gong and the Male Cult. Others are more restricted—such as the second taro myth (which is known only in Gabumi, Saing and, to some extent, Aiyawang), the bullroarer myths for the inland and coastal areas, and the myths (which are found only in the inland) for dogs' teeth and Siasi beads. Again, rights to myths and deities can cut across linguistic borders. The inland bullroarer deity is believed to live in N'dau territory and the slit-gong deities outside Ngaing territory to the west. Meanderi originally came from Asang, west of Ngaing territory. In the same way, Yabuling is accepted as the inventor of the Male Cult ceremonies not only by the Ngaing but also by the M'na, N'dau and Neko, and nowadays even by the Sengam, Gira and Som.[14] But there is a recognized area to which each myth and deity belong. It is said that any attempt by outsiders to use religious secrets which they have not purchased formally—especially those associated with important ceremonial and economic undertakings (such as the secret names for Yabuling, Meanderi, the Cloud Man, the bullroarer deities, and the inland deities for Siasi beads and dogs' teeth)—are regarded as theft and met with strong opposition.

(b) The spirits of the dead: life after death

The spirits of the dead (kabu or asapeng) are not regarded as creators of any part of the culture but as the protectors of their living descendants. Their role as such is discussed in a later context. Here we are concerned only with their conceived nature and mode of existence.

The Ngaing do not distinguish terminologically between distant ancestors and spirits of the recently dead. They call both kabu or asapeng (which are only local dialectical variants). But they concentrate their interest almost exclusively on spirits of the recently dead: of men and women whom they can still place in their known genealogical structure. Although they admit that distant ancestors are able to intervene in human affairs, they dismiss the idea as quite improbable. They forget the names of individuals above the third (and very often the second) ascending generation and hence do not expect the spirits of such persons to show much concern for remote descendants. Nor do they conceive of a pool of generalized or undifferentiated ancestral spirit power. Distant ancestors, therefore, are ignored in the present account.

There are, however, two issues about which there is no uniformity of belief. First, some Ngaing claim that the breath (*kitang*) and shadow (*ananuang*) are manifestations of a living person's soul, which after death continues as an immaterial being unless it wishes to appear as a *kabu* or *asapeng*—that is, assume visible corporeal form as a human, bat, rat, snake or glow-worm. Others deny this belief. They claim that it is a Christian importation and that after death there is no immaterial soul but only a corporeal *kabu* or *asapeng*, which either remains invisible or assumes any of the forms listed above.

Second, there is no general agreement about where spirits live after death. Variations in belief correlate with differences in burial custom. In the past, bodies were left to rot in old slit-gongs or bamboo coffins. The bones were removed when dry. In some areas (Aiyawang and Sibog), they were placed in the sanctuary of the dead man's patrilineally inherited war god; in others (Gabumi and Saing), near his patriclan sacred pool, believed to be guarded by a minor deity; and in others (Sor and Paramus), somewhere on his hunting land, from which the spirit was thought to find its way to the sanctuary of its matriclan war god.

These differences of belief, however, are not of fundamental importance. The spirits are always associated with a deity of some kind, either a war god or the guardian of a sacred pool. They can be invoked at the sacred pools, even when they are not supposed to be living near them, and they are said to roam the bush and visit human settlements. They are seen by their living relatives, especially in dreams but also during waking hours. Furthermore, although their way of life is only vaguely conceived, they are invariably thought to be interested in material goods. In view of this, argument about the exact nature of the dead is largely academic. In the past, personal property was placed with the corpse for the spirit's use. Even now, whenever spirits are said to have practical dealings with the living, they are consistently described both as corporeal—with the normal human attributes of flesh, blood, bone and hair—and as wearing ordinary clothes and ornaments, and carrying ordinary tools and weapons. (From now on, therefore, the term *spirit* or *spirit of the dead* refers primarily to the *kabu* or *asapeng* conceived as a corporeal being.)

(c) Ritual: the control of the cosmos

In Ngaing ritual, the important beings are the deities (other than Parambik) and the spirits of the dead. The people believe that they can achieve full control over the world around them only by ensuring their support, although occasionally they use pure sympathetic magic as an alternative. The secrets of ritual are revealed to boys when they are initiated into the ceremonies of the Male Cult. The totems are unimportant in this context except for the purely protective ritual already mentioned.

(i) *Ritual to the deities and sympathetic magic.* The Ngaing say that during the creation of the culture each deity, either through a dream or personal association, gave human beings all the vital information about his or her particular invention. The deity taught both secular and ritual techniques of production. Ritual techniques (*pananak* or *mana*) involved two principles: the symbolic repetition of certain actions performed by the deity; and knowledge of an esoteric formula based on the secret name (*wawing buingna*) of the deity or of the part of the culture he or she introduced.

The distribution of rights to ritual correlates with that of the myth with which the ritual is associated. Thus ritual may be used in areas far distant from the sanctuary of the relevant deity. The members of each patriclan have rights to ritual for the following: warfare; manufacture of slit-gongs; bullroarers and hunting; weather control; agriculture; pig-raising and Male Cult ceremonies; and sorcery. Inland groups, as noted, claim special ritual for dogs' teeth and Siasi beads.

Correct performance of ritual is assumed to grant automatic success in any important undertaking. The deity must give immediate aid unless the human operator bungles the formula. Ritual procedures are illustrated here for warfare, hunting, agriculture and sorcery.

In the past, the leader of a raiding party took certain leaves from the sanctuary of his war god,[15] breathed a spell over them and fed them to his warriors, who also shouted the god's name as they attacked. This ensured that the deity would give them strength for battle.

The bullroarer is used mainly before hunting expeditions not associated with feasts in honour of the spirits of the dead. On these occasions, the leader breathes a spell over the bullroarer and whirls it in the bush, out of sight of women and children. The deity will drive the game towards the hunters. When the dead are to be honoured, the bullroarer is carried in a net-bag as a hunting talisman but must never be whirled.

For agriculture there are three forms of ritual. They are used with extreme care in gardens planted specially for an exchange, although the procedure is more perfunctory for crops intended solely for household consumption. Only the full forms of the ritual are described.

The first form is associated with the Meanderi myth and is used in the 'red' taro belt. The garden leader makes a shrine of stones (*sijik*) in his own plot. He then performs a purely magical act, rubbing a *galip* nut on the shrine and digging sticks so that its flavour will permeate the crops. He next plants outside the shrine an *atatagat* branch to symbolize the staff carried by Meanderi on her journey. Finally, he plants in or near the shrine shoots of the crops she gave to human beings. At the same time he silently breathes a spell to the goddess[16] and audibly invokes the spirits of departed kinsmen who worked the land in the past. (Their role is discussed later.) Occasionally food offerings are left at the shrine for the goddess and spirits, although this is not regarded as essential.

The second form of ritual is used in the areas where there is only the inferior 'white' taro. Although people there regard Meanderi as the creator of both kinds of taro, they have never had her secret name for ritual purposes but only spells based on sympathetic magic. The visible ritual techniques are exactly the same as above but the silent spells are addressed to the mango and *galip* trees so that the crops will be as prolific as their fruit and nuts.

The third form of agricultural ritual is performed in Gabumi, Saing and Aiyawang on the basis of the second taro myth. Again, the visible ritual is much the same as described but the silent spells incorporate the secret names of the Cloud Man and his wife.

Finally, there are sorcery and love magic. They are exceptional in that they have no specific myths of origin. Moreover, although all Ngaing are aware of the techniques involved, they do not consider them of very great importance.[17] The techniques for both are based on sympathetic magic. Sorcery (*nayang*) is of a type very common in Papua and New Guinea. The sorcerer steals something which has been part of, or in contact with, his victim and either burns it or heats it over a fire according to whether he intends to cause death or illness. Similar procedures are used for love magic.

(ii) *Ritual to the spirits of the dead.* As the protectors of their living descendants, the spirits of the dead are regarded as extremely important in human affairs. They bring messages about the future, ward off illness, confer special benefits in warfare, hunting and agriculture, and in the inland give presents of valuables. But their goodwill must be ensured by according them special honour.

Thus all mortuary ceremonies—attendance at a funeral, formal weeping, exchange of property and disposal of the bones—are designed to show the spirit the sense of loss his relatives feel. Members of hunting and raiding parties, as well as performing the ritual already described, carry with them relics of departed relatives—a lock of hair and finger bone tied to a bullroarer, and the jawbone or skull. The spirits are offered food and invoked before the party sets off. They are thought to accompany their descendants into battle or to the hunt, deflecting enemy missiles or driving up plenty of game and seeing that their kinsmen's arrows reach the mark. Again, as mentioned, part of planting ritual is the invocation of, and offering of food to, the spirits. They are looked upon as the true guardians of the land they worked: they do not actually promote the growth of crops but protect them from disaster, mainly incursions of wild pig.

The spirits of the dead are specially honoured, however, during celebrations of the Male Cult: the Harvest Festival and the Kabu Ceremony. The Male Cult is governed by very strong taboos: women and uninitiated boys are prevented from seeing the inner secrets; the bullroarer may not be whirled but only carried as a hunting talisman; and those participating in the cult must maintain peaceful relations with their enemies or the spirits will be angry.

The Harvest Festival[18] takes place early in the year when the crops in the new gardens are ready for eating. The spirits of the dead, having helped to bring them to maturity, must be thanked. They are formally invited to the settlements and offered part of the first fruits.

In the late afternoon before the festival begins, the men of each patriclan go to their sacred pools, where they wash and decorate their gourd trumpets. They perform ritual to ensure that Yabuling and the deity of the pool[19] will send back the spirits of dead patriclan members, whom at the same time they invoke to follow them to the settlements. As soon as it is dark and they cannot be seen by the women and children, the men return home leading the spirits by playing their patriclan melodies on the trumpets. The appearance of glow-worms and bats is especially auspicious for they are assumed to be incarnations of the spirits.

The spirits are escorted to the cult house. As they enter, their personal call-signs are beaten out on the slit-gongs. Then specially cooked food—including meat and fish—is set out in bowls decorated with dogs' teeth and Siasi beads in each house. Each family head invites the spirits of his immediate patrilineal forebears to eat.

Absolute silence is maintained while the spirits eat and rest. The festival is resumed next day. There are exchanges of food between affines, cross-cousins and any persons in each other's debt, and for several nights the spirits are kept in the cult house, where music is played in their honour. They are then escorted back to the sacred pools.

The Kabu Ceremony is more elaborate and of longer duration. It is celebrated during the dry season (April–November), when there is plenty of food in the gardens, in conjunction with the pig exchanges solemnizing marriage, birth, initiation and death.

The ceremony begins when the parties to the exchange, each helped by the members of his patriclan, have assembled sufficient pigs, valuables, food and game. Members of each group wash their trumpets and bring up their spirits to the settlement in exactly the same way as described above. They also decorate the cult house with their patriclan ornaments and some of the food to be distributed. In the meantime, the women and children remain in hiding. But when the work is finished, they are invited to inspect it.

During the first night of the spirits' appearance, a dance (ola) is held in the settlement, both men and women participating. It is concluded at daybreak, often with ritual to help fishermen. The trumpets used as musical accompaniment during the night are returned to the cult house so as not to be seen by the women and children. But the men of one team, wearing head-dresses of carved wooden fish, continue to dance, while others from the opposite team shoot arrows at their head-dresses. Successful marksmanship is regarded as an omen that the spirits will ensure large catches of fish.

Thereafter the formal business of the exchange is conducted. Pigs are killed and cooked, and in the late afternoon the rest of the food to be distributed is assembled outside the cult house. After the exchange, the men eat in the cult house and the women either outside it or near their own homes.

Meanwhile, men not involved in the work of the exchange play trumpets and slit-gongs in the cult house. After people have eaten, the music is intensified. No food is offered the spirits at this time but pig fat is rubbed on the trumpets and slit-gongs to please them. From now on music is played every night from sunset to sunrise. Women and children, although debarred from the cult house, are expected to dance to this music outside. The music stops during the day and people are free to go to work. At this time also ritual is performed for the growth of pigs. Yabuling's secret name is breathed over a trumpet, which is played over a bowl of cooked food. This is given the pigs to eat.

The Kabu Ceremony concludes with a final dance in the settlement. Early next morning the men escort the spirits back to the sacred pools. In the past, the whole ceremony could last as long as three months, additional exchanges between different principals being held during that period. Today, however, the Administration has limited its duration to a month.[20]

(iii) *Birth and initiatory ceremonies.* Special ritual for the welfare of human beings is performed at the times of the first and second marriage exchanges and, for males, during initiation into ceremonies honouring the spirits of the dead.

Girls are prepared for marriage during their first menstruation. They are tended by their mothers-in-law and other fathers' sisters, who teach them general marital duties, a few minor garden spells and probably methods of abortion.[21] They are now told that the music in the cult house is not the voices of the spirits (as they have been led to believe hitherto) but is produced by the men on trumpets and slit-gongs.

The first marriage exchange takes place when a girl has completed her first menstruation and goes to live with her husband, and the second when she has given birth to her first child. On these occasions, the bride or mother and child stand over a fire built under green mango leaves, and are later showered with sparks. The strength of fire and smoke is supposed to enter the woman's breasts and so benefit her children. Together with some of her own and her husband's relatives, she helps break up a green tree trunk so that her children's joints may be supple. Finally, in the Sor, Paramus and Amun area, when the first child is a male, the mother stands with it behind a wooden shield, into which her own and her husband's kinsmen, dressed in war regalia and shouting war god names, shoot their arrows. This is supposed to help the boy become a great warrior. (In the above ceremonies, kinsmen of both husband and wife are always expected to take part.)

Initiation for males takes place in either late childhood or early adolescence.[22] The ceremony is conducted as follows: First, the boys' fathers and maternal uncles bring up their respective patriclan spirits to the cult house of the boys' settlement. Second, the boys are shown the sacred instruments and taught the Yabuling myth by their mothers' brothers. Third, they are segregated for about a mónth and taught to play the sacred instruments. They are also given a symbolic beating by their mothers' brothers. Fourth, in Amun only, the mothers' brothers perform the operation of penile supra-incision on the novices. Other Ngaing settlements do not have this custom, which belongs properly to the peoples of the beach.[23] At the end of the month's segregation, the boys are dressed in fine ornaments and formally presented to the women. Thereafter exchanges are carried out between the patriclans of the novices and those of their mothers' brothers. The spirits are honoured in the usual way.

The ceremony has two aims: first, it is supposed to ensure that the novices become healthy and attract wives. The symbolic beating and, in Amun, the act of penile supra-incision give them strength. They are now also under the special protection of the spirits of the dead. Second, it is a period of education. During the month of segregation the boys observe rigid taboos on washing, food cooked in water and various types of meat. They eat only dry taro, either roasted or cooked in bamboo containers, and a little sugar cane. The taboos are essential for learning not only the secrets of the Male Cult but also the other aspects of religion described. The novices are now introduced to the myths and especially the ritual to which their patriclans have rights. If they ignore the taboos, the teaching will be useless and even dangerous. They will never use the spells successfully, and they will be afflicted with boils and other illnesses should they attempt to use them. When their training is extended into later life, they have to observe the taboos again for their own protection. Those who show the greatest ability in learning, and the greatest prowess in using, the ritual eventually become leaders. Those novices who do not undergo longer periods of training for leadership know their patriclan mythology, the Yabuling myth and the elements of the associated ritual, but never become expert practitioners.

We may summarize the respective importance of men and women in religion thus: Under normal conditions, all adult males have a wide knowledge of mythology (their matriclan totemic myths and those to which they have title through their patriclans) and of the principles underlying the esoteric techniques used by their leaders. They also play a full part in the Male Cult. Women know only their matriclan totemic myths and the special ritual taught them before marriage; and they participate only in the external ceremonies of the Male Cult.

3. THE MEANING OF NGAING RELIGION

Ngaing religion is analysed from two points of view: its social function and the intellectual assumptions underlying it. The first involves only the objective view of the outside observer. The second involves also the subjective view of the people themselves.

(a) Social function

In this context, we consider the general hypothesis that religion validates and reinforces the cosmic order by means of myth (explanation) and ritual (control or manipulation), and that the degree to which it is used for either of these purposes reflects the value people attach to, or the anxiety they feel about, various aspects of their way of life. From the foregoing account, it can be seen that in Ngaing religion the emphasis on mythology and ritual is uneven. This is illustrated by examining the relationship between religion, on the one hand, and the physical environment, economic resources and the social structure, on the other.

The overall physical environment receives very little attention. The heavenly bodies are completely ignored. The Ngaing feel no need to account for their existence as they are not a seafaring people. Again, the origin of the earth is dismissed in a sentence and no ritual is performed for its continuance. The earth is regarded as changeless: it can be taken for granted.

Economic resources, however, are very heavily emphasized. Their origin is explained in a most detailed mythology. Furthermore, their continuance and exploitation cannot be left to chance. This is an obvious cause of anxiety. Hence ritual must be performed to ensure that gods and spirits protect crops from danger and bring them to maturity; make fish and game abundant; make slit-gongs sound the right note; and so on. Again, the degree of anxiety, and hence of elaboration of ritual, varies according to the degree of hazard and need in any situation. For instance, crops planted specially for an exchange are more carefully protected by ritual than those intended only for household consumption. In the inland, where climatic conditions are uncertain, weather ritual is more important than on the coast, where they are more stable. In the inland also, where the flow of marine valuables can fail to meet the demand, the people claim to make good the deficiency by means of special ritual, which the coastal Ngaing, being nearer the source of actual supply, do not possess.

The relationship between Ngaing religion and society is more complex. There is no single myth explaining the origin of the structure in its totality. This is satisfactory for a people who, like others in the Madang District, do not conceive that there can be forms of society other than their own. They take its overall pattern for granted.[24] Furthermore, there is little correlation between allegiance to deities and group membership.

This does not mean, however, that there is no recognition that key parts of the social structure must be validated and reinforced. Thus, in the first place, some myths explain the origin of separate aspects of the total system. Parambik created the war gods, in most cases the symbols of the bush groups. Each totemic myth accounts for a dispersed matriclan and hence important relationships between patrilocal groups. Yabuling, by creating pigs and gourd trumpets, indirectly validated important groups and relationships within the structure: the patriclan, the group which co-operates in the Male Cult ceremonies; the affinal and kinship relationships which provide the framework for exchanges solemnizing marriage, birth, initiation and death; and the recognition of near equality between the sexes. The Yabuling myth subtly reflects the limited but real participation of women in the Male Cult. In the myth, women were the first to use the trumpets and were forced to surrender them only because they defiled them with menstrual blood. In real life, although they may never see the trumpets, adult women are allowed to know of their existence; they are an integral part of the dance (ola) team; and they dance in the settlement while the men play music in the cult house.[25] Again, they must always be invited to inspect the cult house after it has been decorated.

In the second place, ritual directly or indirectly reinforces the structure at its weakest points. The health and fertility of human beings generally are guaranteed by birth and initiatory ceremonies. Localized groups are maintained and perpetuated by means of ritual: the bush group by war ritual and sorcery; and the patriclan by joint rights to ritual property and co-operation in the work of honouring the spirits of the dead. A man's ties with other members of his matriclan are stressed when he receives initiatory services from, and performs mortuary services for, his mother's brothers. He and they are reminded of their common totemic allegiance. Cross-cutting relationships between patriclan and patriclan within the bush group, and between bush group and bush group within the wider structure, are strengthened by the emphasis on co-operation between husband's and wife's kin in birth ceremonies, the necessity of avoiding conflict during celebrations of the Male Cult, and the reciprocal and equivalent duties between mothers' brothers and sisters' sons, and fathers' sisters and brothers' daughters, in initiatory, menstrual and mortuary rites.

(b) Intellectual assumptions[26]

Within the Ngaing epistemological system, we may define two broad categories of knowledge: secular or empirical knowledge, which is actually possessed; and sacred knowledge, which has no empirical foundation but is believed to have been revealed by the deities.

In relation to the resources at their disposal, the Ngaing have accumulated a modest but sound body of secular knowledge, which they use with considerable efficiency. This is exemplified by their practical knowledge of agriculture, and their skill in the manufacture and use of the slit-gong as a means of communication. Using our own analytical concepts, we may say that this knowledge is the result of human endeavour. For what it is worth, it is the people's own intellectual achievement.

The Ngaing themselves, however, do not interpret and evaluate their secular knowledge in this way. Except in minor matters, they dismiss the principle of human intellectual discovery. All the most valued parts of their culture are believed to have been invented by the deities, who taught men not only the ritual but also the empirical techniques for utilizing them. Thus in the two taro myths, Meanderi and the Cloud Man actually showed men how to plant crops (secular knowledge) and to perform the proper ritual (sacred knowledge). It was the bullroarer deity who placed the sacred instrument in the old woman's net-bag but prevented her from finding the right method of whirling it. He gave this knowledge to her grandson as well as teaching him the relevant esoteric formulae.

This concept of revelation by deities dominates all discussions about knowledge. Even pure sympathetic magic is explained in this way. Birth ceremonies, because of their emphasis on strength and prowess in battle, are said to have been invented by the war gods. Sorcery and love magic, which have no myths of origin and are regarded as of little importance, and the ordinary sympathetic techniques used for agricultural ritual at Sor, Paramus and Amun are conveniently ignored in general conversation. But when challenged, the people attribute their existence to Parambik.

Furthermore, not only is the whole complex of knowledge believed to be derived from the gods but also within the complex it is sacred knowledge that is emphasized as paramount. Secular techniques are, indeed, described as *knowing*, but only at a very elementary level— as something which, given time, everyone can assimilate. The hard core of knowledge is regarded as the mastery of esoteric formulae and symbolic actions associated with them. This can be seen in the traditional processes of education and in leadership.

In the first place, by Western standards, a boy's upbringing is very informal. After an initial period of instruction in basic social usages, he is left to do much as he pleases. He is frequently indulged and rarely disciplined. Many of his amusements at this time, however, are directly imitative of his elders' activities: mock dancing, hunting expeditions, football games and so on. Often, out of boredom, he accompanies his parents to work in the gardens, at a house site or elsewhere, and copies them in what they are doing. He is never discouraged and, as he grows older, comes to be accepted as a member of adult work teams. By the time he has reached adolescence, with a minimum of formal instruction, he has mastered a large part of the secular knowledge of his society.

This, however, is not rated as a high intellectual achievement. True knowledge is acquired only during and after initiation. But what a boy learns at this time has little to do with secular techniques. He is introduced to mythology and ritual: the knowledge which guarantees help from the deities and spirits of the dead, and mastery over occult forces.

In the second place, although personal pre-eminence in important activities is the cornerstone of leadership, it is derived from the mastery of sacred rather than secular skills. The leaders are those who are believed able to ensure success by the performance of ritual. They are the men who *know*. They can direct the activities of others— those who do *not know*—to the best possible advantage. Physical inferiority and temporary poverty are not necessarily handicaps. Attainment of the position depends primarily on talent and patience to learn, and courage to accept responsibility. Otherwise the greatest obstacle is failure in an undertaking because of unforeseen circumstances. Thus in any set of novices, factors of ability, personality and chance eliminate all but the steadfast and lucky. In each generation, such men are relatively few. There are normally no more than one or two leaders in each patriclan so that rivalry tends to limit the geographical and social range of their influence. But there is no feeling that membership in one group completely precludes following the leader of another. A really energetic man, whose consistent success has demonstrated his complete mastery of sacred knowledge, may attract followers from outside his own patriclan. They may join him because they have no leaders of their own or even because of his obvious superiority over those whom they have.[27]

This predilection for sacred knowledge might suggest a high degree of mysticism in Ngaing thinking. But this would be an interpretation in Western terms. In fact, Ngaing thinking is extremely mundane, as can be seen by reconsidering the spatial and temporal dimensions of their cosmos.

The Ngaing are typical of those non-literate peoples who, as Bidney (1949: p. 333) has pointed out, make no distinction between the realms of what we call the natural and supernatural. Gods and spirits are human in character and emotions, and are part of the ordinary physical world. Man sees himself as the focal point of the two systems of relationships described: between himself and other human beings, and between himself and gods and spirits.

The pragmatic quality of both systems of relationships is understood and expressed in roughly the same terms. A man fulfils his social obligations in order to make other persons with whom he has human relationships 'think on him' (*inahok ra-*) and fulfil their obligations towards him in their turn. Similarly, the aim of ritual is to make deities and spirits 'think on' human beings and confer benefits on them.[28] But the activities of gods and spirits in helping mankind have no mystical quality. They are believed to take place on the same plane of existence and are, therefore, just as real as those of human beings working together at any joint task. Thus although the Ngaing regard work in any important undertaking as a compound of secular and ritual techniques, they assume that both have the same validity. Both derive from the same source (the deities) and both involve co-operation between beings who inhabit the same geographical environment.[29]

In its temporal dimensions, the cosmic order is conceived as essentially

fixed and static. There is no historical tradition. Adapting Evans-Pritchard's terms (Evans-Pritchard 1940: p. 94), we may define two
kinds of time: ecological time and cosmic time. The former represents
the annual succession of the seasons but has no real chronological
utility. Time depth can be measured only in relation to the recognized
age of the cosmos. Thus cosmic time may be regarded as known
genealogical time plus the period of antiquity: the period of the
emergence of the physical environment, totemic ancestors, human
beings and their culture.

Even cosmic time, however, has little chronological utility. The
depth of empirically recordable genealogies is not only very shallow
(no more than five generations even when informants' children are
included) but also kept more or less constant. With each new generation distant forebears are forgotten. The period of antiquity is in a sense
timeless: there is no clear concept of any order of creation. Although
the basic physical environment is assumed to have come into being
at the very beginning, thereafter no one event is described as having
preceded another. Food plants, artefacts, domesticated animals,
ceremonies and human beings emerged at random.[30]

Again, not only the overall mythology but also the individual
myths reflect the absence of the concept of time depth. There is no
tradition of a gradual advance from a rudimentary to a more elaborate
way of life. This can be seen in two ways. First, each part of the
culture is described at the time of its invention in exactly the same
form as it is now. Second, each myth depicts the people's culture
during the period of antiquity as quite recognizably up to date and
complete except for that part of it the relevant deity has to introduce
and explain. In short, the way of life of antiquity is the way of life of
today and will be the way of life of tomorrow as well. Therefore,
the relationships between men, gods and spirits within the cosmos
are finally established: all have their unalterable roles to play towards
each other.

By the same token, the body of knowledge, as the people see it,
is as static and finite as the cosmic order within which it is contained.
It was brought into the world ready made and ready to use. It can be
augmented only by further acts of revelation by old or new deities.
Moreover, it is hardly surprising that the epistemological system has
fossilized in this way. The religion is intellectually satisfying for it
operates within a framework which normally guarantees its validity.
Because of the relatively monotonous repetition of economic and social

life, there is hardly any event which cannot be explained by or attributed to it. The whole visible world—the annually ripening crops, and the fertility of pigs and human beings—far from allowing it an aura of mysticism, proclaims that it is solidly based on empirical fact. There is no need—indeed, no room—for an independent human intellect.

4. CONCLUSION

The material presented can be summed up as follows: The Ngaing see their cosmos as an integrated physical whole, in which the existence of gods, spirits of the dead and totems is real in exactly the same sense as that of human beings and animals. Religion—man's beliefs about, and conceived interaction with, gods, spirits and totems—can be interpreted in two ways. From the outside objective point of view, it is a system which validates the cosmic order. From the people's own subjective point of view, it provides a body of knowledge which completely overshadows the principle of human intellectual inquiry and is regarded as absolutely reliable for explaining the existence of the cosmos and controlling its affairs. The criterion of true knowledge is the mastery of ritual, which is rendered effective by the observance of taboos and which ensures for men beneficial relationships with gods, spirits and totems. This is the basis of leadership.

From either point of view, however, Ngaing religion does not represent a fully worked out system. It is not concerned equally and impartially with all aspects of the cosmos but only with those of primary and practical importance. It is essentially a working religion. Whatever the people regard as changeless (the basic physical environment and the overall form of the social structure) and whatever does not impinge on their way of life (the sun, moon and stars), they either gloss over or ignore. They feel no need of detailed knowledge by which to explain and control these things. Religious belief and action are elaborated only for those parts of the culture which cause anxiety: affairs in which there is a considerable degree of risk, in which setbacks cause social disruption and of which, therefore, man must satisfy himself that he has complete understanding. Thus the themes which the religion emphasizes most clearly and consistently are the successful exploitation of economic resources, the acquisition of scarce valuables, the welfare of human beings and pigs, and the strengthening of specific relationships vital for the continuance of society.

Nevertheless, in spite of this limitation of intellectual interest, the attitudes and assumptions underlying Ngaing religion are very tenacious and can be adapted to suit new situations. Fifty years of European contact (direct and indirect) have made virtually no impression on them. During this period the two main changes in the people's way of life have been the importation of steel tools and cotton cloth, and the introduction of Christianity. In common with other peoples of the southern Madang District, the Ngaing reacted to the changes in terms of their traditional values and concepts. Dominant themes similar to those already described emerged in their new way of life. European goods were highly valued. They were a great cause of anxiety: the people wanted larger supplies than those which they enjoyed. But being ignorant of the processes by which these goods were made, they again interpreted their source in terms of creation by a deity and their acquisition in terms of ritual. God and the spirits of the dead in Heaven made the new wealth. Church services, rendered effective by the observance of new taboos (against polygyny and sorcery), would guarantee delivery. Furthermore, as Heaven was believed to be in Australia, the cosmos, although enlarged, still retained its essential physical unity. Dealings between God and man were believed to have a completely pragmatic reality.

The interest in Christianity, however, did not mean the elimination of the old gods. They remained powerful in their own sphere (the traditional culture). Thus when it was recognized that Christianity would not bring them the new wealth, the Ngaing were able to revert to their own religion with a minimum of intellectual dislocation. Although some secrets had been forgotten, the fundamental attitudes and assumptions were unimpaired. It was only a matter of reinstating old gods who had been temporarily neglected. This subject has been analysed more fully in a separate publication.[31]

NOTES

[1] My thanks are due to the Australian National University for providing funds for my field work among the Ngaing (eight months in 1953 and six months in 1956); and to the Department of Territories (Canberra) for enabling me to revisit the area during January 1958, when I was on the staff of the Australian School of Pacific Administration, Mosman, N.S.W.

[2] Approximate population figures for the other groups mentioned are: Sengam 600; Gira 220; Som 150; Neko 180; M'na and N'dau unknown. I am indebted to the Administration of Papua and New Guinea for this information.

[3] During the so called Yali Movement of 1948; see Lawrence (1954; 1955; 1964).

[4] My material on war ritual and sorcery was given entirely by informants. I have also indicated other statements drawn from the same source.

[5] The Nankina-Mot section of the Rai Coast has no clay deposits. Pots have to be imported. Siasi beads are small shells pierced with holes so that they can be strung on thread. The trading system mentioned here once linked Siasi, Madang, the Rai Coast, the Huon Peninsula and probably the coast north of Madang. Between Madang and the Rai Coast it is now largely defunct, the last exchange having taken place in 1953, although the network of relationships survives. I use the present tense when discussing the system (and also warfare) for reasons of consistency and space. For a somewhat fuller description of the trading system between Madang and the Rai Coast see Lawrence (1964); and for references see Neuhauss (1911: *passim*) and Hannemann (n.d. a: p. 10 and n.d. b: p. 4).

[6] The terms 'red' and 'white' refer to the colours of the layers immediately beneath the outer rinds of the two types of taro.

[7] In most cases, each modern Ngaing village consists of the inhabitants of a named bush area concentrated into a single settlement. For the beginning of this process, see Aufinger (1940-1).

[8] Except for the Pig and Betel-nut matriclans, whose members are said to have relaxed the taboos for obvious reasons.

[9] Except of course, for the Pig and Betel-nut matriclans.

[10] Translated as *masalai* in Pidgin English.

[11] Informants were quite unable to explain the significance of Parambik's name. They merely reiterated the vagueness of his identity, although they claimed that he was always somewhere within Ngaing territory. For this reason, and also because he is not given a separate designation by the people themselves, I class him as a deity (*tut*) rather than as a culture hero, as his present lack of interest in Ngaing affairs might suggest. In contrast, among the Sengam and Som, the primal god (Barnun and Balaulau = myth) is far more positively conceived. He has an esoteric name, which is used in agricultural ritual.

[12] Meanderi's distribution of 'red' and 'white' taro as described in the myth correlates exactly with their actual distribution in Ngaing territory today.

[13] In contrast with other societies in Papua and New Guinea, in which women are not supposed to know that music emanates from sacred instruments. Cf. Read (1952a: p. 6).

[14] Hannemann (n.d. b: pp. 6-8 and 9-10) quotes separate origin myths for the Male Cult among the Sengam. Nowadays the Sengam invariably refer to Yabuling as the creator of the Male Cult. This may be due to losses from Sengam religion under mission influence.

[15] Except in Sor and Paramus because of the distance of the sanctuaries of their war deities. In this area, materials for war ritual are taken from the bush. They include bark of a black palm said to have been made to grow by the war god of Saing, one of the creators of the bow and arrow.

[16] In Maibang and Gabumi Meanderi's secret name is used; in Aiyawang, the secret name of the *wirijabi* creeper, which she is said to have planted there; and in Sibog, the secret name of her daughter, who is believed to have remained there on the return journey.

[17] During my fourteen months with the Ngaing I witnessed only one accusation of sorcery. In contrast, among the Garia of the Bagasin Area sorcery accusations were a regular occurrence.

[18] I was unable to observe a celebration of the Harvest Festival. The following account, apart from the section on the washing of the trumpets at the sacred pools, was taken from informants.

[19] In Gabumi, Maibang and Kilang, Yabuling's secret name is used; in Aiyawang, that of the *rombong* shrub, said to have been planted there by Yabuling.

In Sor and Paramus, the people have no secret name for Yabuling but claim that the performance of the other ritual at the sacred pools will cause him to send up the spirits.

[20] Owing to its close association with the Cargo Movement during and after 1948; see Lawrence (1954; 1955; 1964).

[21] I could not fully confirm this statement in the field. Men claim that women have the monopoly of methods of abortion. Women are unwilling to give away information. My informants, however, believed that the secrets were passed on to a girl just before marriage.

[22] I was unable to witness an initiation ceremony. The following account was taken from informants.

[23] For accounts of circumcision in the southern Madang District see Aufinger (1941) and Bodrogi (1953).

[24] This is typical of native parochialism in the southern Madang District. Garia and Ngaing were quite unable to accept differences between their two cultures, and even the Ngaing were unaware of the considerable variations in their own.

[25] Men often complain that they are not allowed to rest from playing music in the cult house because the women are so keen to dance outside.

[26] I have discussed this subject generally in Lawrence (1959; 1964).

[27] This is especially true today. The temporary eclipse of the traditional religion between 1933-48 left many patriclans without leaders or with leaders of very little status.

[28] See Lawrence (1954: pp. 10-11), where similar concepts among the Garia are discussed.

[29] In the same way, sympathetic magic unleashes forces which are essentially part of the physical environment.

[30] See Evans-Pritchard (1940: p. 108) for a discussion of the same problem among the Nuer.

[31] See Lawrence (1964).

K. O. L. BURRIDGE

Tangu, Northern Madang District[1]

TANGU live in hilly country about fifteen miles inland from Bogia Bay on the north coast of New Guinea in the Madang District. Comprising some two thousand souls distributed through approximately thirty settlements of varying sizes grouped into four named neighbourhoods, they are traditionally hunters, gatherers and gardeners who now supplement these basic subsistence activities by going away to the coast and European settled areas to work for cash. At one time they were concentrated into fewer but larger and more exclusive local communities whose members spoke a common language, shared clubhouse rituals, dances and myths, and who were interrelated through a strong network of internal trading and exchange relationships based upon actual or putative kin ties. But a variety of factors interacting over the last sixty or seventy years has resulted in the present dispersed settlement pattern, the disappearance of the clubhouses—formerly centres of ritual activity—and the virtual disappearance of the social groups and regulative categories known as the *gagai* and GAGAI.[2] Mission and effective administrative influences date from the middle 'twenties, though there were many much earlier contacts with Europeans. In 1951 Tangu engaged in cargo cult activities.

Some Tangu are Christians,[3] some are baptized pagans, many pagans have taken to Christian or European ways, and even the most conservative find it difficult to describe the religious institutions of the past. A coherent system of symbols, dogma, rituals and practice which some might call 'Tangu religion' does not exist. Yet despite conversions to Christianity and other minor local differences in culture, a body of behaviour in which all Tangu participate to a greater or lesser extent has survived, or has been produced by, the three or four generations of trouble and disturbance to which they have been subject.[4] General attachment to a few important and interrelated notions and activities delineate a common way of life, a single moral order generally determined by the observance of strict reciprocities in social relationships. All over Tangu first loyalties are to the self, and to the household in terms of which the abilities, desires and ambitions of an individual may be developed and matured. Common ground in the meaning and significance rather than in the particular mode of marriage, the formation of the household, and siblingship lend point to the frequent intermarriages between members of different local groups, co-operation between households, and the numerous and regularly maintained trading and exchange relationships. Over a wide range of other matters, however, consensus is often limited. Effective economic and political solidarities tend to be on a small scale and temporary merely; households shift residence fairly frequently; communities are only loosely organized; there is room to manoeuvre, to opt out of particular arrangements; ambiguity of allegiance and support is itself a desideratum for the ambitious if not for the less able.

As between the generations among Tangu strict reciprocity in relationships cannot exist. And an examination of such myths and stories as survive, as well as the circumstances once attendant on clubhouse rituals, show that the bulk of traditional Tangu religious institutions were attached to relationships of filiation and were mainly concerned with the problems associated with the growth and maturation of individuals into the reciprocities of the moral order. These particular aspects need not be considered here, nor is there space to do so.[5] The present discussion is confined to the more general features of the nexus between the moral order which is characterized by reciprocal relations, responsibility and the controllable, and a variety of non-reciprocal and largely uncontrollable elements which may be summed up as the 'divine' order.

For Tangu the moral order is unique to the human condition. But elements of the divine intervene in human affairs from time to time. And when these divine elements do so intervene, whilst they do not change the guiding principle on which the moral order rests, reciprocity in relationships, they have the effect of altering the particular constellation of relationships within which individuals express their reciprocities. Ultimately, therefore, the moral order as it exists at any particular moment must proceed from the divine. Yet it cannot be said without considerable distortion that there are any gods, goddesses, deities or even culture heroes which are in any meaningful sense creative, causative or regulative. Outside the Christian context the idea of 'worship' is absent. Social life is regulated by human beings. Though there are certain partial exceptions, in principle the divine is unmanipulable.

The divine consists of, briefly, the *ranguma* or sorcerer who, though human, has become non-reciprocal and perhaps uncontrollable; that part of the human which, existing in life, survives physical death and is represented as maturing through several stages—all of them essentially non-reciprocal states; natural phenomena and the denizens of the wild, non-reciprocal elements; and a class of being known to Tangu as *puoker* (sing. *puok*) which, if anthropomorphic, are also non-re-ciprocal. Since, however, myths relate the adventures of certain kinds of *puoker* and are themselves considered to be the creations of *puoker*, and dreams are considered to proceed from the divine and often figure the dead, both myths and dreams as entities in themselves may be considered to belong to the divine. Like other aspects of the divine, but excepting the spell and the *ranguma*, man cannot manipulate myths and dreams for his own ends—though of course he may try.

1. MORAL RELATIONSHIPS

Tangu are ethnocentric, suspicious of each other, more so of strangers. By day their settlements are deserted. Households, con-sisting of a man, his wife or wives, their natural and adopted children, and perhaps an ageing parent of either spouse—who eat, live, and work together as a team—are in the surrounding countryside, in the forest or on grassy downs, in their hunting lodges, tending their several scattered gardens, or visiting kinsfolk or friends. Only at dusk, or on festive occasions, or when some specific community task is afoot, is any substantial proportion of a settlement present. Com-munity life rests mainly upon the relationships of a pair of spouses with their actual or putative siblings: the co-operative relationship is described as one between married siblings of the same sex, and trading and exchange relationships are described as existing between married siblings of different sex. Or, married siblings of the same sex are in actual or potential co-operating relationships, and married siblings of different sex are in actual or putative trading or exchange relationships. Apart from tasks which are carried out under the direction of ad-ministrative officials or mission catechists and boss-boys, the work a household does goes into subsistence, trading, food exchanges, feasts and feasting and dancing exchanges. The latter, occurring regularly during the harvesting months between two principal but temporary groups of co-operating households to which other households attach themselves, define the active membership of a local community in any one year. During these feasting and dancing exchanges, which are group exchanges, *br'ngun'guni*—a debating and talking in public assembly, and the explicit and proper occasion for discussing future community arrangements, making claims or announcements, airing grievances, disputing and arguing—takes place.[6]

Although a household is free to choose a trading or unitary exchange relationship as convenience or an actual kin relationship requires, the formation of co-operative alliances and group exchange relationships, while partly depending on residence and kin affiliation, and always described in the kin idiom, tends more often in fact to flow from the activities of hard-working and influential men, managers, who by oratory, cunning, knowledge, experience, skill at handling others, and making good their claims to an ability to produce quantities of food-stuffs, are able to persuade other households into forming a co-operative relationship with them. Their chief but not sole opportunity occurs during *br'ngun'guni* when, either formally at a feasting and dancing exchange, or contingently when a fair proportion of a settle-ment is present and the moment seems propitious, they try to make their names as skilled debaters, food producers and worthy managers. The alliances so formed, however, are not stable. Their composition changes over a relatively short period of time and depends on the relationships between managers—and between managers and others—whose inherent competitiveness provides the dynamic of the society whilst at the same time preserving a major structural division of any community into two roughly equivalent halves in an exchange or oppositional relationship.

Several factors combine to maintain this balance. The critical axiom which governs all Tangu relationships through a variety of contents, bases and motives is amity. No vague and emotional good-will, amity depends on and is expressed by equivalence, a principle of moral equality which must be continually reaffirmed and reiterated lest someone become dominant. Without equivalence there can be no amity in Tangu. The focal assertion of equivalance is at food exchanges at every level whether the exchange is completed in a day, weeks or months. And since all food exchanges are required to be equivalent, and prestige and influence are reflected in the amount produced, a manager, household, or group of households may only attain such prestige as is implicit in the production of the opposition. Further, because no exchange of foodstuffs can be precisely equivalent, the acceptance without argument of a particular exchange as equivalent indicates true amity and moral equivalence. When such a situation obtains between a pair of households they are said to be *mngwotngwotiki*, truly equivalent: neither household may engage in activities in relation to the other which might imply either a co-operative or an exchange relationship between them. *Mngwotngwotiki* lapses when an act or word on either side is deemed to belie the equivalence between them.[7]

Becoming *mngwotngwotiki* is comparatively rare. More often exchanges are challenged as a matter of course and *br'ngun'guni* ensues. Such action is approved. *Br'ngun'guni* is as it were 'designed' to allow disputation in public. It is a device, closely dependent on that ambiguity in relationships which allows scope for manoeuvre and challenge, by which Tangu can find approximate and overt equivalence with one another. Participation by the assembly, members of which interject, taking the part now of one, then of the other; a pragmatic gauging of the real political and economic consequences of an act or words spoken; and the threat or fear of retaliation through sorcery—these are the main factors which, related to the maintenance of amity and equivalence, keep an issue within bounds. Shame also plays a part, but on the whole a minor one. The main deterrent lies in damaging withdrawals of support, and particularly in the fear that a man whose pride has been injured may resort to sorcery to get even with an antagonist by making him sick—thus preventing him from working and so maintaining his stature through productive ability. A man who cannot hunt, or till his garden, cannot provide what is necessary to an exchange, cannot maintain his reciprocities.

What Tangu approve and require is that men should show their equivalence with each other in public, under amity, in terms of food production, oratory and personality, through *br'ngun'guni*. They appreciate keen talk, barbed words, the act that needles. But they cannot abide the decisive, unanswerable shaft. A flexible approach and tactical variety in disputation which leave room for another to equalize are applauded: the man who obstinately insists on his point earns little esteem and breeds suspicions. He who works hard in field and bush, and who is at the same time capable of maintaining equivalence and amicable relations with others is a good man, more able in himself to become better yet. Others respect and even admire him. But should a man attempt to demonstrate, say, a superior working capacity by making an unequal exchange, he is regarded as culpable.

Tangu allow for particular deviations from the forms of tradition or expectation by judging issues in their subsistence against amity, equivalence and due process of *br'ngun'guni*. What they deplore and very much fear is that a man may try to realize his desires outside *br'ngun'guni* by using the methods, both mystical and otherwise, characteristic of a sorcerer, a *ranguma*. A manager, the epitome of the good man who is also able, has to remain fit and maintain amity and equivalance fully exposed to a watchful public under conditions of acute strain. Consequently, more than others, managers are not only vulnerable to the temptation to take advantage of sorcery, but they are, accordingly, the more readily suspected of doing so. For maintaining equivalence requires a hypercritical attitude towards the actions and words of others; and Tangu, deeply concerned for their equivalances, are extremely sensitive to what might be construed as an insult to, or an invasion of, their personal integrity as men. Authority over others in one of their number is anathema. Managers may guide or steer; and this they do in virtue of their ability to produce quantities of foodstuffs for feasts and exchanges and maintain amity and equivalence under stress. They have no authority. Equivalence, expressed in the equivalent prestation, is the radical note of being in the moral order.

Tangu are happiest in their gardens or hunting lodges where they are free from the more obvious reminders of their obligations towards others. When households gather together opportunities for comparisons arise, tensions grow, and the atmosphere ripens for a quarrel. Ambiguities as well as undercurrents of personal and emotional discord—all readily translatable into political issues within the managerial process—make the situation one of inherent conflict which must be controlled. Just that sense of release from the obligatory prestation of the redemptive process, is contained in the meaning of *mngwotngwotiki*. For by connoting unobligedness within the terms of morality, the moral and divine are merged and form one.

2. THE MORAL COMMUNITY

The maintenance of overt amity and public equivalence by, or in spite of, regular food, feasting and dancing exchanges, and through *br'ngun'guni*, conveniently sums up the core of the Tangu ethic. And *br'ngun'guni* itself links amity and equivalence with, on the one hand, prestige, influence, industry and organizing ability, and on the other with the good man, the manager, who is himself the most exposed to temptation. But there can be no guarantee that all men are either able or willing to translate their aspirations into oratory and equivalent productions of foodstuffs. Further, the fact that men and women become sick, and then die, long before they reach old age reveals to Tangu the presence of a power which they cannot control and which dominates them in a way their community morality cannot. That this power may kill is of consequence: that it may, working in men, cause them to kill, or induce sickness in, others is of more immediate concern. For, whether as 'vehicles' or 'originators' the acts of men are the interest of members of the community. Killing or inducing sickness is non-reciprocal behaviour and, irrespective of final consequences, wrong or evil. For Tangu the problem of evil resolves itself into the problem of the non-reciprocal man, the *ranguma* (pl. *ranguova*). 'When the *ranguma* came into the world,' Tangu say, quoting a myth, 'he was the last man out of the hole in the earth. He brought with him poison and [the means and ability to cause] sickness and death. He was arrogant and proud, and proclaimed that all things were his.'

The *ranguma* is the epitome of the non-reciprocal man, the man who will not engage his reciprocities as do others. If in some contexts the word translates conveniently as 'sorcerer', and in others as 'witch', only too frequently 'criminal', 'assassin', 'scapegoat', 'non-conformist' or 'unusual' might be more accurate. Though Tangu themselves point out that there are different kinds of *ranguma* they make no other linguistic distinction: the one category suffices. Used of men, not of women, almost always of a particular man at a specified time, less often of a man all the time and only rarely of a co-ordinated group of men,[8] the word *ranguma* describes a type of person who may always become a particular individual. A man may be thought of as a *ranguma* but only in certain situations does the thought become explicit: in different circumstances he may be regarded as any other man—a good father, a hard worker, a careful husband. A *ranguma* is *imbatekas*,[9] a word with a wide range of translations including evil, wicked, bad, eccentric, useless, odd, unusual, unfortunate, awesome, remarkable, queer or singular but which, in its most precise sense, connotes the non-reciprocal, the uncontrollable. Any act, situation, or being which does not belong to the normal, preferred, expectable, commonplace order of society or nature may be *imbatekas*. A two-headed dog would be *imbatekas*, a kinless person is *imbatekas*, and so too are unusually severe storms, thunder and lightning, enormous snakes, patches of forest, earthquakes, boars that kill men, too much food at a feast, and those who provide too much food at a feast. On the whole, though not precisely, *imbatekas* corresponds to what we have called the divine: that which is singular or odd or non-reciprocal; that which defies reciprocal obligation.

A *ranguma* is *imbatekas* because he is essentially non-reciprocal, because he is a 'bad' man doing 'wicked' things in an evil way; because more often than not he is, or is expected or considered to be, an outsider, a stranger,[10] one who does not in any full sense of the term 'belong' to the moral community; because since all ordinary folk would, rightly, regard a *ranguma* with extreme distaste, he must be exceptional who would be a *ranguma*; because not only does a *ranguma* not conform with the community ethic but, since he is thought to have powers denied to the majority of ordinary folk, his very non-conformity may and often does bring about a situation of moral conflict. His activities may entail normal reciprocal persons behaving non-reciprocally. By insisting that a *ranguma* is a man, however, and not an idea or concept, Tangu are able to exert some measure of control over what one might be tempted to call the Principle of Evil. But Tangu do not see it this way. To them the *ranguma* is a man who has become *imbatekas*. And since he is a man a *ranguma* lays himself open to being dealt with as such. Providing he can be seen, Tangu are not slow to retaliate with a spear or a club. If he can be identified as a particular man he may be killed or persuaded to pay compensation. On the other hand, though some times and situations are more inviting than others, a *ranguma* is always considered to have the initiative and no one knows just when he will act or what methods he will use. Consequently, foreknowledge, discovery and identification are of prime importance.

A *ranguma* is habitually thought of as a tall, bony man with red-rimmed eyes and the splay hand and long fingers of a strangler; he is surly and unsociable, walks by himself. Not all red-eyed men are *ranguova*—but it behoves one to be careful in dealing with such men. A secretive and churlish fellow is quickly suspected of being a *ranguma*. Why else, Tangu ask, does he not stop to gossip as other people do? Lonely men with chips on their shoulders tend to brood over their fires, smoking, and their eyes become bloodshot: such men, Tangu aver, are dangerous. A *ranguma* is a thief, not one who merely seizes the opportunity to pick up an axe carelessly left aside, but the sort who plans a theft and who is prepared to break open and enter a hut when the owners are away. Unlike the adulterer who, sharing his wrongdoing with the woman, is willing to shoulder such responsibilities as may flow from the act, a *ranguma* deliberately, ruthlessly lures a good wife into his arms. Only a *ranguma* could, or would, intentionally cause sickness in another or initiate a killing outside open warfare or feud. A *ranguma* has within him what others have not: both the desire and the ability to do such things, either for his own ends, or on behalf of those who may have similar desires but not his abilities. And the means he uses, Tangu consider, may be potent charms or spells, rites or gestures, actual poisons to be found in the bush, strangulation, the spear, or a club. Thus, if to a European the translation of '*ranguma*' would depend upon a *post hoc* assessment as to how and in what context a *ranguma* is supposed to have acted, to Tangu each of the different kinds of *ranguma* has that in common with the others which justifies the use of the single category, *ranguma*.

A *ranguma* is feared, especially at night when counteraction is difficult. Women and children, who cannot in any case retaliate themselves, are considered particularly vulnerable. In daylight a *ranguma* may hide near the gardens or walk in the bush on the lookout for unaccompanied women and children. At night he is expected to creep into the environs of a settlement seeking his opportunity, and he may crawl under the floorboards of a hut to entice the womenfolk out. A careful man whose wife or daughters are not sleeping well, or who hears a rustle underneath, thrusts his spear down through the gaps in the flooring—in case. No man walks abroad after nightfall, not even to answer a call of nature, without a light or a weapon. To be without a light is suggestive of covert designs, and having a light is both evidence of innocent intentions as well as an aid to seeing a *ranguma* and so being able to retaliate if attacked.

Tangu anticipate trouble from a *ranguma* when they know a *ranguma* is in the vicinity; and they expect a visitation from a *ranguma* when there is trouble in the village. During feasting and dancing exchanges especially, when *br'ngun'guni* takes place, a *ranguma* is considered to be watching. Normally the members of a community prefer to think of a *ranguma* as not being one of themselves. The most dangerous *ranguova* are thought to live in the areas neighbouring Tangu, and no Tangu will travel to or through these places unless he has a sister or a friend[11] who lives there, and who will protect him. Within Tangu itself *ranguova* are considered to come from another neighbourhood, another settlement. There are, however, certain men whose ancestry is questionable, or who are over-taciturn or non-conformist, or who have been identified as *ranguova* in the past, who are 'well known' as *ranguova*: their activities are whispered about, but only rarely are they openly accused. Being partly, if not wholly, of the community, and deemed to possess at least something of the powers of a *ranguma*, accusation without the kind of evidence which will carry the support of the community entails an undue risk. Besides, such men are useful. Their reputed knowledge of the habits of *ranguova* may be employed to kill other *ranguova*, the community may use them as scapegoats, and merely to be seen talking to one may instil caution in an exchange partner who is going a little beyond his equivalences.

A *ranguma* killer, though by no means always identified as a *ranguma* proper, is usually suspected of being very like a *ranguma*. He is bolder, more cunning, more patient, more skilled in bushcraft than others. He knows mystical ways of detecting the approach of a *ranguma*, and he has the will and capacity to surprise and kill a *ranguma*. An ordinary man is capable of retaliating against a *ranguma* but he cannot, as a *ranguma* killer can, take the initiative and ambush a *ranguma*. Some killers, indeed, are 'retired' *ranguova*, men who were once thought to be wicked but who, now, act in defence of good men. More often in the old days, but rarely today, a *ranguma* killer was one who had 'eaten *ranguma*', *ranguma brami*,[12] a man who in company with others of like mind had ritually eaten—so it is said—either a dead baby, or a live toad, and a species of chestnut,[13] and who rubbed brows and eyes with nettles to make them hot and red. The purpose of the rite, it seems, was to invest a man with the desire, will and ability to kill in cold blood. Any man, in passion, may wish for the death of another, or kill if sufficiently provoked. A *ranguma* eliminates with professional precision.

The *ranguma* killer is not a regular night watchman: he stands his guard on certain occasions only—when his skin becomes 'hot' or 'creeps', when a *ranguma* is thought to be prowling, when there is trouble in the village, when there has been a quarrel, when an air of tension and crisis in relationships becomes obvious to all. And while the killer protects the community from a suspected *ranguma*, it is also true that he prevents disputants from surprising each other and perpetrating an unnecessary or even irreparable injury. That is, in situations of stress, when it is felt that a man will not, as he should, resort to *br'ngun'guni*, and might interpret the law for himself, then the idea that a *ranguma* is present becomes immanent. The task of identifying who the *ranguma* is, however, while always supposedly urgent, only really becomes so if disquiet continues. For most of the time a *ranguma* is, perhaps, an imaginative projection, personifying evil: and as such he prevents ordinary men from behaving, outwardly, as though they themselves were *ranguova*. But when his intent becomes concrete the responsibility for saying that this man or that man is a *ranguma* becomes more insistent.

When a man falls sick he cannot work, he is unable to meet his co-operative obligations, he cannot make proper exchanges, and he has little basis for successful participation in *br'ngun'guni*. Sickness may wreck any man's plans for the year, and if a manager is forced to spend his days on his pallet instead of in his gardens or in the bush, temporary if not permanent ruin is inevitable. A manager must keep fit in order to produce the food on which his prestige and influence ultimately depend. Headaches, colds, boils, cuts, bruises or fractured limbs may be but are not necessarily taken to have been caused by *ranguova*. When a man vomits, however, and vomits the next day and the day after; when boils continue to erupt and he cannot eat, has diarrhoea, and begins slowly to waste away, then assuredly a *ranguma* is causing it—and the sick man must make a confession. Almost any ailment will occasion a searching of conscience and confession to a kinsman, friend, or old man.[14] For no such disability is considered to be wholly an accident. A prior transgression is probably responsible. And whether a sickness is considered to flow directly from a wrongdoing —as with most sexual misdemeanours—or from defying the powers of a protective spell—as may happen in cases of theft or trespass— confession externalizes and expunges guilt on one side and also obliges a human initiator of the malady to negative the power of his spell. Ordinary men will feel so obliged. But a *ranguma*, typically, will not. He is without pity, essentially non-moral, nasty. Thus, once a sickness has been diagnosed as the work of a *ranguma* it becomes imperative for the community to make him subject to morality by identifying him as a man and forcing him to stop. Yet who but the sick man, or the *ranguma*, or the *ranguma's* employer, may judge whether or not the confession is complete?

A victim may start by protesting his innocence, threatening revenge, or pleading for mercy. Then, as the illness continues, successive confessions will elicit the names of wronged persons who, through being talked about, assume standing as popular suspects. If this know-ledge in itself does not ease the situation, members of the victim's community may resort to spoliation of the suspects' gardens, incitements to fight, or counter-magic. Such methods failing to persuade the *ranguma*, or his hirer, to desist, and the victim still surviving but continuing sick, the community is forced to look inwards to itself. Unable today to resort to open war or feud, insistence on the guilt of an outsider can only lead to a complete rupture of relations between one community and another. So, men skilled in dreaming the identity of a *ranguma* are pressed into service. For several days dreamers and victim confer with one another, discussing their dreams and possible suspects, and eventually they decide who the *ranguma* must be. Usually the 'odd man out', the man who is *imbatekas*, is fixed on. Once identified, the supposed *ranguma* is physically coerced into confessing his guilt, and then made to pay compensation—which is later repaid by the sick man when he recovers and is able to return to work. If, in theory, a *ranguma* is quite capable of striking an innocent, Tangu find it hard to believe that an adult is without stain. On the contrary, since anyone may be a wrongdoer it is necessary first to search one's own conscience. Then, so soon as guilt is admitted, the automatic consequences of a wrongdoing are negatived and others contained in the moral order are put under obligation to neutralize the power of their spells. Confession by the *ranguma* or his hirer both erases their guilt in the affair and is an acknowledgement of being subject to morality. And the compensation exchange that follows not only maintains public equivalence—confession for confession, payment for payment—but reiterates again the triumph of morality.

Whatever the complaint may be the statement that a *ranguma* has thieved, trespassed, or is trying to commit adultery, or is determined to cause sickness or death, recruits the support of the community. A man who feels insufficiently secure, unwilling or unable to venture into *br'ngun'guni*, can always turn a personal problem into one of community interest by remarking on the presence of *ranguova*. Men and women going about their daily work keep a sharper lookout, *ranguma* killers stand their guard at night, a situation of nervous tension and preparedness is brought into being. No ordinary thief, trespasser or adulterer would risk himself: the odds would be against him, and the penalty might be a spear in his side. Neither amity nor public equivalences are challenged; indignation and the impulse to retaliate are channelled outside the community; community solidarity is renewed. Often the tension is such that if there is a wrongdoer in the community he will confess and make restitution. Otherwise, anxiety

Q

and suspicions gradually relax until it becomes clear that that particular *ranguma* is either quiescent or has gone elsewhere. Death caused by a *ranguma*, on the other hand, brings about a situation which, in the modern context, may not even itself out for years. For though some-one may have confessed already it becomes clear, on the death of the victim later, that a mistake has been made. The *ranguma* who kills is surely an outsider. Though the kinsmen of the dead man may feel reasonably certain of the identity of the *ranguma*, or his employer, they cannot simply put a spear into him for fear of the police. Nor, in the face of denials of guilt, may they extract compensation. The alternatives are to await a suitable opportunity to commit a murder which the police will be unable to handle, or to employ another *ranguma* to cause sickness, and finally death if the sickness fails to elicit a confession. Since, however, no *ranguma* can guarantee success within a specified time limit, and he also would prefer to avoid answering to the police, the matter is normally long drawn out.

If to an outside observer the *ranguma* appears in most contexts as a useful fiction, created *post hoc* to explain or account for certain situa-tions, for both Christians and pagans in Tangu he is part of a total reality. And he is more than simply a thief, trespasser, adulterer, criminal or murderer. He is a moral being, self-willed and arrogant, who exemplifies hubris. These qualities in him are troublesome, and therefore wrong or evil. They justify Tangu bracketing together sorcerer, criminal, witch, scapegoat or non-conformist simply as *ranguma*. There are those who readily confess to being *ranguova*: it makes them feared. And if it is true that a man who realizes that he is going to be forced to confess might just as well do so before he is beaten, Tangu argue that only a *ranguma*, or a man like a *ranguma*, would actually make such a confession and thereby, wittingly or un-willingly, gain an ascendancy over his fellows. Tangu think of themselves as living a regular and traditional kind of life based upon particular standards and rules. Into this ordered scheme a *ranguma* enters, bringing with him envy, hatred, quarrels, sickness and death. Most men, Tangu say, are ordinary men, good conformists. Here and there, however, are men who have deliberately chosen to be wicked, or who in spite of their better selves cannot control that which is in them. These men are *imbatekas*, and they cause trouble. Tangu allow that any man might become a *ranguma*, and that all men are prone to arrogance or greed, selfishness or lust. But whereas most men will shun or attempt to curb expressions of such vices, a *ranguma*, purposely or otherwise, has the ability to develop, exploit, and manipulate those tendencies towards non-reciprocity which probably exist in all men. That a man is a *ranguma*, or like one, enables the community to take positive action. Once he is identified as a man whom one has known since boyhood it becomes possible to treat him with an appearance of charity. The process of identification pulls the *ranguma* into the moral order until his confession makes him a part of it. Outright condemnation is reserved for the unknown outsider.

It will be clear that the *ranguma* belongs to and sustains a moral order based on egalitarian reciprocal relations. Thus though European techniques of hygiene and therapy may have had an effect on the incidence of sickness among Tangu, they have made no impression on the axiom that *ranguova* exist. Once a sickness has been diagnosed as due to the activities of a *ranguma*, many Tangu will refuse medical treatment from Europeans: it makes nonsense of the reciprocities involved and can only encourage the *ranguma* to have done without delay. Traditional techniques make it possible to draw the *ranguma* into the moral order and persuade him to undo his work. The prime axiom is that *ranguova* exist and do what they do. If, Tangu say, they were like Europeans then things would be different: they would not be plagued by *ranguova*. Certainly: if they were like Europeans, they would be living within the terms of a quite different moral order.

Christians among Tangu tend to see in the *ranguma* a mani-festation of the Devil without properly distinguishing between a *ranguma* who is always a man, and the Devil who was never a man. But the equation has a certain practical value, and both Christians and pagans use prayers, holy water, and the Sign of the Cross as counters against *ranguova*. Though Christians have adapted themselves to the Christian confessional, the latter, secret and expressing a peculiar relation between man and the divine, is not necessarily linked to the reciprocities of the moral order. Hence a *ranguma* does not recognize confession to a Christian priest: confession ignores the reciprocities involved. Traditionally Tangu were, and to a certain extent still are, concerned not so much with a man's 'conscience' as with his clear and overt surrender to the reciprocities of the moral order. Thus while traditional Tangu forms of confession express a moral relationship only, in using the Christian as well as the traditional forms of con-fession Christians in Tangu are simply bowing to necessity. For if they now have an additional allegiance, they are still as involved in reciprocities as are others. Though only an unmitigated *ranguma* would continue through to the kill, this is precisely what any *ranguma* might do. That is why he is a *ranguma*, and why he must be identified as a man.

3. THE DIVINE AND THE MORAL

So far as non-reciprocity is manifested in men the process of selecting a man to be a *ranguma* is an attempt to assert the moral as the appropriate mode of being for humans. Nevertheless, a *ranguma* is *imbatekas*. He is not simply 'bad', 'criminal' or 'wicked'. He prevents most men from being like *ranguova*; his actions keep the ethic alive and vigorous in men's minds; he precipitates moral conflicts; he provides other men with opportunities for developing their moral strengths. In the further consequences of his actions a *ranguma* may be a power for good, a servant of the ethic. Let loose in society he carries a germ of the infinite and completely non-moral. He kills not because the customs of the society may oblige him to do so but because it is in him to kill. And since it is possible that he may never be identified he may escape the moral net in which other members of the moral community are caught. So far as Tangu can know a *ranguma* in his particular acts he is culpable. Through his self-will and arrogance he usurps the divine. Confession, the humble admission of fault and rejection of hubris, makes him a part of the moral order. Yet, principally because a *ranguma* does usurp the divine, more than other men he participates in, and manifests, what is divine.

Storms, floods, thunder, lightning and earthquakes, not being men or personalized, are non-moral, distinct from the moral order, outside or beyond or above morality. But Tangu invest them with a punitive or corrective role. Always on the fringes of the meaning of *imbatekas*, severe manifestations are certainly *imbatekas*. Though a few men are believed to possess spells which enable them to 'call on' the rain, make it cease, or prevent it from falling, these phenomena conjure presentiments of evil and tribulation, and are generally considered to be beyond the control of man.[15] When a thunderstorm occurs guilty consciences are pricked—not so far as a confession, perhaps, but into mentally noting a past misdemeanour. Not necessarily directed against any individual, but to the community as a whole, storms and earthquakes are a reminder to man to mend his ways. *The* earthquake, Tangu assert, hearking to their myths, will happen only once more. Then, with accompanying thunder, lightning, rain and floods the world will turn turtle. Just such a storm ends many myths, and just such cataclysms herald radical changes in myths—the act or omission which starts mythical beings on the road to becoming men, creation itself. Both in life and in myth thunderstorms and earthquakes are associated with the presence, and particularly the killing, of large snakes or snake-like beings; large snakes are associated with patches of bush that are *imbatekas*; to enter a portion of the bush described as *imbatekas* is almost sure to bring on a thunderstorm or earthquake; after minor earthquakes investigations are started to discover who has killed a large snake; stories about *ranguova* usually include a storm as introduction to the situation in which a *ranguma* sets about his malevolent work; and while in one cycle of myths the snake is a creative, beneficent influence until it is killed and eaten—when troubles start—in another it is a monster upon whose death peace and safety depend. *Imbatekas*, a key word in the culture, draws meaning from the associative complex of *ranguova*, storms, thunder, lightning, earthquakes and snakes; classifies the anomalous, the unconstrained; includes the generative, originating spark as well as that which is punitive, but finally evokes forebodings of danger and trouble. Tangu do not venture to places that are *imbatekas* because, they say, they might not be able to deal with the consequences. The same hazard attaches to the unequal prestation.

The class of beings known as *puoker* are non-human and non-reciprocal: when they intervene in human affairs they are dubbed as *imbatekas*. They cannot be countered, manipulated, persuaded. When a man stubs his toe on a root, or falls from a tree, and hurts himself thereby, he may say that a *puok*, resident in root or tree, caused his hurt. And the *puok* is *imbatekas* because the man cannot get even with it. Such *puoker* are all about one, existing in a generalized sense, only becoming particularized when they cause damage. But there are also *puoker* the results of whose activities are more regularly and consistently evident. One such kind of *puok* is the *pap'ta*, a water being which is generally accorded a punitive role. A *pap'ta* has no personal or individual name, and men have no control over it. They cannot plead with it, placate it or enforce its service. Normally thought of as attacking trespassers, a *pap'ta* may, however, strike at anyone. If a man walks in a stream, or fishes in it, and then develops a boil on the inside of his thigh, the *pap'ta* residing in the stream is considered to have caused it. The boil is lanced when ripe, and when he recovers the victim avoids that part of the stream where it is judged that the *pap'ta* struck him.[16] It obviously disapproved. Should he, however, enter the same part of the stream again with no ill effects the conclusion is that the *pap'ta* now has no objections. And because it is as capricious as that a *pap'ta* may have an oracular as well as a punitive role. Thus, when a man is trying to create fishing claims in a stream, a point in his favour is that, since he has not suffered from boils after walking in the water, the *pap'ta* does not object to him. On the other hand, a *pap'ta* is not precluded from attacking a man who has fished in a stream so long as he can remember. For though it is thought that a *pap'ta* generally strikes at trespassers, no man who, otherwise, has undoubted claims in certain waters, will continue to hold to those claims in the face of what he considers to be a series of determined attacks by the *pap'ta*. Ultimately, therefore, a whimsical *pap'ta*, unobliged by morality, can decide who is a trespasser and who is not.

To relate a myth is to talk about *puoker* and, Tangu maintain, myths were not made up by men but by *puoker* themselves. Long ago, when certain *puoker* became human, the stories were there in the minds of the ancestors, who handed them down through the generations. Myths contain truths, or truth. However well or imperfectly the ancestors knew, or living men and women know their myths, each is thought to have an ideal form and content. And both in telling their myths and criticizing their bards living people, like their forebears, attempt to come as near as they can to the ideal—and the implied truths—even though whilst in possession of the truths they may not comprehend them. In a similar way Tangu consider that dreams reveal truths. It is for men to try and understand what these truths are. Neither myths nor dreams, it is thought, flow directly from the will and purpose of man. They exist or are experienced irrespective of particular intentions. Though it may be given to some to dream more effectively than others, and while one or two may have a more exact knowledge of myths, no man may dream what he thinks he wants to dream, he is unable to say precisely what he will dream, and myths themselves come down through the ages as though they had a 'life' of their own.

The *puoker* of myths are neither men nor women though they are named and cannot but be anthropomorphic in certain particulars. But, not being human, they are, consequently, not bound by the terms of the moral order. *Puoker* never have trouble from *ranguova*, thieves, trespassers or adulterers. Nor are they bound by amity and equivalence. With a single exception they do not debate and talk in public (*br'ngun'guni*).[17] As they appear in myths *puoker* are sexed, and may be babies, youths, maidens or adult. They have kinsfolk, they hunt, gather, garden, cook, dress and live very much as Tangu do today. But they are not organized into communities. The idea of the village community appears only abstractly, in the background. Unlike Tangu themselves, *puoker* are individuals merely, unburdened by the cares of society and its morality. Their disembodied penises and vulvae move and copulate by themselves, they marry their sisters, kill their wives, eat stones, feast without working, grow up in a trice, travel great distances. . . . And while it is true that men may impute particular reasons for the activities of *puoker*, or glean a meaning from the symbolism, or perceive a reflection of their own inner feelings, on the face of it what a *puok* does it does for no reason—whimsically, impulsively. Only those who live in a moral system need to have reasons for acting, and need to impute a reason or meaning in the acts of a *puok*. Why should a *puok* have a reason for doing anything? If Tangu are asked why so-and-so did such-and-such they shrug their shoulders and answer '*Puokake*! [He/she/it] is [a] *Puok*!' Nevertheless, what is told in a myth may have an oracular significance. By scrutinizing the myth Tangu may confirm for themselves, or perceive an alternative to, current activities and beliefs.

While *puoker* manifest themselves to men mainly through their activities in myths, those who most often reveal themselves in dreams are dead kinsmen, usually a father or elder brother. Normally referred to in the kin idiom simply, such a visitant, a 'ghost', may also be identified as an ancestor, *nduor*—though the latter word is generally reserved for remoter forebears and has a community rather than kin connotation. Though ghosts are thought to have some sympathy for the problems of men, since they are 'dead', cannot 'die' again, and are not fettered by time and space, they are not expected to behave as though they were bound by the same rules as the living. While they may remonstrate or admonish they are not usually aggressive: generally they appear in dreams to advise. But no one can know precisely in relation to what point of reference the advice is being given. Thus should a man as a result of a dream determine to give a feast, and things turn out unexpectedly, the dreamer does not blame the ghost for wrong advice. He blames himself. He knows already, and accepts, that the dream may be a trick or deception, or that he may have interpreted the advice wrongly, or that there may be some other consideration for which the disaster is a necessary preliminary. Not all dreams, however, feature a ghost. Sometimes a man will dream of a pig, a feast, yams, copulation, or wake with a cry, sweating and trembling, having dreamed of a *ranguma*. Yet whatever the dream may be it appears patent to Tangu that a man cannot lie down and dream what he might like to dream; and that when he does dream it is up to him to take notice. He must act on the dream. For a dream carries an imperative, is never experienced for nothing, and tends to realize the future. If a man dreams of a pig he may build a trap, visit the trap he has already set, or confidently await the pig he is expecting in an exchange. If he dreams of a *ranguma* he takes precautions against a *ranguma*. If a ghost comes to see his live kinsman it is not for the former to explain himself but for the dreamer, who needs reasons, to work his way to an answer in terms of his own fears, motives, ambitions and social experience. Though a man might seek advice from a ghost, not only can he not put the ghost under any compulsion, but the advice he may get might well prove or appear disastrous. Interpretations of a dream as well as the subsequent action-decision are made and reached in terms of the relationship the dreamer sees between his dream and his moral experience and sophistication.

There are two classes of being which Tangu classify as *puoker*, but of whom today they know little: the founding ancestor of an ancient settlement site, the founder (*angai'ek*, pl. *angai'eker*), and the specifically named patron, perhaps associated with the *gagai*.[18] Presumptively a first ancestor, a founder as such is, strictly, neither man nor *puok*. He, or it, belonged to a locality and marked, it seems, a transition from the world of *puoker* to the world of man—unlike an ancestor of the living, *nduor*, who is perpetually in passage from the world of man to that of *puoker*. Founders are associated with those parts of bush or forest thought to be *imbatekas*, and are said to have entered into pythons or large snakes the better to deal with trespassers. A founder's attachments were to land, to stable associations of social groups with particular lands. A patron, on the other hand, while he might be identified with a particular founder, seems to have been more mobile, attached to a social group rather than to land, associated with clubhouse rituals and pig sacrifices and, more pertinently, with the relationship between father and son.[19]

Neither founder nor patron seems to have been susceptible to the pleas of men, and neither is asked for help or consideration in any matter today. Such requests are reserved for ghosts, God, the Holy Ghost, Jesus Christ, the Virgin Mary and some saints. Always becoming man after having participated in *br'ngun'guni*,[20] and properly neither *puok* nor man nor ancestor but *puok* and man and first ancestor, because a founder could act on man through a large snake, he made men aware of themselves and of the rules by which they were bound in community. Yet, since trespass often occurs today, there are only a few pythons in the forest, no one can actually remember anyone being killed by a python, and settlement—once concentrated and relatively static—has become mobile and dispersed, it has become evident to Tangu that a founder remains more ' or less satisfied with having founded an ancient settlement site. He, or it, belongs to a lost past. And the same is true of the patron. Relevant to clubhouse ceremonial, clubhouses have disappeared. Attached either to the *gagai* or to a male patriline,[21] since these internal groupings have dissolved into their constituent households, and households only cohere into groups in *ad hoc* ways, the patron has little relevance today. He is occasionally symbolized in a dance mask.

If the representations of founder and patron are casualties attributable both to the migrations which Tangu underwent in the early years of this century, as well as to the general disruption of traditional life following European penetration, those representations which affect an individual as such or the community as a whole, rather than a group within the community, still have some relevance. Ancestors, ghosts, myths, dreams, *puoker* in general, the *puoker* of myths, the *pap'ta* and the *ranguma* are still very relevant. They bear upon reciprocities as founder and patron do not.

The Tangu word for 'think' or 'ponder' is *gnek'gneki*. In the past men only seem to have been deemed possessed of a *gnek*, a word which may be translated as 'soul' or 'mind' but which is probably best thought of in its context simply as *gnek*. After death the *gnek* became a ghost. Women, who were thought not to have a *gnek*, became *niemur*, sprites. Today, however, both men and women are held to have *gneker*. But while women cannot become ghosts after death, men may become *niemur*, sprites, before proceeding to the stage of ghost. Eventually, it is supposed, the *gnek* becomes a *puok* or like a *puok*. Thus while the progression is, roughly, *gnek*-sprite-ghost-*nduor-puok*, an ancestor thought of as a man who once lived is *nduor*, relevant to the community as a whole, the *gnek* of one who has finished with life and the living becomes a *puok*, and the *gnek* of one recently dead, not yet thought of as either *nduor* or *puok*, becomes a sprite and, in the case of a man, a ghost.

Though ghosts are generally considered to have passed beyond the stage of sprite, sometimes a sprite may appear in a dream as a ghost does. A dream in this context is an experience between the *gnek* of a living man and the *gnek* of a dead kinsman, which is *as* a ghost if not quite a ghost. Generally, a sprite cannot itself be seen though it can see the living and may manifest itself as a rat, a noise, or a whitish luminous glow which moves over the tops of trees. A sprite croons softly, like a melancholy dove; it crackles and sighs in the bush, slithers loose pebbles down a hillside, mutters in the eaves of a hut, and pokes its way into the vulva, tickling it. Mischievous, pinching the legs of the living, a sprite is neither harmful nor punitive. When a man is working and lays down his axe to have a smoke, and then cannot put his hand on his axe when he resumes, a sprite is considered to have moved it or taken it away. If one is sitting on a log, or a stool, and the log slides, or the stool topples, a sprite is up to its tricks. Upon a death the hut of the deceased is vacated for a few nights and food is left in the half shell of a coconut: the sprite, usually in the form of a rat, eats the food. When a man dies or is killed kinsfolk watch at the graveside to see whether the sprite will appear and tell them something about the death. If it is thought that a person has been killed by a *ranguma*, kinsfolk proceed to an oracular rite, putting names to the sprite, and obtaining negative or affirmative answers by the way in which the pebbles in a bamboo barrel are rattled by the sprite.[22]

Through his *gnek*—which survives his bodily death, passes out of the moral order, develops and later becomes wholly a part of the order considered divine—man participates in divinity, is aware of it, and apprehends something of the conflict in himself which gives him access to it. For Tangu man is a moral being, unique, aware that he is aware, therefore responsible. Other beings are not, and cannot be, responsible. Yet man must have come from somewhere, and Tangu say that man was originally made from the flesh of a pig. A pig was once the sacrificial animal often identified with certain aspects of man, or representing certain aspects of men. Even today important feasts—births, betrothals, weddings, funerals and anniversaries—must contain pork. No feast has importance without pork; it is an insult to omit to provide pork at a feast; *ranguova* are certain to operate if pork is not scrupulously apportioned; no one really blames a fellow who hires a *ranguma* to act against a man who has not fairly and appropriately divided his kill. Pigs are suckled at the breast, severally named, talked to, allocated slit-gong signals, credited with much the same kind of intelligence that man has, and mourned when, in the case of domestic pigs, they are killed. But a pig does not have a *gnek*. It is killed and eaten, and absorbed into man, making him strong. If a man did not have a *gnek*, he would be just like a pig. Dead men, dead bodies, are referred to as pigs: the *gnek* has been loosed from the flesh and has become a sprite or ghost. The remains moulder just as a pig's would. When in the past the fore-arms of slain enemies were eaten by the victors, this was done, ex-plicitly, not so much to participate in the personality of the dead man—for the *gnek* had become a sprite—as to assuage hunger.[23]

Between the *gnek's* awareness of divinity, and participation as or like a pig, lies the whole man who participates like a pig, has awareness through his *gnek*, and can articulate his awareness in speech. For Tangu speech, the ability to communicate, to talk and talk well, is the manifestation of man's power over himself and the material world about him. To *br'ngun'guni* is to talk with effect both within and to the community. By sounding his slit-gong a man speaks to the members of his own and other communities. Originally, Tangu say, quoting a myth, the slit-gong could speak for itself. But, because of a primordial stupidity, man now has to labour to make a slit-gong and cause it to speak for him. In former times a slit-gong was made with due care and accompanying rituals, and a large feast and the sacrifice of a pig were required to render it efficient as an instrument.[24] Today, although the constructional and initiatory rituals have dis-appeared, a slit-gong still talks for a man as, if not more powerfully than, his voice does. A man mourns on his slit-gong, and announces feasts, complaints, claims, anger, threats, confession, warnings, dances, the births of children, betrothal, marriage, the killing of a pig or cassowary. And whether a slit-gong signal constitutes the announce-ment of an event or intention, or is an invitation, request, plea or simply the expression of a mood or disposition, it is always a publica-tion, a definitive statement from which a man retreats at his peril. Hence, if a slit-gong originally came from the divine, it articulates the activities of the *gnek*, thought, and does so within the terms of the moral order. The user of a slit-gong should be responsible, aware of reciprocities in community life.

4. ACCESS TO DIVINITY

Tangu are much more concerned with day-to-day tasks, ex-changes, feasts, dances, maintaining equivalence and their fears of *ranguova* than they are with the divine which, having no rewards to offer, does not smile, will not bargain or exchange, cannot be manipulated. Manifestations are either oracular, at best shedding fresh light and other shadows on problems which man has to resolve for himself, or, fitfully, they bring retribution and punishment. Death releases man from the rewards, punishments, prestations, prescriptions, restrictions and preferences characteristic of the moral order: whatever he has done with his life the *gnek* becomes a sprite and eventually a *puok*; *he* becomes an ancestor. Yet when there is some conflict of mind, and myths are told, dreams dreamed, and thunderstorms and earthquakes occur, or when they encounter large snakes, hear a noise in the stillness, see a glow on the hillside, or a rat, Tangu realize the existence of divinity, ponder on it, and are aware of it. The pig from whose flesh they were made is a symbol of their animal nature; the slit-gong which speaks for a man and reflects his public behaviour and mood betokens awareness through speech. And the word, formulaically uttered as in a spell, usually conjoined with a rite, in all a charm, has power.

When Tangu want something to happen, or not to happen, they resort to charms. The test of efficacy is pragmatic. New charms which have been revealed in dreams, or which have been elicited from encounters with other New Guinea peoples, missionaries and Europeans in general, are continually replacing those which all have in common, or which men have inherited from their fathers or mother-brothers, or which women have inherited from their mothers. Neither the community rituals handed down by the ancestors, nor the private charms inherited from kinsfolk are sacrosanct: they are abandoned if they seem ineffective. When a man sets traps in the forest he cordons the area with saplings lashed to tree trunks, blows his spittle on the barrier and utters a formula. Trespassers are expected to sicken. A second charm following upon the sickness and subsequent confession of the trespasser will nullify the efficacy of the first. Only a more powerful charm, such as a *ranguma* might possess, will enable a trespasser to pass unscathed. Love potions, conception, contraception, success in the hunt, a bountiful harvest, protection from *ranguova*—a catalogue of the number and variety of charms, rites, and rituals does not belong here. The 'turnover' is substantial because Tangu experiment with the Sign of the Cross, holy water stolen from the mission, garbled English phrases, the written word and other expedients. And though, generally, to stand a chance of being effective a new charm should be obtained through a dream, on the analogy of the inherited charm which, if actually gained at second hand is thought originally to have been revealed in a dream, Tangu are willing to test those formulae which they come across and which seem to them to be effective at least for those who seem to be using them.

In most contexts in Tangu mystical and pragmatic techniques form an inextricable amalgam producing 'effectiveness'. But much depends upon situation. While ageing managers, for example, search for more charms in order to compensate for their ebbing physical strength, younger men point to grey hairs and skimpy limbs. If established managers sometimes tend to attribute their current fortune to secret, mystical knowledge, and even to consistently good advice from a ghost, others prefer to allude to their bulging muscles and hard-working wives—only admitting a *ranguma* to have a special and more effective access to mystical sources than they have themselves. Ultimately, however, since in some contexts the charm by itself is considered to be effective, the power to do or undo resides in the charm, the power of the divine in the word.

5. CONCLUSION

The terms 'moral' and 'divine' represent contraposed categories of power or behaviour relevant to the Tangu situation. Moral powers are those which men exert upon each other in community life, which are able to, and do, generate an equal and opposite reaction. Divine powers are those to which man in community has no reply, and which he classifies and represents to himself in particular ways, distinguishing varieties of types of non-reciprocal or as-though-self-willed behaviour. Since the world is represented as proceeding from the divine, the divine is everywhere. Self-willed, creative, the divine is before men were, and will not be obliged. Man, the moral being, is unique in creation. He is both pig and *gnek*. Often self-willed he is also subject to morality. He both participates in, and is aware of, the divine. He has channels of access to the power that resides in the divine. However self-willed, and so divine, they may be initially, the acts or omissions of men and women in community are made to earn their deserts, and the consequences are dealt with, in terms of the moral order or not at all. After death the struggle between morality and self-will is ended. Whatever a man may have done with his life the *gnek* is released from the flesh and becomes wholly a part of the divine—where morality as such is irrelevant.

Outside the Christian context Tangu do not represent to themselves any of those beneficent powers or purposes which may be found in other religious systems. They are most deeply touched by expressions of that in men which lies either completely within, or wholly outside, the requirements of equivalence. Being *mngwotngwotiki*, transcending the prestatory relationship, is an approximation with, or an imitation of, the divine. It represents a state of unobligedness within the terms of the moral order, self-willedness in conformity with morality, redemption.

Through charms, primarily through the spell, the word man has access to some of the power residing in the divine. By scrutinizing his myths and dreams he is given the opportunity to perceive and resolve moral problems. And so it is with other manifestations of the divine: they act upon him non-reciprocally, forcing him into this or that line of action so that immanent in the divine is a new moral order based on the self-same moral principles. But when access to the divine is used contrary to morality it is anomalous, rebellious, a usurpation of the divine, an attempt by a man to be himself divine, wholly self-willed.

It is possible that in the past there were rituals, now forgotten, which expressed a warmer and more intimate contact between Tangu and the divine. But it does not seem likely. And today, despite the contrary and melting influences of Christianity, and though their cargo activities pointedly suggest an attempt to come into a closer and more mutually sympathetic relationship with the divine, Tangu remain generally preoccupied in their day-to-day lives with the *ranguma*, the man who is *imbatekas*. Unlike other manifestations of the divine, and despite his self-will, he may be put under obligation and forced to surrender to the moral order by confession.

NOTES

[1] My thanks are due to the Australian National University under whose generous auspices field research was carried out in 1952.

[2] See Burridge (1957b).

[3] About 55% of Tangu are nominal Christians. Some have lapsed; others never had much to lapse from. Many pagans attend religious instruction at school, go to Mass, and adopt a variety of Christian usages without being baptized.

[4] See Burridge (1960).

[5] Work on this matter, which is circumstantial and contained in myths, is in progress.

[6] See Burridge (1957c).

[7] As between a pair of households *mngwotngwotiki* is explicit. As between groups of households the relationship is impracticable: exchanges would cease altogether.

[8] In the old days *ranguova* worked in gangs as well as singly.

[9] Or *'mbatekas*.

[10] The word for stranger is *rangama*, so like *ranguma* that it provides many opportunities for playing on either word at the expense of the other.

[11] See Burridge (1957a).

[12] *Brami* = eat, partake of. The word is used of eating food, drinking water, smoking, suckling from the breast.

[13] These chestnuts have close associations with *ranguova*, and when gathering them people take very careful anti-*ranguma* precautions.

[14] Confession to a kinsman implies a bias of interest. Confession to a friend or old man, both of whom are removed from the interplay of exchanges and reciprocities of the person concerned, is confession to a disinterested party.

[15] Rainfall is variable, irregular and, indeed, capricious—a feature which is probably due to the conformation of the country. Thunderstorms are fairly frequent; and so are minor earth tremors.

[16] Such boils are quite common.

[17] In a myth the founder (*angai'ek*) does participate in *br'ngun'guni* (see p. 243 below).

[18] This portion must be as necessarily vague as Tangu are. The position can be sharpened with access to Tangu myths but, as will be seen, the point is of small relevance here.

[19] A scrutiny of Tangu myths shows this to be probable.

[20] See footnote 17 above.

[21] Again, this feature is revealed in a scrutiny of Tangu myths.

[22] The pebbles are put into a bamboo barrel which is held tightly by two persons, arms outstretched in tension, by means of two crossed staves lashed to the barrel. The latter being delicately balanced, and the muscular tension extreme, any positive reaction of the holders to a direct question is likely to cause their arms to tremble and so rattle the stones in the barrel.

[23] Some men still live in Tangu who were cannibals. While they expatiate on the delicacy of human flesh and the satisfaction to be got from eating it, there is no hint that they hoped to absorb anything of the dead man's personality.

[24] See Burridge (1959b).

R. B. LANE

The Melanesians of South Pentecost, New Hebrides[1]

P ENTECOST is a narrow island about thirty miles long and five or six miles wide. The people whose religion is described here inhabit only its southern quarter. Although no part of their territory is distant from the sea, the primary orientation of the people is to the land. They are horticulturists depending on their crops, taro in particular, and upon products of the forest for their major sustenance. In pre-European times, the bulk of the population dwelt inland. Today most villages are near the sea.

The culture of the area was basically uniform with minor differences from village to village. Somewhat sharper contrasts distinguished the eastern villages from those of the west. The region is part of the Central New Hebrides culture area which has been described by Deacon, Layard and others. Northward on Pentecost, the cultures gradually change until in the far north contrasts in language, culture and physical type are major. South Pentecost is culturally more closely related to the island of Ambrym a few miles to the south than it is to North Pentecost.

In pre-European times—and to a certain extent today—South Pentecost was an end of the road. Main centres of cultural elaboration were on islands lying to the west and north. South-west Pentecost was subjected to cultural influences from the west via Ambrym and from the north via the west coast. By and large south-east Pentecost remained isolated and little influenced by the main streams of development elsewhere.

European contact began late in the eighteenth century and led to a rapid decline in population. Missionary activities commenced almost at the time of contact, but conversion to Christianity is not yet complete. The present population totals about 400 persons of whom 130 are non-Christians. The bulk of the latter live in four villages near the east coast. The non-Christian population consciously maintains a relatively unaltered aboriginal culture, albeit with reduced flourish owing to diminished population and to contact with Europeans. The materials considered in this study, unless otherwise specified, are drawn from an essentially functioning aboriginal culture.

The people of South Pentecost recognize no category of culture comparable to that which we label religion, nor do they have any institutions which are primarily religious. The phenomena dealt with here permeate much of the culture. I have abstracted those bodies of material which seem to me to be most related to what we conceive to be religion. By themselves these materials do not form a coherent system within the culture. However, I have deduced what appear to be logical underlying patterns. These patterns are in many ways speculative, but they provide a reasonable interpretation of the recorded data.

In the following presentation, I proceed from the general, covert and deduced framework to the particular and overt; from underlying principles through belief to observed practices. The reader is cautioned that a degree of orderliness appears as a characteristic of the analysis. It may be implicit in the system, but certainly it is not an explicit feature of the observed data.

I. WAYS OF THINKING

Melanesians have been called pragmatists and this characterization seems reasonable for the people of South Pentecost. In addition, I would stress their empirical outlook. At first glance, this appears to do injustice to the facts. There is no experimenting in the conventional sense. Tradition and convention are important in structuring the life of the individual and of the group. However, tradition and convention are guides rather than controls. They are not rigid boundaries forcing conformity. Their influence is always tempered by evidence accumulated by the individual via his own senses. One looks to the past for guidance, but not at the expense of the present.

Excluding the realms of ritual and ceremonial the individual is free to accept, reject or interpret information from all sources in the light of circumstance and personal inclination. Every event is a test of tradition and convention. Each bit of information received and each day's occurrences are experiments through which validity is checked. If this is the case, are not beliefs daily confounded? Within the native frame of reference, the apparent correlation between belief and reality is sufficiently close for few conflicts to arise and for discrepancies to be

R

easily rationalized. If each individual acts as critic and judge for himself, should we not expect wide variations in thought and behaviour? Variations exist but they do not override the collective unity of thought and opinion. The close similarities in background and experience of all members of the society restrict the range of variability.

In addition, while it is true that individuals analyse the available data and reach their own conclusions, they do so to a considerable extent as members of a collective: Analysis takes place in formal and informal group discussions. Individual conclusions are not necessarily disclosed in public and they may only become apparent through subsequent actions.

To understand this, let us consider the outlines of a specific example. W. was working alone in his garden. The work was routine and his thoughts were wandering. Suddenly he became conscious of having heard a strange whistling. It may have been a bird or it may have been imagination, but on the other hand spirit-beings often whistle. While considering these possibilities, his imagination already stimulated and his eyes and ears alert, he heard a crackling noise and saw or thought he saw something move away along a shadowy path from the garden. Now upset, he stopped work and returned to the village.

In the evening around the cooking fire in the communal men's house where every event of the day is brought forth, re-created, and dissected for the edification and pleasure of the group, he presented his experiences. As is usual, every variety of opinion was expressed, both pro- and anti-spirit-being. The discussion went on through most of the night. Similar incidents were recalled and reconsidered at length. Spirit-beings were discussed in detail. The ultimate consensus of opinion was that W. had actually had an encounter with a spirit-being. Private opinions, solicited subsequently, were much less uniform running from complete acceptance to complete rejection of the possibility.

The pertinent point is that W. did not come home and say that he had seen a spirit-being. He came home and described everything that had happened or that seemed to have happened and presumably reached his own decision only after hearing the public discussions of the evidence. In such discussions, through subtle interplay between speakers and audience, problems are worked out. Influenced by who is present, moods, and evidence, people arrive at their decisions. In the case cited above, public acceptance of the idea that a spirit-being had been seen (whether the majority privately concurred or not) gave the belief a certain dignity and it can be used as proof in supporting comparable past and future interpretations.

Each incident involves a judgement which predicates the course of future judgements. A body of similar decisions grows based on traditional criteria. As long as the facts of each new case are in accord with the beliefs thus formed, people tend to accept, not automatically, but as though each case were what in fact it is, a new case. Minor contradictions may be ignored as exceptions to the rule for the weight of past evidence is heavy. If evidence is consistently out of accord with traditional judgement, there is a good possibility that belief and practice are altered in consequence.

I have suggested that the individual is free to act on the basis of his own decisions. This is true providing only that the actions are not so atypical and anti-social as to be inimical to the group. Even if the latter should be the case, unless actual physical danger to the group were involved social pressure and social isolation are normally the only means of controlling non-conformity.

The beliefs which result are not developed in precise and systematic detail, nor are they woven into an overall scheme. Contradiction is of no concern. Only when belief is translated into ritual and ceremony do organization and precision predominate.

2. BASIC BELIEFS

(a) Animate versus inanimate

Two native terms *mir* and *maet* may serve to classify all things, although the people themselves are not normally concerned with such classification. Interest tends to focus on the specific rather than the generic. These two terms are usually translated as 'living' and 'dead' respectively, although a more accurate rendition might be 'animate' and 'inanimate', since included as *mir* are not only things which we class as living but also things which seem to exhibit characteristics of life or which are assumed to have been alive at one time. In native thought almost anything can be animate and nothing is irrevocably animate or inanimate.[2]

The basic criterion of animateness is an appearance of volition and of independent movement, although this characteristic does not of itself ensure that any particular thing possessing it will be considered animate. Animals, including man, and plants are usually considered animate. Inorganic things and natural phenomena such as stones, water and winds are not ordinarily thought of as animate but may be so considered under special and fairly common circumstances. A stone which rolled down a hillside might or might not be considered animate. If it struck someone or something in its descent both independent movement and volition might be inferred and the stone regarded as animate. Alternatively, if it were suspected that a spirit-being had propelled the stone no assumption of animateness would accrue.

An immobile but unusual stone which is unlike others in the vicinity is assumed to have moved to its present location from elsewhere. Therefore, it was once animate, perhaps a spirit-being or a human being, and may still be animate. Myths are commonly associated with such stones.

A human corpse is considered animate as long as it or parts of it continue to exist in recognizable form. The recognizable form may be material (a body) or non-material (a ghost or spirit-being). This helps to explain why skulls are preserved, and slivers of human bone used as 'poison' arrow points are considered potent.

The seas on the east (windward) and west (leeward) coasts of the island are respectively animate and inanimate for the eastern sea is always turbulent and dangerous whereas the western sea is usually quiet and safe. Thus it seems that things are animate which particularly activate the human mind and senses. The falling stone demands alertness. The unusual stone stimulates thought. The earthquake and landslide arouse fear. In effect those things which animate people are animate. The condition of animateness depends upon human recognition. Considering this, it is not surprising that things are not classified in a hard and fast way and that there is confusion and vagueness. The act and fact of classification depend upon circumstances. A ghost is animate only so long as it is recognized or remembered. It does not die; it simply ceases to exist as a factor in the affairs of human beings. Animals and plants which are insignificant in the lives of men are not thought of as either animate or inanimate.

There is no clear and simple answer to the question of what causes motion and volition. Fire and heat are certainly associated with animateness in the minds of the people, but it would be going beyond the evidence to assign to these a causative role. The people of south Pentecost are simply not concerned with precise relations and explanations.

(b) The soul

Every human being has a soul, but ideas regarding its nature are not clearly formulated. There is a connexion between soul, shadow and reflection, all being *manun* or *nunun*.[3] The shadow and reflection are related to the soul, but are not equated with it. The soul is most often described as an amorphous image of the exterior body. There is disagreement as to when the soul enters the body. This difference of opinion may reflect Christian influence, since Christian and younger non-Christian informants claim that it is in the body at birth, whereas older informants claim that it is acquired after birth. Assuming that the latter idea is the aboriginal belief and since the soul can leave the body during life, it seems reasonable to say that the soul maintains rather than activates life. An extended absence of the soul causes unconsciousness or insanity. According to those informants who believe that the soul enters the body after birth, the entrance takes place at about the time when the infant can be said to be developing an independent personality. In general, the South Pentecost concept of the soul incorporates much that we include within the concept of personality. In addition, there may be a belief in a second soul, but information about this is very vague.

There is uncertainty regarding the derivation of the soul. In some cases the soul is that of an ancestor. Such reincarnations may be recognized because the individual exhibits physical or mental traits like those of the ancestor. When an infant cries incessantly, it is assumed to be a reincarnation. The parents name ancestors until the infant hears his original name and ceases to cry. That name is then given to him again. In other cases the fact of reincarnation never becomes evident.

There is no agreement as to whether animals other than man have souls. Many informants believe that pigs may have souls. The pig is the most important animal on South Pentecost and lives in a symbiotic relationship with man. Pigs share the household dwellings, the daily food, are made pets of, and are crucial on all ceremonial and ritual occasions. In the New Hebrides no other animal is so endowed by nature and by man with personality. In view of this it is not surprising that they are sometimes considered to have souls.

(c) Death

The explanation of death, beyond such immediately apparent causes as sorcery, attack by spirit-beings, illness, old age, accident

and the like, is absence of sufficient power to maintain an overtly
animate state. When a person dies the event is usually ascribed to an
attack by a sorcerer or a spirit-being. If the victim has not sufficient
power to ward off the attack, or if his power is circumvented, death
results. Overtly it appears that the victim has died of illness, of old
age, by accident or from a variety of other causes. If a man is killed
in a fight, the same reasoning prevails. It is recognized that he
died of injuries received in the fight, but had he had sufficient power
with which to defend himself, the injuries would not have been
fatal.

Nearly all deaths are explained within this framework, but there are
a few exceptions. Suicide, an accepted means of escaping unbearable sorrows or suffering, is self-determined. Further, malaria and
various diseases of the respiratory system are regarded as due to over-
exposure to sun and rain, and death from them is considered to be
'natural'.

If a person appears to be near death, his friends and relatives gather
around him in order to protect him from spirit-beings and sorcerers
who may be responsible for his condition. Even if the latter are not
involved initially, they may take advantage of a situation in which
there is a potential victim whose powers are weakened or who is too
distraught to defend himself. The presence of the noisy crowd frightens
away spirit-beings and sorcerers who prefer to attack in solitude. In
addition, the collective power or vitality of the group is thought to
sustain the patient. The crowd remains either until the crisis is passed
and the patient is on his way to recovery or until death occurs. After
death the soul, particularly if it remains in or returns to this world, is
called *aramaet*, a 'ghost'.

(d) Power

One of the central concepts in South Pentecost thought is the notion
of power. Just as weakened power invites death, so all successes and
importance in life are attributed to adequacy or abundance of power.[4]
This is an intangible metaphysical energy which enables an individual
to perform in superior or unusual ways. It is a quality or attribute
whose presence is necessary for success and the presence of which
is attested by success. An abundance of power is not an assurance of
success, but it is a necessary prerequisite—a complement to human
effort. Power is impersonal and amoral and if incorrectly or carelessly
handled it is dangerous to the possessor. It appears that it is generated

rather than tapped. It is not all-pervading nor does it have any continued existence apart from its sources.

Power, as an energy which can be generated, is closely associated with heat. Articles impregnated with power are often stored where heat will reach them (as in the roof thatch directly over a cooking fire) so as to preserve and increase their potency. Power is often activated by holding the object from which it emanates close to a fire or by rubbing the object until it is warm. The superior quality of Ambrym sorcery is attributed to the presence of an active volcano on that island. While power can be generated, it cannot be created from nothing. It must be possessed before it can be increased, or perhaps more correctly, before it can be made increasingly potent.

Power is usually concentrated in charms which are used for specific purposes. A spiral shell owned by the crab sib* may be rubbed on the tusk of a boar to ensure that the tusk will circle properly. A bone relic kept by the yam sib is placed in a special garden to ensure a bountiful yam crop. In addition to their specific uses, the charms generate a general aura of power in accordance with their nature. For the most part this emanation is positive, promoting well-being, fertility, and peace.

The term *mana* is unknown in South Pentecost and no single term in the language refers to a unified concept of power. In general, the term *loas* seems to apply to power which one has by virtue of sib membership. It is power bequeathed to members by the founding ancestors. The corporate nature of sib power is seen in intersib competitions which take the form of trying to outstrip or thwart one's rivals. If one group is giving a feast, it is taken as read that a rival group will try to interrupt the occasion by such tactics as making rain.

Bivari is the term employed for power acquired by an individual and used primarily for his own benefit. This power may be acquired from a spirit-being in the following manner. A man alone in the forest is accosted by a spirit-being which usually appears in animal form. The man falls unconscious and while he is in this state the spirit-being either bestows power on him or arranges for a subsequent meeting in the man's home. In the latter event, the man recovers, returns home, purifies himself and arranges for privacy at the appointed time. This time the spirit-being appears in human form and explains its nature and capabilities and the ways in which the man may exploit

* In this symposium, the terms *sib* and *clan* may be regarded as synonymous—Editors' Note.

these. It instructs the recipient in ritual, incantations and songs and directs him to the spot where he will find the charm containing the power he is to receive. Some men contact their tutelary spirit-being at will; others never see them after the initial encounter.

The original encounter with a spirit-being is usually a matter of chance. Deliberate questing in lonely places is unusual, for a meeting with a spirit is as likely to bring injury or death as benefits. Despite the attractions of individual power, few men are willing to risk a deliberate encounter.

Although the power acquired always has a degree of general utility it is usually employed for specific purposes. The use correlates with the animal form of the spirit-being. Thus, according to native belief, power derived from pigs and snakes assures success in the graded society and in making and preserving peace. Eels bestow power for success in pig-breeding and in raising tusked boars.

Individual power is given in perpetuity. Upon the recipient's death, his eldest son ordinarily inherits the charm with its attendant power. Use of the power can be sold to anyone. This transfer involves preparing coconut milk and at the same time going through the motions of 'grating' and 'milking' the charm. The power 'extracted' is mixed with the coconut milk. This mixture is rubbed over the body of the purchaser and over any equipment that the latter intends to use in conjunction with the power. This transfer of power in no way reduces the potency of the original charm.

(e) Sacredness

Power implies also a sense of 'forbidden', 'dangerous', and 'sacred' ideas which I will subsume under the last-named term. The precise relationships between power and sacredness are not clear to me. The commonest designation for sacredness is *kon* which also denotes hardness, strength, tribulation and masculinity. A participant in a ritual or a man of high rank in the graded society is *kon*. A tabooed tree or a sacred spot is *kon*. The term is used in reduplicated form, *konkon*, to refer to saltiness or bitterness. Salt water is an important ingredient in ritual and consecration. It is used to exorcise and to sanctify a new dwelling. Suffering may be a prerequisite to sacredness as when the body is whipped with stinging nettles in an initiation. Things which are *kon* are dangerous, forbidden, and to be approached with caution. They are to be avoided by the unsanctioned, the un-initiated and the untutored.

(f) Sex and sex symbolism

Another series of attributes, virility-sexuality-fertility, is also related to power. The term most frequently used to describe them is *bwari*, one of the terms for power. *Bwari* is primarily a masculine trait, active rather than passive. This accords with the cultural convention that power is primarily associated with men rather than with women.

Sexual symbolism is a major feature of the culture. There is little if anything in the native scheme which is not classified by sex. Ocean and sky are male; the earth female. The soils of the east coast are male because they are relatively hard and dry whereas the softer, moister soils of the west coast are considered to be female. The sun is masculine; the moon feminine. Yams are male and taros female. Bows and arrows are male; baskets female. Hardness, angularity and penetration are male characteristics; while softness, roundness and receptivity are feminine. The parts of artefacts are commonly designated by terms for sex organs. Thus the handle of a canoe bailer or a paddle is called a penis and these are frequently carved in detail to show circumcision and testicles. Ceremonial clubs are similarly embellished. Economic activities such as gardening are likewise viewed in sexual terms. Women fill the holes in which tubers are planted but men wield the digging sticks because the act of jabbing them into the ground is metaphorically viewed as sexual penetration.

The people are concerned with sex symbolism because it is a concomitant to fertility. Amusement and pleasure are derived from this symbolism as in *leng* dances when men impersonate women and wear half coconut shells representing breasts. Nevertheless, personal sex life is not a topic for casual conversation because as an aspect of power it is treated circumspectly. Despite their intimate relationship, sexual activity profanes power in ritual and ceremonial contexts and is forbidden at such times.

(g) Magic and ritual

Gurian includes beliefs and practices which we would call magic. In addition much, if not all, ritual can be subsumed under this term. *Gurian* involves recitation of formulae and performances of acts in specific sequences in order to influence such diverse phenomena as weather, crops, and love. Objects as a source of power may be involved in ritual. Both imitative and contagious techniques are employed. Success depends upon accuracy of performance, the power of the practitioner, the power of the subject and deliberate or accidental interference by extraneous forces such as spirit-beings or active power in the vicinity.

Gurian may be utilized in a wide variety of activities and everyone has some practical knowledge of the techniques. Individuals who know more *gurian* and possess greater power acquire a semi-professional status as ritualists and sorcerers.

(h) Sorcery

Sorcery, *mlinik*, is distinguished from other forms of *gurian* mainly in the intent to injure. Christians and non-Christians in the area still believe in the efficacy of sorcery. It is commonly thought that the practice is not so widespread today as in the past because of the sudden deaths of sorcerers in epidemics before they passed on their knowledge to others. At the same time, new techniques have diffused from neighbouring islands with the breakdown of aboriginal barriers to travel and this complicates the problem of defence against sorcery.

The techniques involve pointing, burying charms in paths, and manipulating human refuse. Pointing may be accomplished with a human bone arrow point, sometimes also with a miniature bow. The point is drawn back four times while directed toward the victim and an incantation is uttered: '(name of victim), may the ghost of the man whose bone this is destroy you'. Fever and death are thought to result. A variant technique requiring a more skilled performer with greater powers utilizes neither arrow point nor bow. The sorcerer concentrates power in his fingernail which is thrust toward the victim four times. This is a particularly dangerous practice for should the sorcerer accidentally touch himself with his charged fingernail he would die.

Another type of sorcery required the aid of an accomplice. The practitioner carried a power-charged object between his teeth or in a small basket. His aide preceded him as a scout to drive all living things from the path or failing that, to warn off the sorcerer, for the power carried by the latter would enter the first living thing it encountered. Once in the vicinity of the victim, the power-charged object was shaken four times in his direction and the power was thus discharged.

Some sorcerers are shape-shifters, *abile*, who rape women, steal children and otherwise harass or injure people. Sorcerers' cults, one feature of which is shape-shifting, are said to occur on Ambrym where they are known as *bwile*. A secret society complex recently introduced to South-west Pentecost is called *nabwil*, but informants deny that shape-shifting is associated with *nabwil*. The trait evidently predates this complex in South Pentecost.

Sorcery techniques, like other forms of *gurian*, are acquired by inheritance or purchase. Some persons inherit techniques but refrain from using them because they are not disposed to practice sorcery, whereas other men avidly seek to acquire such knowledge. The former are in a difficult position because it is practically impossible to keep such abilities secret, and pressures to use them are placed upon these persons by others in the community. At first these may be only for legitimate ends, as in punishment or elimination of wrongdoers in the community or against enemies of the community, but corrupting temptations are great and unprincipled use often follows. Once a person indulges in sorcery, involvement in counter-attacks and feuds results.

Sorcery is viewed with mixed feelings. While many informants profess disapproval, they also recognize it as a means of effecting social control within the community and as an integral part of defences against aggression from outside. In a very real sense, fear of retaliation through sorcery serves to inhibit overt hostile acts. There is a paradox which is more apparent than real in that some informants attribute the supposed current decline in sorcery to the virtual cessation of inter-group and inter-personal physical conflict. To the enthnographer it is a moot question whether sorcery has increased or decreased with the advent of European administrative control.

There have always been deterrents to sorcery. Fear of sorcerers is not and presumably never has been universal. There are accounts of men who coped with sorcerers by direct physical retaliation. People recognize that sorcery is not inevitably effective but depends in part upon the state of mind and the power of the intended victim. There is always the possibility that an intended victim is an unwilling heir of magical techniques heretofore concealed and thus able to ward off the power and direct it against the attacker. Should such counter-sorcery or an accident interrupt a practitioner, the power involved would rebound and destroy him.

Anyone may become a sorcerer, although motivation varies enormously. Some people are vicious and wilfully malevolent; others attempt to use their dangerous powers for the benefit of kin and community. The danger lies in the fact that once a sorcerer becomes accustomed to inflicting injury, however worthy his motives, the temptation grows to injure at the slightest provocation, or perhaps with none at all. Native views on this subject, although they may appear somewhat self-contradictory, are not beyond our understanding. Power in the hands of well-intentioned people may be useful, but power tends to corrupt.

The dangers of perversion do not lie only in the corrupting influence of power. In one tale a sorcerer while attempting to locate his victim encountered his own daughter by chance and accidentally discharged the power, thereby killing her. As a result of this tragedy he became embittered and totally malicious.

Power both attracts and repels its practitioners. In discussing sorcery, almost everyone grants benefits and deplores excesses. Individuals see more of one or the other, probably depending upon whether they consider themselves to be beneficiaries or victims of sorcery.

In theory, sorcery was directed toward individuals who were not members of one's own sib or village. In fact, actual personal relationships were more of a force in determining victims than formal relationships. Although they were considered improper, attacks both within the sib and within the village were known.

(i) Existential belief

The assumptions which the people make about their total environment are embodied in explanatory myths which deal with the origins and behaviour of material and non-material phenomena of marvellous character. The myths are cited as authority for belief and practice in both secular and sacred realms. In one sense they are in the public domain and everyone has some knowledge of these myths. On another level, certain myths are the private property of individual sibs and theoretically there exists a proper and complete form which is never divulged to non-sib members. This secrecy is due to the assumed potency of words and specific combinations of words as receptacles of power.

The myths, discrete and often contradictory, provide no coherent or unified framework of belief. This is hardly surprising in view of their semi-private nature and the discrepancies disturb no one. The past is divided into various eras of existence but these are not neatly arranged in chronological sequence. The historical past extending indefinitely to cover the period of human existence merges and overlaps with an era of 'time belong story', an aoristic period with events but without historical continuity.

There are no cosmic origin myths. Aboriginal belief commences with the cosmos fully formed and consisting of three parts, the sky world, this world and the underworld. Little is known of the sky world and it is not important to human beings. Some of the culture heroes came from there and some of them have returned there.

The underworld is the land of the dead. Despite its importance to human beings it is not much better known than the sky world. The underworld is definitely under the sea and perhaps also under the land. It is entered through a rock in the sea off the southern tip of the island. A male ogre symbolically associated with spiders guards the entrance to the underworld, challenging and testing all ghosts who try to pass into this realm. Should they fail in the tests, they are devoured by the ogre.

There is little knowledge of or concern with the nature of life in the underworld. It is evidently much as in this world, neither very good nor very bad.

Prior to European contact, the real world of the people of South Pentecost was limited to the places visible from their own hills and beaches. Clockwise from south to north the islands of Lopevi, Ambrym, Malekula and Aoba can be seen. Of these only Ambrym, about nine miles distant, was really known. The other visible islands were for the most part simply outlines on the horizons.

The ocean is believed to be flat and dotted with islands. It is thought that islands beyond the horizon cannot ordinarily be seen because, although the ocean is flat, the islands are concealed by constantly surging waves.

Originally there were no seas and no islands, only dry land. According to a sib myth, a woman working in her garden left her children near their house warning them not to touch a particular taro plant. The children became hot while playing and tried to pull leaves from the forbidden taro to use as umbrellas. Instead, they pulled up the whole plant. Water poured from the hole where the plant had been. It rapidly covered the lower lands until only the mountain tops remained to become the present islands.

For practical purposes the world of the individual was restricted to his own and immediately adjacent districts. Unless a person had specific friends or kin to go to, he did not venture lightly beyond his own territory. The treachery of strangers and the dangers of magical and physical attack were taken for granted. The only overseas travel was for trade southward to Ambrym where there were sibmates and northward along Pentecost for trading and raiding. Places beyond were as far from everyday reality as the sky world.

(j) Spirit-beings

Spirit-beings are timeless phenomena. They are not frequently met with, although they may appear anywhere and are believed to be fairly numerous. In all important activities rituals are performed to drive out or ward off spirit-beings. This routine precaution does not imply the presence of spirit-beings in the locality, but merely a recognition of this possibility.

The reader may wish for more precise judgements regarding native belief as to the prevalence of spirit-beings, but greater precision would be spurious. One informant may see or sense spirit-beings behind every tree, while another may accept them as a reality but deny every claimed confrontation. One person may claim frequent confrontations, whereas another may know of encounters only as hearsay. No one denies the existence of spirit-beings, but their nature and characteristics preclude any agreement as to numbers.

Spirit-beings are sentient beings capable of assuming many forms which may be either material or non-material. In character and behaviour they are not remarkably different from human beings except that they are less likely to reflect emotions. Also, they have great supernatural powers and not being bound by the natural conditions that circumscribe human beings, they are more likely to act dangerously, harmfully and maliciously.

In a casual way, spirit-beings are categorized. The most common type are *armat en sanga*. They are light coloured and incorporeal and are usually encountered in lonely places. They may assume human form and seduce people, death resulting from such encounters.

Another type, perhaps as common but more malicious than deadly, are *lipsipsip*, dwarfs who dwell in trees and in stones. Usually they ignore human beings, but if offended they may cause injury to people or to their belongings. They are cannibalistic and if sufficiently aroused or hungry will kill and devour human beings.

Ghosts are conceptually spirit-beings especially when they remain, as some do, in this world. The line between human beings and spirit-beings becomes blurred at some points. A man of highest rank in the graded society transcends human limitations and could as well be classed as a spirit-being. A sorcerer with shape-shifting abilities is not far removed from a supernatural being.

(k) Culture heroes

In the beginning there were no men. A coconut tree in the sky world gave birth to Barkulkul, the major culture hero, and to his five brothers, the most important of whom was Marelul. The brothers descended to earth and settled at Revrion on the south-east coast. The site is now sacred and no gardens are planted there.

The brothers lived together in a communal men's house for there were no women. One day Barkulkul threw a roasted fruit at one of his brothers striking him on the penis. When the brother pulled the fruit off, his penis came off with it and he became the first woman.

The woman established a separate dwelling house and each of the remaining brothers visited her in turn to borrow fire, water and wood for use in the men's house. She addressed each of them by a different kinship term (for example, father, brother, mother's brother) until at last Barkulkul arrived and she addressed him as husband. They became man and wife and set up a separate household.

One day Barkulkul decided to visit Ambrym. Before leaving he placed a string figure over his wife's vagina by affixing the outer loops around her thighs. When he departed, his brother Marelul shot an arrow which penetrated the thatch roof of Barkulkul's dwelling house. On her invitation, Marelul entered to retrieve his arrow and had intercouse with Barkulkul's wife. In replacing the string figure Marelul and the woman inadvertently reversed the design. Upon his return from Ambrym Barkulkul noted that the design had been disarranged and questioned his wife. She explained that she had removed it to relieve herself. Barkulkul was not satisfied and that evening in the men's house he proposed to his brothers that they all make sand tracings in the ashes of the fire. Marelul alone produced the design represented in the string figure. The next day Barkulkul invited Marelul to accompany him on a trip, and tricked and killed him.

In five days Marelul was resurrected but the others could not stand the odour of decay which emanated from him. Their reactions angered Marelul so that he decided to return to the sky world and everlasting life. Barkulkul and some of the others accompanied him. Those who remained lost the powers of eternal life and became the ancestors of human beings. Some informants believe that instead of going directly to the sky world, Barkulkul travelled first to other islands. When Europeans first arrived there was an initial but soon discarded idea that they were returning culture heroes. Some of the favourable reactions to Americans during World War II stemmed from the fact that their convoys arrived from the north-east, the direction in which Barkulkul had departed. Most informants believe that Barkulkul is now in the sky world where he is a passive observer of mankind.

In addition to myths associating Barkulkul and his brothers with the origins of woman, the kinship system, adultery, death and numerous features of the local landscape, accounts concerning the activities of various sib ancestors must be included in any consideration of culture heroes.

One sib traces its origin to a man who fell from the sky world through a hole while he was catching crickets to be used in a bird trap. He fell on the dance plaza of a village and his container of crickets was knocked from his hand and shattered. Before this time there had been no crickets on earth and, as a corollary, no night. People had had to work all the time with no rest. The escaped crickets began to sing and this produced night. The stranger remained for a while, married, and sired offspring who were the first members of this sib. He then returned to the sky world.

The ancestor of the pig sib is responsible for the origin of this animal, which is the largest native mammal and of utmost importance in both native economy and ceremonial. The original myth of the pig sib relates that the ancestor was climbing a tree when the rough bark splintered against his testicles causing them to swell. He rested at home but they continued to swell. He instructed his relatives to place stakes in the ground and to affix ropes to these. His testicles grew larger and larger until they eventually burst. Out of each testical ran five pigs, each of a different description. Several of the pigs were caught and secured to the stakes; the rest escaped and swam away to other islands. This story is thought to explain the origin and distribution of various strains of native pigs in the New Hebrides.

The culture heroes were essentially human but they differed from modern human beings in virtue of their complete possession and control of such attributes as power, sacredness and virility. For this reason they had capabilities far beyond those of modern men. These culture heroes did not make the world although they did shape parts of its surface and some of its superficial features. In addition they were responsible for various aspects of human life, society and culture. Those who did not become ancestors of human beings departed long ago and ceased to be involved in earthly affairs. They are not sanctified nor is any great concern devoted to them.

3. PIGS

Pigs are the supreme objects of sacrifice and are important in all major ceremonial and ritual contexts. South Pentecost is part of the larger New Hebridean area in which boars are artificially treated in order to produce circling tusks. The upper canines of the boar are removed to allow the lower canines to grow unimpeded in a circle. The circling tusk, though much admired and predicating the value of the boar, was not so important as in other areas. Size and quality of the animal were also valued. The native attitude is well expressed in the Pidgin remark, 'Tooth he good, but man he no kai kai tooth'. (The tusk is fine but one can't eat it.) As a result of this attitude, boars were rarely allowed to live beyond the first circling.

After the pig is sacrificed, the tusks have little value except as ornaments and they are retained for this purpose by the sacrificer.[5] The person to whom a sacrificed pig has been dedicated displays a cycas palm leaf in his *mal* (communal men's house) where it remains for several years. It is a visible symbol of his close relationship with the sacrificer and a reminder of his obligation to make a return sacrifice at some later date.

It is difficult to determine precisely the inner meanings of the sacrifice of pigs. The pig represents both power and fertility. The claim made by Layard that the sacrificer and the sacrificed pig merge and share identity is undoubtedly justified, as is his suggestion that the pig is the symbol of the sacrificer and that a metaphysical drama of death and rebirth is involved.[6]

One result of this identification is that the power and fertility of the sacrificed pig accrue to the sacrificer and to the person to whom the animal is dedicated. When a pig is dedicated to a living or dead person and sacrificed at a graded society performance, a bit of food is fed to the sacrificer and a bit of the same food is fed to the pig. The meaning of this procedure is clarified by reference to the way in which a special formal friendship is instituted between two men. Each cooks food and in turn places some of his food in his own mouth and then places another bit in the mouth of the other man. Such friends are from that point considered brothers and would never fight or injure one another.

The economic aspects of the sacrifice are important. Pigs are of the utmost value. A large amount of time, effort and resources goes into their breeding and maintenance. Their sacrifice is literally a sacrifice of a significant part of the donor's life. The sacrifice of the pig is a voluntary resignation of something of great value to honour those to

S

whom the animal is dedicated. The flesh of the sacrifice nourishes the recipient and its non-material counterpart nourishes the ghosts of the recipient's sib. This nourishment is in part a matter of actual food with its accompanying spiritual attributes of power and vitality, but it is also nourishment in the sense that the sacrifice preserves the memory of the living and deceased recipients.

4. SIB AND LAND

Society consists of sibs, villages, an indefinite surrounding world of known extra-local kin and apart from these, strangers who were always potentially dangerous and viewed with suspicion. The sibs have an eternal existence independent of presently existing personnel and they are inseparable from the land and the environment. The fiction is that however few the living members may be, a sib never dies out. A few members always survive to perpetuate it. With the disastrous losses of population due to European contact, many sibs are reduced to a few last survivors and a subtle process of salvage may be observed involving transfer of personnel, equation of related sibs and reinterpretation of independent existence. The people are thus able to maintain their credo in the face of an apparently obvious loss of particular sibs.

Through gardens and natural products the land sustains the people and thus the sibs and the people in turn must maintain the land. The responsibilities of land and people are reciprocal and this view is accompanied by deep emotional attachments similar to those which have been observed elsewhere in Melanesia. Gardening is not only a means of obtaining food, but a satisfying end in itself. The specific origins of sibs lie in miraculous births from culture heroes, spirit-beings, plants or animals all intimately associated with or products of the land. Sibs are known by two names, one indicating the totemic affiliation and the other the locality of origin. The local name is the one ordinarily employed. Some sibs stem from the sea and some originated on Ambrym but each of these nevertheless is bound to a particular locality on South Pentecost by strands of mythological association.

The yam sib ancestor is credited with the origin of the tuber which figures in all ceremonial and upon whose cultivation the native calendar is based. According to the origin myth the ancestor of the yam people was paring his nails one day when he tasted one of the parings and found it to his liking. He instructed his relatives to dis-member his body when he died and to bury the parts in a garden which they were to prepare. He told them how to arrange stick supports for the vines which would grow from his remains. When he died they followed his instructions. The remains which they planted took root and grew, becoming the first yams. They varied in shape and consistency according to the part of the ancestor's anatomy from which they developed. Long hard yams are supposed to have developed from the long bones of the legs and arms, and short, round, soft yams from the heart and entrails; while certain stubby yams with protuberances resembling a fist with fingers are said to have originated from the ancestor's hand.

From the sibs come the bulk of power, ritual, and knowledge which enables their members to survive and to thrive. The yam sib controls magic which promotes the growth of this tuber, the pig sib possesses knowledge about pig-breeding and these powers and techniques may be used for the benefit of non-sib members as well. The sib is a network of people inextricably bound together by common origin, common interest, and by a common dedication to the idea that the sib rather than the individual is the important and meaningful reality. Its human personnel consist of the living, the dead and the as yet unborn. As long as the sib survives, the individual is in a metaphysical sense immortal. Life is only one phase of sib existence and all members living and dead have mutual responsibilities. Children are born, grow to adulthood, become elders, ultimately die and become ancestors. Some of these become at least for a time earthly ghosts or spirit-beings. Others enter the land of the dead and are ultimately forgotten. Still others are reincarnated and the cycle continues. At least for those who are reincarnated, life and death are not two distinctly different things but are parts of a never-ending cycle. Persons who are reincarnated are unusually important people for they embody prestige and experience beyond that gained in a single earthly existence.

5. LO SAL

The discussion of sibs may serve to introduce one of the important institutions of South Pentecost culture, the rites of *lo sal*. These rites, the name of which may be translated as 'the way' or 'the path', have been interpreted by Tattevin as ancestor worship, a cult of the dead.[7] Although partially correct, this is a limited and somewhat misleading view.

The rites consist, for a man, of sacrifices of pigs and presentation of gifts or payments on public and ritual occasions to members of his mother's sib and the sib of his wife. Throughout his life a man presents mats and pigs to his mother's brothers. From the time of his engagement until the birth of his first child, he periodically makes gifts of pigs and mats to his wife's parents. After the birth of his child, a man gives pigs and mats to his wife's brothers, the mother's brothers of the child, thus starting a new cycle which the child will continue throughout his lifetime. When the man dies, his son periodically gives pigs to the mother's brothers of the deceased. Thus, when the son is immature the father provides the necessary gifts to the mother's brothers of the child. When the father is deceased the son reciprocates by providing sacrifices to the mother's brothers of the father.

The natives assign specific reasons to the various exchanges in these cycles. Thus a man makes gifts to his wife's kinsmen in order to recompense her sib for the labour she expends in bearing and caring for his offspring. In our terms the payment to the woman's sibmates can be interpreted as validating the patrisib affiliation of the child. When a son provides pigs to his deceased father's maternal uncles, he says he does it to ensure that the soul of his father safely reaches the land of the dead and remains there. He enlists the aid of deceased members of his wife's sib to secure entrance to the land of the dead for a member of his own sib.

This pattern of obligatory gift-giving and payments may be regarded first and foremost as a means of cementing and maintaining relationships with those kin who are not sibmates but whose aid and support are vital. These are, in effect, one's village mates and extralocal kin, almost the totality of local society.

Whether the offerings are to specific living or dead individuals, they are always offered to these individuals as representatives of their sibmates living and dead. Informants say that fulfilment of these obligations 'makes the way smooth' and this is probably the essence of *lo sal*, the smoothing of the path in intersib relations in both sacred and profane life.

6. GRADED SOCIETY

The graded society, *warsangul*, is the key ceremonial institution of South Pentecost. It is the overt framework which serves as the public focal point for the various beliefs and practices considered here. Power, virility, the aid of supernatural beings—all of these elements are necessary adjuncts for all human activities, but it is in the activities of the graded society that they find culminating purpose. The graded society has been described by many students of New Hebrides culture and that of South Pentecost is essentially the same in pattern as that of adjacent areas.[8] There is a series of grades through which a man advances by means of payments, sacrifices, and the performance of ritual acts. The grades are progressively more difficult to achieve and each successive one is characterized by more complex ritual and by greater obligations and duties and also by greater privileges and prerogatives.

The grade-taking is done at public ceremonials sponsored by the candidate and his kin. The ceremonial includes dancing and feasting in which all the candidate's village mates and guests from surrounding villages join. The names of the grades vary somewhat from place to place as do the number of grades. Today there are ten grades. Some of these have subdivisions which must be taken separately and some grades may be repeated several times before a higher rank is reached.

Associated with the men's graded society is a less elaborate women's graded society. There are three basic grades with subdivisions and each of the grades may be repeated at different times in different ways. The taking of these women's grades is sometimes linked with the achievements in the men's society by a woman's son or husband.

The graded society is not a 'society' in the sense of a formal corporation or association having definite functions, nor does it ever act, except incidentally, as a unit with specific aims. The most important feature of the grades is that they define a person's rank in the total society. The rise is portrayed symbolically for men in the ceremonial passage through the *mal* (communal men's house). There are four fireplaces in the *mal* and, although the ceremony of grade-taking is the spectacular and materially expensive phase of the progress, the successive purchases of the rights to use the fireplaces are the more significant steps. When the right to use the fourth fireplace is purchased, the candidate kindles a new fire on the hearth. Layard has commented briefly on the significance of fire in the religious life of the New Hebrides and in the graded society, pointing out its sacred importance and its symbolic association with power and life.[9] My information supports his suggestions. As noted previously, fire is definitely related to life and power in South Pentecost. In the rekindling of the fourth fire there is a symbolic association with 'rebirth' or with a transition to a new state of existence. The rekindling of the fourth fire serves to mark a man's completion of grade-taking. Such a man has transcended earthly existence. He is a living ancestor. A person of the highest rank is in many ways freer from restrictions than others for he is not bound by the rules regulating the conduct of ordinary mortals. He can ignore day-to-day restrictions which bind others. The same situation obtains for a woman of the highest rank.

The progression through the ranks of the graded society which is a measure of a man's achievement is equated with the attainment of height. This symbolism is quite clear in the higher grades. In these the key acts are the ascent of a ladder, first on the sacred hillock at the edge of the dance plaza, then alongside the *mal*, then by the side of a dwelling house, and ultimately ascent from the ladder to the roof of the *mal* where the rank-taker stands alone above the heads of all the assembled people completely divorced from the ground. Such a person has been elevated by his own efforts and by the support of his kin until he stands on the peak of the sacred structure. There is no greater height to achieve. Appropriately the term for the completion of rank-seeking is *tan manok*, ground/finished.

It should be emphasized that this elevation of the individual is not solely his own glory. Indeed, excessive personal ambition and competitiveness are considered undesirable. Rather, the individual is a representative of his sib; it is only through the support of his sibmates that his achievement is possible. His climb has lifted his sib to a position of greater power and prestige. This is the ultimate success to which men aspire.

The effects of this success extend beyond the sib. The individual's success enables his wife, and in certain circumstances his mother, to achieve higher ranks and thus bring prestige to their sibs. It also engenders mutually profitable exchanges with the wife's sib and that of the mother. Ultimately it is an achievement reflecting upon the whole area, for individuals, sibs, villages, neighbourhoods—all contribute to the success of their high-ranking men. Their co-operation in these efforts serves to bind them together and to strengthen the unity of groups in a society in which, apart from kinship bonds, the cohesive ties are few.

Although it is not in accord with the ideals of the graded society, competition is one of its by-products and may produce discord and strife. Jealousies are aroused among competitors and a successful person is a natural target for sorcery or, very rarely, physical attack. Competition and discord are at least partially controlled by the fact that one of the graded society's important underlying ideas is peace.

The elaborate economic preparations for performances are most efficiently made in a peaceful environment. Fighting is tabooed during a performance and during the sacred period following it, and this taboo is respected by all. This is in part because of ritual sanctions and in part because the society is universal. The totality of ranks is a series of brotherhoods, the highest of which in particular have common interests cutting across local group boundaries. As a man rises in rank, he ordinarily becomes more preoccupied with peace and more of a force in efforts to prevent and settle fights. A very high man does not participate in combat and his person is usually safe from physical attack. This is partly because of his sacred nature and his great power and partly because he is actively concerned with maintaining the long periods of peace necessary for the performance of the rites and ceremonials of the higher ranks.

It can be seen that the graded society is an important factor in social and political control in the total society. For the latter, it is essentially the only mechanism for that purpose. Political organization is weak and nebulous in South Pentecost. In theory, in any village all initiated males have a say in any decision affecting the group. However, within the general framework of equality, seniority is influential. The components of seniority are age, experience and power, the combination of which inevitably adds up to high rank in the graded society. The expression of this influence is a potential and there is great individual variation in its use. Some high men openly exercise their authority but most wear a cloak of humility and dignified preoccupation, their concern being ideally devoted to matters beyond the ken of ordinary men. They prefer to work through others from behind the scenes.

The influence of such men has a broader and more concrete base than status and prestige. Through a lifetime of exchanges, negotiations and labour a high-ranking man accumulates wealth upon which other men are dependent for their success. A high man's personal contacts and community of interests with men of comparable grade beyond the boundaries of his own neighbourhood can be put to specific uses, one of which is to arrange execution of undesirables within the community. High men are senior sib members. They have the fealty of their juniors and through these some call upon the loyalty of their wives and their respective sibs. High-ranking men control sib knowledge, which includes power and ritual, and in addition they are demonstrated possessors of great personal power.

7. OTHER CEREMONIAL INSTITUTIONS

There are two other ceremonial institutions which although important in the culture do not add significantly to our understanding of South Pentecost religion. The first of these is secret societies. One of these, the *tamate* society, was found throughout the area and was related to the yam harvest. The others, forming a complex of graded secret societies, were fairly recently introduced from Ambrym and were found only on the south-west coast.

The second institution was that of *gol*, a ceremonial performance held at the time of the yam harvest. It involves the construction of an impressive wooden tower from which performers dive head first, their legs secured to the tower by lianas. Recent popular articles have described this unique performance as a test of manhood and imply a licentious context. These interpretations are a product of journalistic imagination. Prestige accrues to those who jump from the highest positions on the tower; but all males young and old participate. Both the tower and the diving are associated with sexuality and virility, but these notions permeate most aspects of the culture and have no special emphasis here. The people themselves stress the therapeutic benefits of diving rather than anything else. They claim the diving invigorates them and removes fevers and accompanying aches and pains accumulated during the preceding wet season.

8. COMMENTARY

It is frequently asserted that religion is an explanatory and operational system which provides a means of coping with the unknown. Proponents of this view suggest that religious phenomena are most in evidence at times of crisis, when events are unexpected, uncontrollable or considered to be dangerous.

With reference to this idea, it is pertinent to note that what is regarded as a crisis or as unknown or uncontrollable may be culturally defined. We are accustomed to regard circumcision in primitive cultures as an important *rite de passage*. In South Pentecost circumcision is attended by a negligible amount of ritual and ceremonial in comparison with rank-taking in the graded society. Similarly the native would claim that he has knowledge and control in many areas in which we judge that he has none.

Religious activities in South Pentecost usually involve time and precise preparations. In circumstances perceived as crises, these are apt to be overshadowed by direct non-religious actions. In the case of mysterious intruders such as shape-shifters, the response is to seize weapons and take direct physical action. In a dangerous hurricane taboos and ritual are ignored as everyone takes immediate co-operative action for survival. The only instance in which women ever entered the communal men's house at Bunlap was during a severe hurricane when the entire village gathered in this structure after dwelling houses had been demolished. It is also worth noting that in the case of a widespread catastrophe such as a major hurricane, people are less likely to attribute the disaster to machinations of sorcerers or spirit-beings. A little rain shower may be the work of a sorcerer, but a major storm is likely to be considered as simply a natural catastrophe. On South Pentecost there are relatively few natural phenomena for which there are serious explanations and people are not greatly exercised about problems of the origin, nature or meaning of major phenomena such as storms, earthquakes and eclipses which obviously affect friend and foe alike.

Unexpectability is not an important consideration. In aboriginal times although the occurrence of specific events could not be predicted, given the relatively unchanging environment and stability of the culture, relatively few events would be unprecedented. The advent of Europeans was certainly an unexpected event, but apparently religion did not play an impressive part in attempts to deal with Europeans. Sorcery was attempted against them but the results were patently so unsuccessful that it was soon abandoned in favour of more pragmatic and empirical approaches.

Finally it may be noted that many areas involving unknowns such as the sky world and the underworld are of little importance or concern.

What are in our terms supernatural phenomena can be dangerous but are not necessarily so. If they are dangerous, they may or may not be feared. Such dangers are taken for granted among the hazards of life. Fear is normally aroused only when danger is immediate and personal. In most situations the supernatural is treated with cautious calm.

I have not focused to any extent on the relationships between religion and the individual. There are no religious specialists qualitatively set apart from the rest of the population. Everyone has more or less of a grasp of the essentials of religious belief and practices and everyone can more or less act for himself in his own religious life.

Quantitative differences exist. Some people have so much more knowledge, skill and power that others solicit their services. High men in the graded society might be classed as specialists, but their special knowledge accrues because of their position in the social structure and not because they are qualitatively different.

There are no doubt individuals in South Pentecost who have a greater interest in religion and who experience religion more intensely than others; but, because of the nature of the society and of the religious life, this is not obvious. The approach to religion is matter-of-fact and ritualistic rather than emotional.

At ritual and ceremonial high points, it is true that individuals involved reach peaks, or rather plateaus, of emotion which might be related to the concept of the 'religious experience', but one can never escape the impression that this emotion is subordinated to and controlled by the necessity to perform ritual correctly. The intensity of emotions seems to arise from the necessity of performing the ritual without error.

Considering the problem of the individual in another way, I have noted that there is a wide latitude for individual acceptance of belief. Action upon the basis of individual variation is more circumscribed. Even the most sceptical acquiesce in the rituals and ceremonials which make up so much of the overt religious activity. Participation, regardless of belief, takes place for a variety of reasons. Among the most cogent is responsibility to the group. Whatever one's beliefs about the efficacy of an action, the first obligation is not to self but to group. It would be most irresponsible for an individual to act in a way that the majority of a group felt to be inimical to their well-being and all but the most anti-social would feel constrained to conform outwardly. The stress at the performance level on repetition, ritual rather than belief, makes this conformity easier. It is mechanical repetition of forms which counts rather than the attitudes of the performer.

In conclusion, it seems clear that the main objective of South Pentecost religion is to supplement other techniques in manipulating and controlling animate phenomena. The ultimate purpose is to create and perpetuate satisfactory relations within the inner circle of kin, to cope with dangers from outside, and to ensure successful existence for the group and, within the framework of the group, for the individual.

9. RECENT CHANGES

It was noted initially that the patterns described here are no longer those of the majority of the people of South Pentecost. The bulk of the population are Christians.

The conversion to Christianity has not involved a total rejection of the old and total acceptance of the new except on superficial levels. Two mission groups are important in South Pentecost, the Roman Catholic Church and the Church of Christ. Catholic missionaries have discriminated against aboriginal beliefs and practices selectively, incorporating, tolerating or forbidding in accordance with their judgement as to the compatibility of particular features of native culture with Catholic dogma and European values. The Church of Christ missionaries have followed a policy of forbidding or discouraging any beliefs and practices associated with what they believe to be the native magico-religious system or which appear to them to be in conflict with European-Christian morality.

As a consequence of these different approaches, aboriginal beliefs and practices survive to a greater extent among Catholics than among members of the Church of Christ. However, the Church of Christ people have by no means abandoned all aboriginal beliefs. Most Christian natives continue to believe in the effects of aboriginal ritual and in the efficacy of sorcery although they indulge in little of the former and profess to disapprove of the latter. Weather control through ritual remains an active interest for all groups and new techniques are even today imported from the Small Islands off Malekula.

The dissociation of Christians from aboriginal traditions does not involve rejection of aboriginal ideas as false or erroneous, but rather an acceptance of a system empirically demonstrated to be more practical in the contact situation. It is not a matter of 'true' versus 'false' so much as a utilitarian choice between two alternative procedures. In the same perspective, non-Christians adhere to their system not because they believe that it is more valid but because, assessing the contact situation differently, they believe that the older ways continue to offer a better solution to their problems.

Although most Christians seemingly accept the basic theological doctrines of Christianity without question, many are presently sceptical about the formal aspects of Christianity. They are increasingly concerned with such questions as: Why does each church claim that only it has the 'true' word? Are differences in ritual and organization meaningful? They are disturbed and disillusioned by the gap between Christian belief and behaviour, particularly as it is evidenced in the differences between missionaries and local European laymen.

The people have always been prone, to some extent, to judge the various missions materialistically, and the tendency appears to be increasing: '. . . are good because they teach us English', '. . . have the best medicine'. The spiritual elements of Christianity are often subordinated to the above sorts of considerations.

As the people become more sophisticated, they begin to question the suppression of various facets of aboriginal culture and there is an incipient though unorganized move towards a revival of interest in certain features of aboriginal life. This 'revivalism' is not, at present, a deliberate rejection of Christianity and European culture. Natives concerned with such problems do not, for the most part, see any possibility of or point in attempts to move backwards.

The people of South Pentecost have never been involved in cults or nativistic movements although they are familiar with such movements in adjacent areas. In general both Christians and non-Christians are sceptical of the profit of such movements and of the motives of their leaders. Although dissatisfied with present conditions of life, they still hope for progress and change within the existing social and religious framework. This is particularly true for the non-Christians and only slightly less so for the Christians.

It is not easy to understand why radical solutions to their problems have received little favour. The people have been relatively fortunate in the Europeans with whom they have had close contact, and they have had some shrewd and forceful native leaders. Without the latter, they would have been much more susceptible to the influence of cults and nativistic movements. However, it should also be noted that if their present beliefs and practices do not seem to lead them in the direction they desire to go and if they do not receive more active and enlightened European guidance than they have had in the past, they will probably not hesitate to explore other courses of action. They remain pragmatists and empiricists.

NOTES

[1] The data incorporated in this report were collected in the New Hebrides in 1953-54 during a field trip supported by a Fulbright grant and conducted under the auspices of the Australian National University and during a subsequent trip in 1957-58 under the Tri-Institutional Pacific Program (University of Hawaii, Yale University and Bishop Museum) supported by the Carnegie Corporation

of New York. The author gratefully acknowledges the support of the institutions concerned.

[2] The terms 'animate-inanimate' are themselves not entirely satisfactory. The root *maet*, for example, occurs in the terms for ghost and for some types of spirit-beings which are animate. For convenience I employ the customary translations 'living' and 'dead' beyond this section, making it clear by context whether the terms are used in our sense or in the native sense.

[3] On the west coast the soul is *nunun*; the shadow and reflection are *manun*. On the east coast all three are *manun*.

[4] There is little difference between Codrington's (1891: p. 191) use of the term 'mana' and my use of the term 'power'. I avoid the former term because of the confusions which have developed about it in the subsequent literature.

[5] This does not conflict with the earlier statement that the tusks preserve the animateness of the sacrificed pig. The treatment of relics is often casual and the fact of animateness does not of itself give value. Even the skulls of ancestors, outside of ceremonial context, might be handled with no overt reverence or awe, and they were knocked about and broken, sometimes by children, in the communal men's house.

[6] Layard (1942: pp. 255 ff.).

[7] Tattevin (1926: pp. 411 ff.; 1927: pp. 82 ff.).

[8] See Deacon (1934), Guiart (1951) and Layard (1942). Tattevin (1927; 1928) gives a fairly detailed account of the graded society on South-east Pentecost.

[9] Layard (1942: p. 232).

BIBLIOGRAPHY

BIBLIOGRAPHY

Allen, M.	1967	*Male Cults and Secret Initiations*, Melbourne University Press.
Aufinger, A.	1940–1	'Siedlungsform und Häuserbau an der Rai Küste Neu Guinea', *Anthropos*, 35-36.
	1941	'Einige ethnographische Notizen zur Beschneidung in Neu Guinea', *Ethnos*, 6.
Baal, J. van	1966	*Dema*, The Hague, Nijhoff.
Barth, K.	1960	*The Humanity of God*, Richmond, Va., Knox Press.
Bateson, G.	1936	*Naven*, Cambridge, Cambridge University Press.
Berndt, C. H.	1953	'Socio-cultural change in the Eastern Central Highlands of New Guinea', *Southwestern Journal of Anthropology*, 9.
	1954	'Translation problems in three New Guinea Highland languages', *Oceania*, 24.
	1957	'Social and cultural change in New Guinea', *Sociologus*, 7.
	1959	'The ascription of meaning in a ceremonial context in the Eastern Central Highlands of New Guinea', in Freeman, J. D. and Geddes, W. R. (eds), *Anthropology in the South Seas*, Auckland, Thomas Avery.
	n.d.	'The Ghost Husband: Society and the Individual in New Guinea Myth', in Jacobs, M. (compiler) and Greenway, J. (ed.), *The Anthropologist looks at Myth*, Austin and London, University of Texas Press.
	1966	Myth in Action (Ph.D. Thesis, London School of Economics, University of London: reoriented volume for publication elsewhere, titled *Myth in Conflict*.)
Berndt, R. M.	1952–53	'A cargo movement in the Eastern Central Highlands of New Guinea', *Oceania*, 23.
	1954a	'Reaction to contact in the Eastern Highlands of New Guinea', *Oceania*, 24.

T

Berndt, R. M.   1954b   'Kamano, Jate, Usurufa and Fore kinship of the Eastern Highlands of New Guinea', *Oceania*, 25.

1954c   'Contemporary significance of prehistoric stone objects in the Eastern Central Highlands of New Guinea', *Anthropos*, 49.

1955a   'Cannibalism', *World Science Review* (December issue).

1955b   'Interdependence and conflict in the Eastern Central Highlands of New Guinea', *Man*, 55.

1956   'Anthropology and education', *Educand*, 2.

1957a   'The changing world in New Guinea', *Australian Quarterly*, 29.

1957b   'An anthropologist looks at literature', *Meanjin*, 16.

1958   'A devastating disease syndrome: Kuru sorcery in the Eastern Central Highlands of New Guinea', *Sociologus*, 8.

1962   *Excess and Restraint*, Chicago, University of Chicago Press.

1964   'Warfare in the New Guinea Highlands', *American Anthropologist*, 66, Special Publication: New Guinea.

1969/71   'Political structure in the Eastern Central Highlands of New Guinea', *Anthropological Forum* 2, republished in Berndt, R. M. and Lawrence, P. (eds), *Politics in New Guinea*, 1971.

Berndt, R. M. and   1971   *Politics in New Guinea*, University of Western Australia Press.
Lawrence, P. (eds)

Bidney, D.   1949   'Meta-anthropology', in Northrop, F.S.C. (ed.), *Ideological Differences and World Order*, New Haven, Yale University Press.

1953   *Theoretical Anthropology*, New York, Columbia University Press.

Blackwood, B.   1935   *Both Sides of Buka Passage*, Oxford, Clarendon Press.

Boas, F.   1938   *The Mind of Primitive Man*, New York, Macmillan.

Bodrogi, T.   1953   'Some notes on the ethnography of New Guinea', *Acta Ethnographica*, 3.

Brown, G.   1910   *Melanesians and Polynesians*, London, Macmillan.

Bulmer, R. N. H.   1957   'A primitive ornithology', *Australian Museum Magazine*, 12.

1960   'Political aspects of the Moka ceremonial exchange system among the Kyaka', *Oceania*, 31.

1961   'Leadership and Social Structure among the Kyaka' (Ph.D. Thesis, Australian National University, Canberra).

Bulmer, R. N. H.   1962   'Figurines and other stones of power among
and S. E.   the Kyaka', *Journal of the Polynesian Society*, 71.

Burridge, K. O. L.   1954   'Cargo cult activity in Tangu', *Oceania*, 24.

1956   'Social implications of some Tangu myths', *Southwestern Journal of Anthropology*, 12.

1957a   'Friendship in Tangu', *Oceania*, 27.

1957b   'The Gagai in Tangu', *Oceania*, 28.

1957c   'Disputing in Tangu', *American Anthropologist*, 59.

1957d   'Descent in Tangu', *Oceania*, 28.

1958   'Marriage in Tangu', *Oceania*, 29.

1959a   'Adoption in Tangu', *Oceania*, 29.

1959b   'The slit-gong in Tangu, New Guinea', *Ethnos*, 3-4.

1960   *Mambu*, London, Methuen.

1969a   *Tangu Traditions*, Oxford, Clarendon Press.

1969b   *New Heaven, New Earth*, Oxford, Blackwell.

Bus, G. A. M.   1951   'The Te festival or gift exchange in Enga . . .', *Anthropos*, 46.

Chowning, A.   1958   Lakalai Society (Ph.D. Thesis, University of Pennsylvania).

Chowning, A. and   1965/66   'Lakalai Political Organization', *Anthropological*
Goodenough, W. H.   71   *Forum* 1, republished in Berndt, R. M. and Lawrence, P. (eds), *Politics in New Guinea*, 1971.

Cochrane, G.   1970   *Big Men and Cargo Cults*, Oxford, Clarendon Press.

Codrington, R. H.   1891   *The Melanesians*, Oxford, Clarendon Press.

Crouch, E.   1955   'Notes on Enda Semangko and other Topics relating to the Supernatural' (Typescript, Baptist Mission, Baiyer River).

Deacon, A. B.   1934   *Malekula*, London, Routledge and Kegan Paul.

Dousset, R.   1970   *Colonialisme et Contradictions*, Paris, Mouton.

Draper, D.   1952   'Outline of the Culture of the Enga People' (Mimeograph, Baptist Mission, Baiyer River).

Durkheim, E.   1947   *Elementary Forms of the Religious Life*, Glencoe, Free Press.

Elkin, A. P.   1953   'Delayed exchange in Wabag Sub-district . . .', *Oceania*, 23.

Evans-Pritchard, E. E.   1940   *The Nuer*, Oxford, Clarendon Press.

Firth, R.   1951   *Elements of Social Organisation*, London, Watts.

Forde, C. D. (ed.)   1954   *African Worlds*, London, Oxford University Press.

Fortune, R. F.   1932   *Sorcerers of Dobu*, London, Routledge and Kegan Paul.

     1935   *Manus Religion*, Memoir of the American Philosophical Society.

Frazer, Sir J. G.   1913   *The Golden Bough*, London, Macmillan.

Glasse, R. M.   1959a   'Revenge and redress among the Huli', *Mankind*, 5.

     1959b   'The Huli descent system', *Oceania*, 29.

     1962   The Cognatic Descent System of the Huli of Papua (Ph.D. Thesis, Australian National University, Canberra).

Goode, W. J.   1951   *Religion among the Primitives*, Glencoe, Free Press.

Goodenough, W. H.   1952   'Ethnological reconnaissance in New Guinea', *University of Pennsylvania Museum Bulletin*, 17.

     1953   'Ethnographic notes on the Mae people . . .', *Southwestern Journal of Anthropology*, 9.

     1955   'The pageant of death in Nakanai', *University of Pennsylvania Museum Bulletin*, 19.

     1956a   'Residence rules: a re-appraisal', *Southwestern Journal of Anthropology*, 12.

     1956b   'Malayo-Polynesian land tenure', *American Anthropologist*, 58.

     1961   'Migrations implied by relationships of New Britain dialects to Central Pacific languages', *Journal of the Polynesian Society*, 70.

     1962   'Kindred and hamlet in Lakalai, New Britain', *Ethnology*, 1.

Guiart, J.   1951   'Société, rituels et mythes du Nord-Ambrym (Nouvelles Hébrides)', *Journal de la Société des Océanistes*, 7.

Guiart, J.   1962   *Les Religions de l'Océanie*, Paris, Presses Uni-
                                versitaires.

Hannemann, E. F.   n.d. a 'Village Life and Social Change in Madang
                                Society' (Mimeograph, Madang).

                        n.d. b 'Papuan Dances and Dancing' (Mimeograph,
                                Madang).

Hees, F.   1915–16 'Ein Beitrag aus den Sagen und Erzählungen
                                der Nakanai', *Anthropos*, 10–11.

Herskovits, M. J.   1949   *Man and His Works*, New York, Knops.

Hogbin, I.   1935   'Native culture of Wogeo', *Oceania*, 5.

                        1939a   'Native Land Tenure in New Guinea',
                                Oceania, 10.

                        1939b   *Experiments in Civilisation*, London, Routledge
                                and Kegan Paul.

                        1947   'Shame: a study of social conformity in a
                                New Guinea village', *Oceania*, 17.

                        1951   *Transformation Scene*, London, Routledge and
                                Kegan Paul.

                        1958   *Social Change*, London, Watts.

                        1964   *A Guadalcanal Society*, New York, Holt,
                                Rinehart and Winston.

                        1970   *The Island of Menstruating Men*, Scranton,
                                Chandler.

Höltker, G.   1941   'Die Mambu-Bewegung in Neuguinea',
                                Annali Lateranensi, 5.

Honigman, J. J.   1959   *The World of Man*, New York, Harper.

Horton, R.   1960   'A definition of religion, and its uses', *Journal
                                of the Royal Anthropological Society*, 90.

Kaberry, P. M.   1940–1 'The Abelam tribe, Sepik District, New
                                Guinea', *Oceania*, 11.

Kelly, E.   n.d.   'Socialisation among the Kyaka People of the
                                New Guinea Highlands' (Typescript, Baptist
                                Mission, Baiyer River).

Kroeber, A. L. (ed.)   1953   *Anthropology Today*, Chicago, University of
                                Chicago Press.

Lawrence, P.   1952   'Sorcery among the Garia', *South Pacific*, 6.

                        1954   'Cargo cult and religious beliefs among the
                                Garia', *International Archives of Ethnography*, 47.

                        1955   'The Madang District cargo cult', *South
                                Pacific*, 8.

Lawrence, P.	1959	'The background to educational development in Papua and New Guinea', *South Pacific*, 10.
	1964	*Road Belong Cargo*, London, Manchester University Press and Melbourne University Press.
Layard, J.	1942	*Stone Men of Malekula*, London, Chatto and Windus.
Leach, E. R.	1954	*Political Systems of Highland Burma*, London, Bell.
Leahy, M. J. and Crain, M.	1937	*The Land that Time forgot*, New York, Funk and Wagnalls.
Leenhardt, M.	1947	*Do Kamo*, Paris, Gallimard.
Lowie, R. H.	1920	*Primitive Society*, New York, Liveright Press.
Lutzbetak, L. J.	1956	'Worship of the dead in the middle Wahgi', *Anthropos*, 51.
McArthur, N.	1971	'Men and Spirits in the Kunimaipa Valley', in Hiatt, L. R. and Jayawardena, C. (eds), *Anthropology in Oceania*, Sydney, Angus and Robertson.
Malinowski, B.	1926	*Crime and Custom in Savage Society*, London, Routledge and Kegan Paul.
	1932	*The Sexual Lives of Savages in North-Western Melanesia*, London, Routledge and Kegan Paul.
	1935	*Coral Gardens and their Magic*, Vols. I-II, London, Allen and Unwin.
	1948	*Magic, Science and Religion*, Glencoe, Free Press.
Marwick, M. G.	1964	'Witchcraft as a social strain-gauge', *Australian Journal of Science*, 26.
Mead, M.	1933	'The Marsalai cult among the Arapesh', *Oceania*, 4.
	1934a	'Tamberans and tumbuans in New Guinea', *National History*, 34.
	1934b	'Kinship in the Admiralty Islands', *Anthropological Papers of the American Museum of Natural History*, 34.
	1940	'The Mountain Arapesh. II. Supernaturalism', *Anthropological Papers of the American Museum of Natural History*, 37.
	1947	'The Mountain Arapesh. III. Socio-economic life. IV. Diary of Events in Alitoa', *Anthro-*

pological Papers of the American Museum of Natural History, 37.

Meggitt, M. J.   1956   'The valleys of the upper Wage and Lai rivers . . .', *Oceania*, 27.

1957a   'House-building among the Mae Enga . . .', *Oceania*, 27.

1957b   'Ipili of the Porgera valley . . .', *Oceania*, 28.

1957c   'Mae Enga political organisation . . .', *Mankind*, 5.

1958a   'Mae Enga time reckoning and calendar . . .', *Man*, 58.

1958b   'Salt manufacture and trading in the Western Highlands', *Australian Museum Magazine*, 12.

1958c   'The Enga of the New Guinea Highlands', *Oceania*, 28.

1962a   'The growth and decline of agnatic descent groups among the Mae Enga . . .', *Ethnology*, 1.

1962b   'Dream interpretation among the Mae Enga of New Guinea', *Southwestern Journal of Anthropology*, 18.

1962c   *Desert People*, Sydney, Angus and Robertson.

1964   'Male-female relationships in the Highlands of Australian New Guinea', *American Anthropologist*, 66, Special Publication: New Guinea.

1965   *The Lineage System of the Mae Enga of New Guinea*, Edinburgh, Oliver and Boyd.

Merton, R. K.   1957   *Social Theory and Social Structure*, Glencoe, Free Press.

Murdock, G. P.   1949   *Social Structure*, New York, Macmillan.

Nadel, S. F.   1954   *Nupe Religion*, London, Routledge and Kegan Paul.

Neuhauss, R.   1911   *Deutsch Neu-Guinea*, Vol. I, Berlin, Reimer.

Newman, P. L.   1964   'Religious belief and ritual in a New Guinea society', *American Anthropologist*, 66, Special Publication: New Guinea.

Nilles, J.   1950   'The Kuman of the Chimbu region, Central Highlands, New Guinea', *Oceania*, 21.

Oliver, D. L.   1955   *A Solomon Island Society*, Cambridge, Mass., Harvard University Press.

Parkinson, R.   1907   *Dreissig Jahre in der Südsee*, Stuttgart, Strecker und Schröder.

Parsons, T.	1949	*The Structure of Social Action*, Glencoe, Free Press.
	1952	*The Social System*, London, Tavistock.
Powdermaker, H.	1933	*Life in Lesu*, New York, Norton.
Radcliffe-Brown, A. R.	1952	*Structure and Function in Primitive Society*, London, Cohen and West.
Rappaport, R. A.	1967	*Pigs for the Ancestors*, Newhaven and London, Yale.
Read, K. E.	1952a	'Nama cult of the Central Highlands, New Guinea', *Oceania*, 23.
	1952b	'Missionary activities and social change in the Central Highlands of Papua and New Guinea. I', *South Pacific*, 5.
	1954	'Cultures of the Central Highlands, New Guinea', *Southwestern Journal of Anthropology*, 10.
	1958	'A "cargo" situation in the Markham Valley, New Guinea', *Southwestern Journal of Anthropology*, 14.
Reay, M. O.	1959	*The Kuma*, Melbourne, Melbourne University Press.
Riesenfeld, A.	1951	'Tobacco in New Guinea', *Journal of the Royal Anthropological Institute*, 81.
Ryan, D. J.	1961	'Gift Exchange in the Mendi Valley' (Ph.D. Thesis, University of Sydney, Sydney).
Salisbury, R. F.	1956a	'Unilineal descent groups in the New Guinea Highlands', *Man*, 56.
	1956b	'The Siane language . . .', *Anthropos*, 51.
	1959	'A Trobriand Medusa?', *Man*, 59.
	1962	*From Stone to Steel*, Melbourne, Melbourne University Press.
	n.d.	*There upon the Rock: Political Consolidation in the New Guinea Highlands*, forthcoming.
Schaefer, A.	1938	'Zur Initiation im Wagital', *Anthropos*, 33.
Schmitz, C. A.	1960	*Historische Probleme in Nordost-Neuguinea (Huon-Halbinsel)*, Wiesbaden, Franz Steiner Verlag.
Schwartz, T.	1962	'The Paliau Movement in the Admiralty Islands, 1946-54', *Anthropological Papers of the American Museum of Natural History*, 49.

Tattevin, E.	1926	'Sur les bordes de la mer sauvage', *Revue*
	1927	*d'Histoire des Missions*, 2, 3, 4.
	1928	
Todd, J. A.	1934	'Report on research work in Southwest New Britain. . . .', *Oceania*, 5.
Tylor, Sir E. B.	1903	*Primitive Culture*, Vols. I-II, London, John Murray.
Valentine, C. A.	1958	An Introduction to the History of Changing Ways of Life on the Island of New Britain (Ph.D. Thesis, University of Pennsylvania, Philadelphia).
	1959	'Religion and Culture Change: Reflections on an Example from Melanesia', Address to the Annual Meeting of the American Anthropological Association.
	1960	'Uses of ethnohistory in an acculturation study', *Ethnohistory*, 7.
	1961	*Masks and Men in Melanesian Society*, Kansas, Lawrence.
	1963a	'Social status, political power, and native responses to European influence in Oceania', *Anthropological Forum*, 1.
	1963b	'Men of anger and men of shame: Lakalai ethnopsychology and its implications for sociopsychological theory', *Ethnology*, 2.
Vicedom, G. F. and Tischner, H.	1943–8	*Die Mbowamb*, Hamburg, Cram, De Gruyter.
Wallace, A. F. C.	1956	'Revitalisation movements', *American Anthropologist*, 58.
Wedgewood, C. H.	1934	'Report on Research in Manam, Mandated Territory of New Guinea', *Oceania*, 5.
Williams, F. E.	1924	*The Natives of the Purari Delta*, Port Moresby, Government Printer.
	1930	*Orokaiva Society*, London, Oxford University Press.
	1936	*Papuans of the Trans-Fly*, Oxford, Clarendon Press.
	1940	*Drama of Orokolo*, Oxford, Clarendon Press.
Wilson, M.	1954	'Nyakyusa ritual and symbolism', *American Anthropologist*, 56.
Worsley, P. M.	1966	*The Trumpet Shall Sound*, New York, Schocken.

Wurm, S.   1961   'The linguistic situation in the Highlands
                                   Districts of Papua and New Guinea', *Aus-
                                   tralian Territories*, 1.

INDEX

145°

BISMARCK

ADMIRALTY IS.

Manus

NEW

BISMARCK SEA

GUINEA

VANIMO

AITAPE

Wogeo I.

WEWAK

Arapesh +
+ Abelam
+ Iatmül

Manam I.

BOGIA

Tangu

Karkar I.

Sepik
River

Ramu River

CENTRAL

TELEFOMIN

WABAGA

+ Mae
Enga
+ Kyaka

Mt HAGEN

Metlpa +

Huli +

TARI

MENDI

Bagasin
Garia +
Area

MADANG
Astrolabe Bay

Rai Coast

Ngaing

Kuma
+
+ Chimbu
MINJ
Siane +

GOROKA

+ Gahuku Gama
+ KAINANTU

SAIDOR

Siasi Is.

am River

AMAUA

WEST NEW GUINEA

Strickland River

Fly River

ARAFURA

SEA

NDETTA
+
Orokaiva

RT MORESBY

P

12°

141° E.